We Own The World

Z Reader on Empire

Published by Z BOOKS, a project of the Institute
for Social and Cultural Communications, Inc.

18 Millfield Street
Woods Hole, MA 02543
www.zcommunications.org
zmag@zmag.org

ISBN: 978-1-938824-11-1

TABLE OF CONTENTS

Preface

This *Z Reader on Empire* contains selected articles from *Z Magazine*—from its founding in 1988 to 2012. They cover all the many ways—and institutions—that the U.S. uses to build, maintain, and expand its empire. These include genocide, intervention (military and economic), occupation, structural adjustment, the media, the UN, NATO, drones, death squads, pretexts such as protecting Americans, saving and/or promoting "democracy," "humanitarian" reasons, bribing local officies, appropriating resources, claiming racial dominance, and violating international law as well as the U.S. Constitution.

In the opening piece, "Year 501," Noam Chomsky writes: "As everyone knows, we are entering the 500th year of the Old World Order, sometimes called the Colombian era of world history or the Vasco da Gama era, depending on which bloodthirsty adventurer got there first. Or 'the 500 year Reich,' to borrow the title of a recent book that compares the methods and ideology of the Nazis with those of the European invaders who subjugated most of the world. The major theme of the Old World Order has been a confrontation between the conquerors and the conquered on a global scale. It has taken various forms and been given different names: imperialism, the North-South conflict, core versus periphery, G-7 (the 7 leading state capitalist industrial societies) and their satellites versus the rest. Or, more simply, Europe's conquest of the world...."

"In the post-World War II era, the U.S. has been the global enforcer, guaranteeing the interests of the club of rich men. It has, therefore, compiled an impressive record of aggression, international terrorism, slaughter, torture, chemical and bacteriological warfare, human rights abuses of every imaginable variety."

Edward S. Herman notes in the second piece, "The Global Empire," that "the New World Order (NWO) gives daily manifestations that a new, more centralized, sophisticated, but blatantly hypocritical phase of imperialism has evolved in which trade, aid, loans, debt management, proxy armies, techno-wars, and international 'law' are deployed to keep Third World countries in a dependent status."

The 25 articles presented here expose imperial policies and institutions. In doing so, they indicate important areas for organizing: (1) challenging institutions like capitalism, which demand hierarchical structures of class, race, and gender in order to build an empire that disregards such "externalities" as the environment and human potential; (2) challenging all attempts by the U.S. Empire and its satellite/client states to ignore the will of the population; that is, to fight for, reclaim, and develop new truly democratic structures and institutions, which are counter to the current savage imperialism and democracy deficit.

- Lydia Sargent, Editor
with additional editing by Eric Sargent

Part One

Building an Empire

1.

Year 501: World Orders Old and New

By Noam Chomsky

THE YEAR 1992 posed a critical moral and cultural challenge for the more privileged sectors of the world-dominant societies. The challenge is heightened by the fact that within these societies, notably our own, popular struggle over many centuries has won a mea-

> *As everyone knows, we are entering the 500th year of the Old World Order, sometimes called the Colombian era of world history or the Vasco da Gama era, depending on which bloodthirsty adventurer got there first*

sure of freedom with opportunities for independent thought and committed action. How this challenge is addressed, in fact, whether it is perceived at all on a broad scale, may have fateful consequences.

As everyone knows, we are entering the 500th year of the Old World Order, sometimes called the Colombian era of world history or the Vasco da Gama era, depending on which bloodthirsty adventurer got there first. Or "the 500 year Reich," to borrow the title of a recent book that compares the methods and ideology of the Nazis with those of the European invaders who subjugated most of the world. The major theme of the Old World Order has been a confrontation between the conquerors and the conquered on a global scale. It has taken various forms and been given different names: imperialism, the North-South conflict, core versus periphery, G-7 (the 7 leading state capitalist industrial societies) and their satellites versus the rest. Or, more simply, Europe's conquest of the world. By the term "Europe," we include the European-settled colonies that now lead the crusade—adopting South African conventions, the Japanese are admitted as "honorary Whites," rich enough to qualify. Japan was the one part of the South that escaped conquest and, perhaps, not coincidentally, the one part that was able to join the core, with some of its former colonies in its wake. The idea that there is more than coincidence in the correlation of independence and development is reinforced by a look at Western Europe, where parts that were colonized followed the Third World path of underdevelopment. One notable example is Ireland, violently conquered, then barred from development by the standard "free trade" doctrines selectively applied to ensure subordination of the South—today called "structural adjustment," "neoliberalism," or "our noble ideals," from which we, to be sure, are exempt.

A Bit of History

The early Spanish-Portuguese conquests had their domestic counterpart. In 1492, the Jewish community of Spain was expelled or forced to convert. Millions of Moors suffered the same fate. The fall of Granada in 1492, ending eight centuries of Moorish rule, made it possible for the Spanish Inquisition to extend its barbaric sway. The conquerors destroyed priceless books and manuscripts with their rich record of classical learning and demolished the civilization that had flourished under the far more tolerant and cultured Moorish rule. The stage was set for the decline of Spain and also for the racism and savagery of the world conquest—"the curse of Columbus," in the words of Africa historian Basil Davidson.

Spain and Portugal were soon displaced from their leading role as English pirates, marauders, and slave traders swept the seas, perhaps the most notorious, Sir Francis Drake. Later, the newly consolidated English state took over the task of "wars for markets" from "the plunder raids of Elizabethan sea-dogs" (British historian Christopher Hill). State power also enabled England to subdue the Celtic periphery, then to apply the newly-honed techniques with even greater destruction to new victims across the seas. By 1651, England was powerful enough to impose the Navigation Act, which established a closed trading area throughout much of the world, monopolized by English merchants. They were thus able to enrich themselves through the slave trade and their "plunder-trade with America, Africa, and Asia" (Hill), assisted by "state-sponsored colonial wars" and the various devices of economic management by which state power has forged the way to development.

It should be stressed that the economic doctrines preached by the powerful are intended for others, so that they can be more efficiently robbed and exploited. No wealthy developed society accepts these conditions, unless they happen to confer temporary advantage and their history reveals that sharp departure from these doctrines was a prerequisite for development. At least since the work of Alexander Gerschenkron in the 1950s, it has been widely recognized by economic historians that "late development" has been critically dependent on state intervention. Japan and the Newly Industrializing Countries (NICs) on its periphery are standard contemporary examples.

The same is true of the "early development" of England and the United States. High tariffs and other forms of state intervention may have raised costs to American consumers, but they allowed domestic industry to develop, from textiles to steel to computers, barring cheaper British products in earlier years, providing a state-guaranteed market and public subsidy for research and development in advanced sectors, creating and maintaining capital-intensive agribusiness, and so on. "Import substitution [through state intervention] is about the only way anybody's ever figured out to industrialize," development economist Lance Taylor observes, adding that, "In the long run, there are no laissez-faire transitions to modern economic growth. The state has always intervened to create a capitalist class, and then it has to regulate the capitalist class, and then the state has to worry about being taken over by the capitalist class, but the state has always been there." Furthermore, state power has regularly been invoked by the capitalist class to protect it from the destructive effects of an unregulated market to secure resources, markets, and opportunities for investment, and, in general, to safeguard and extend their profits and power. The Pentagon system of public subsidy for high tech industry is the most glaring example, close to home.

Balance of Payments

It is hardly surprising that the government is seeking new ways to maintain the Pentagon-based industries now that the conventional pretext had disappeared. One method is increased foreign arms sales, which also help alleviate the balance of payments crisis. The Bush administration has created a Center for Defense Trade to stimulate arms sales and has directed U.S. embassies to participate actively while proposing U.S. government guarantees for up to $1 billion in loans for purchase of U.S. arms.

The Defense Security Assistance Agency is reported to have sent more than 900 officers to some 50 countries to promote U.S. weapons sales. The Gulf war was prominently featured as a sales promotion device. Larry Korb, of the Brookings Institution, formerly Assistant Secretary of Defense, observes that the promise of arms sales has kept stocks of military producers high, despite the end of the Cold War, with arms sales skyrocketing from $12 billion in 1989 to almost $40 billion in 1991. Moderate declines in purchases by the U.S. military have been more than offset by other arms sales by U.S. companies.

Such considerations, however, should not obscure the more fundamental role of the Pentagon system (including NASA and DOE) in maintaining high tech industry generally, just as state intervention plays a crucial role in supporting biotechnology, pharmaceuticals, agribusiness, and most competitive segments of the economy.

By IMF standards, the United States, after a decade of what George Bush accurately called "voodoo economics" before he joined the team, is a prime candidate for severe austerity measures. But it is far too powerful to submit to the rules, intended for the weak. No one espoused liberal doctrine more fervently than the British, after they had employed state power to rob and destroy, establishing the basis for the first industrial revolution and their domination of world manufacture and trade. But the passionate rhetoric subsided when it no longer served the needs of the rulers. Unable to compete with Japan in the 1920s, Britain effectively barred Japan from trade with the Commonwealth, including India. The Americans followed suit in their lesser empire, as did the Dutch.

These were significant factors leading to the Pacific war as Japan set forth to emulate its powerful predecessors, having naively adopted their liberal dictates only to discover that they were a fraud, imposed on the weak, accepted by the strong only when they are useful. So it has always been.

Today, the World Bank estimates that the protectionist measures of the industrial countries—keeping pace with free market bombast—reduce the national income of the "developing societies" by about twice the amount provided by official "development assistance"; the term "developing societies" is the standard euphemism for those that are not developing, with a little help from their friends.

The "development assistance" may help or harm the recipients, but that is incidental. Typically, it is a form of export promotion. One familiar example is the Food for Peace program, designed to subsidize U.S. agribusiness and induce others to "become dependent on us for food" (Senator Hubert Humphrey), and to promote the global security network that keeps order in the Third World by requiring that local governments use counterpart funds for armaments (also subsidizing U.S. military producers). Another familiar example of export promotion was the Marshall Plan and other devices of the period, motivated in large part by the "dollar gap" that deprived U.S. industry of an export market, threatening a return to the depression of the 1930s.

More generally, its goal was to avert economic, social, and political chaos in Europe, contain communism (meaning not Soviet intervention, but the success of the indigenous Communist parties), prevent the collapse of America's export trade, and achieve the goal of multilateralism and provide a crucial economic stimulus for "individual initiative and private enterprise both on the Continent and in the United States," undercutting the fear of "experiments with socialist enterprise and government controls," which would "jeopardize private enterprise" in the United States as well (Michael Hogan, in the major scholarly study).

The Marshall Plan

The Marshall Plan also "set the stage for large amounts of private U.S. direct investment in Europe," Reagan's Commerce Department observed in 1984, establishing the basis for the modern multinational corporations, which "prospered and expanded on

> *Harvard economist Lawrence Summers, chief economist of the World Bank, explains that the world's environmental problems are largely "the consequence of policies that are misguided on narrow economic grounds," particularly the policies of the poor countries that "have been practically giving away oil, coal, and natural gas to domestic buyers in hopes of fostering industry and keeping living costs low for urban workers"*

overseas orders...fueled initially by the dollars of the Marshall Plan" and protected from "negative developments" by "the umbrella of American power," *Business Week* observed in

1975, lamenting that this golden age of state intervention might be fading away. Aid to Israel, Egypt, and Turkey, the leading recipients in recent years, is motivated by their role in maintaining U.S. dominance of the Middle East, with its enormous oil energy reserves.

So it goes case by case. "Our idealism" and "American moral leadership" (Henry Kissinger) are the tools of trade of the commissar class in state and ideological institutions. The real world proceeds along a different path.

The utility of "free trade" as a weapon against the poor is well-illustrated by a World Bank study on global warming, designed to "forge a consensus among economists" (meaning, the expert advisers of the rulers) in advance of the Rio conference on global warming in June, *New York Times* business correspondent Silvia Nasar reports under the headline "Can Capitalism Save the Ozone?" (the implication being: "Yes").

Harvard economist Lawrence Summers, chief economist of the World Bank, explains that the world's environmental problems are largely "the consequence of policies that are misguided on narrow economic grounds," particularly the policies of the poor countries that "have been practically giving away oil, coal, and natural gas to domestic buyers in hopes of fostering industry and keeping living costs low for urban workers" (Nasar). If the poor countries would only have the courage to resist the "extreme pressure to improve the performance of their economies" by fostering development while protecting their population from starvation, then environmental problems would abate.

"Creating free markets in Russia and other poor countries may do more to slow global warming than any measures that rich countries are likely to adopt in the 1990s," the World Bank concludes correctly, since the rich are hardly likely to pursue policies detrimental to their interests and they do have many weapons to wield against the poor, including selective use of "free trade" (in the small print, the consensus economists also recognize that "more effective government regulation" reduces pollution, but crushing the poor has obvious advantages).

The same day, the *London Economist* released a confidential World Bank memo by Lawrence Summers in which he wrote: "Just between you and me, shouldn't the World Bank be encouraging more migration of the dirty industries to the [Third World]?" This is reasonable on economic grounds, he explained: for example, a cancer producing agent will have larger effects "in a country where people survive to get prostate cancer than in a country where under-5 mortality is 200 per 1,000." Poor countries are "under-polluted" and it is only reasonable, on grounds of economic rationality, to encourage "dirty industries" to move to them. "The economic logic behind dumping a load of toxic waste in the lowest-wage country is impeccable and we should face up to that."

Summers recognizes that there are "arguments against all of these proposals" for exporting pollution to the Third World: "intrinsic rights to certain goods, moral reasons, social concerns, lack of adequate markets, etc." But the problem is that these arguments "could be turned around and used more or less effectively against every Bank proposal for liberalization."

"Mr. Summers is asking questions that the World Bank would rather ignore," the *Economist* notes, but "on the economics, his points are hard to answer." Quite true. We have the choice of accepting the conclusions, or regarding them as a reduction ad absurdum against the "free market" ideology. Confronted with the memo, Summers said that it was only "intended to provoke debate"—elsewhere he said that it was a "sarcastic response" to another World Bank draft, in the style of Jonathan Swift. Perhaps the same is true of the

World Bank "consensus" study reported on the same page of the *Times* business section. In fact, it is often hard to determine when the intellectual productions of the World Bank and other experts are intended seriously, or as a perverse form of sarcasm. Unfortunately, huge numbers of people, subjected to these

> *Highly developed nations can use free trade to extend their power and their control of the world's wealth and businesses can use it as a weapon against labor*

doctrines, do not have the luxury of pondering this intriguing question. Though not intended for us, "free trade does, however, have its uses," Arthur MacEwan observes in a review of the uniform record of industrial and agricultural development through protectionism and other measures of state interference, notably in the United States: "Highly developed nations can use free trade to extend their power and their control of the world's wealth, and businesses can use it as a weapon against labor. Most important, free trade can limit efforts to redistribute income more equally, undermine progressive social programs, and keep people from democratically controlling their economic lives." Small wonder, then, that neoliberal doctrine has won such a grand victory within the ideological system. The evidence about successful development is dismissed with the contempt that irrelevant nuisances deserve.

Doctrinal and Policy Framework

All of this is a crucial part of the doctrinal and policy framework of the New World Order, as of the old. The English colonists in North America pursued the course laid out by their forerunners in the home country. From the earliest days of colonization, Virginia was a center of piracy and pillage, raiding Spanish commerce and plundering French settlements as far as the coast of Maine. By the beginning of the 17th century, "New York had become a thieves' market where pirates disposed of loot taken on the high seas," historian Nathan Miller observes, while as in England, "corruption...was the lubricant that greased the wheels of the nation's administrative machinery"; "graft and corruption played a vital role in the development of modern American society and in the creation of the complex, interlocking machinery of government and business that presently determines the course of our affairs," Miller writes, ridiculing the ideologists who expressed great shock at Watergate.

As state power consolidated, piracy became less acceptable than graft and corruption, though the U.S. would not permit American citizens apprehended for slave trading or other crimes to be judged by international tribunals. The U.S. would not accept the reasonable standards proposed by Libya's Qaddafi, who has urged that charges concerning its alleged

In the approving words of diplomatic historian Thomas Bailey, Americans "concentrated on the task of felling trees and Indians and of rounding out their natural boundaries."

terrorism be brought to the World Court, a proposal dismissed with disdain by the U.S., which has little use for such instruments. Perhaps, the noted specialist on international law Alfred Rubin suggests, because "the U.S. and its two European friends are seeking a legal basis for some military strike at Libya that might help an incumbent president or prime minister nearing election time."

With American independence, state power was used to protect domestic industry, foster agricultural production, manipulate trade, monopolize raw materials, and take the land from its inhabitants. In the approving words of diplomatic historian Thomas Bailey, Americans "concentrated on the task of felling trees and Indians and of rounding out their natural

boundaries." These tasks were eminently reasonable by the approved standards of political correctness; the challenge to them in the past few years has, predictably, elicited much hysteria among those who regard anything less than total control over the ideological system as an unspeakable catastrophe. Hugo Grotius, a leading 17th century humanist and the founder of modern international law, determined that the "most just war is against savage beasts, the next against men who are like beasts."

George Washington wrote in 1783 that "the gradual extension of our settlements will as certainly cause the savage, as the wolf, to retire; both being beasts of prey, tho' they differ in shape"—though he regarded purchase of Indian lands (typically, by fraud and threat) as a better tactic than violence. Consciences were eased further by the legal doctrine developed by Chief Justice John Marshall: "discovery gave an exclusive right to extinguish the Indian right of occupancy, either by purchase or by conquest"; "that law which regulates, and ought to regulate in general, the relations between the conqueror and conquered was incapable of application to...the tribes of Indians, fierce savages whose occupation was war, and whose subsistence was drawn chiefly from the forest." The colonists, to be sure, knew better. Their survival depended on the agricultural sophistication of the "fierce savages."

Observing the Narragansett-Pequot wars, Roger Williams could see that their fighting was "far less bloody and devouring than the cruel wars of Europe." John Underhill sneered at the "feeble manner" of the Indian warriors, which "did hardly deserve the name of fighting," and their laughable protests against the "furious" style of the English that "slays too many men"—not to speak of women and children in undefended villages, a European tactic that had to be taught to the backward natives.

The useful doctrines of John Marshall and others remained in place through modern scholarship; thus the highly regarded anthropological authority A. L. Kroeber attributed to the East Coast Indians a kind of "warfare that was insane, unending," inexplicable "from our point of view" and so "dominantly emphasized within [their culture] that escape was well-nigh impossible," for any group that would depart from these hideous norms "was almost certainly doomed to early extinction."

This "harsh indictment would carry more weight," Francis Jennings observes, "if its rhetoric were supported by either example or reference," in this influential scholarly study. The Indians were hardly pacifists, but they had to learn the techniques of "total war" and true savagery from the European conquerors, with their ample experience in Ireland and elsewhere.

Respected statesmen have upheld the same values. To Theodore Roosevelt, the hero of George Bush and of the liberal commentators who gushed over his sense of "righteous mission" during the Gulf slaughter, "the most ultimately righteous of all wars is a war with savages," establishing the rule of "the dominant world races." This "noble minded missionary," as contemporary ideologues term him, did not limit his vision to the "beasts of prey" that were being swept from their lairs within the "natural boundaries" of the American nation. The ranks of "savages" included as well the "dagos" to the south, and the "Malay bandits" and "Chinese half breeds" who were resisting the American conquest of the Philippines, all "savages, barbarians, a wild and ignorant people, Apaches, Sioux, Chinese boxers," as their stubborn recalcitrance amply demonstrated. Winston Churchill thought that poison gas was just right for use against "uncivilized tribes" (Kurds and Afghans, particularly).

Noting approvingly that British diplomacy had prevented the 1932 disarmament convention from banning bombardment of civilians, the equally respected statesman Lloyd George observed that "we insisted on reserving the right to bomb niggers,' capturing the basic point succinctly. The metaphors of "Indian fighting" were carried right through the

> *Respected statesmen have upheld the same values. To Theodore Roosevelt, the hero of George Bush and of the liberal commentators who gushed over his sense of "righteous mission" during the Gulf slaughter, "the most ultimately righteous of all wars is a war with savages," establishing the rule of "the dominant world races"*

Indochina wars. The conventions have not lapsed into the 1990s, as we have seen only a few months ago and doubtless will again.

"The task of felling trees and Indians and of rounding out their natural boundaries" also required that some way be found to rid the continent of European interlopers. The main enemy was England, a powerful deterrent, and the target of frenzied hatred in broad circles. It was, incidentally, reciprocated, interlaced with considerable contempt. Thus, in 1865, a progressive English gentleman offered to endow a lectureship at Cambridge University for American studies, a subject then considered too insignificant to merit attention. Cambridge dons protested with outrage against what one called, with admirable literary flair, "a biennial flash of Transatlantic darkness." They feared that the lectures would spread "discontent and dangerous ideas" among uneducated undergraduates, "over whom they would naturally exercise some considerable influence."

Some thought "that the Harvard credentials of the lecturers would guarantee that the lectures be inoffensive," historian Joyce Appleby notes, quoting one don who recognized that the lecturers would be drawn from the class that felt itself "increasingly in danger of being swamped by the lower elements of a vast democracy." Most feared the subversive influence of these lower elements. The threat was beaten back in an impressive show of the kind of political correctness that continues to reign in most of the academic world, as fearful as ever of the lower elements and their strange ideas.

Recognizing that England's military force was too powerful to confront, Jacksonian Democrats called for annexation of Texas to ensure a U.S. world monopoly of cotton. The U.S. would then be able to paralyze England and intimidate Europe. "By securing the virtual monopoly of the cotton plant" the U.S. had acquired "a greater influence over the affairs of the world than would be found in armies however strong, or navies however numerous," President Tyler observed after the annexation and the conquest of a third of Mexico. "That monopoly, now secured, places all other nations at our feet," he wrote: "An embargo of a single year would produce in Europe a greater amount of suffering than a fifty years' war. I doubt whether Great Britain could avoid convulsions." The same monopoly power neutralized British opposition to the conquest of the Oregon territory.

The editor of New York's leading newspaper exulted that Britain was "completely bound and manacled with the cotton cords" of the United States, "a lever with which we can successfully control" this dangerous rival.

The editor of New York's leading newspaper exulted that Britain was "completely bound and manacled with the cotton cords" of the United States, "a lever with which we can successfully control" this dangerous rival. Thanks to the conquests that ensured monopoly of the most important commodity in world trade, the Polk administration boasted, the U.S. could now "control the commerce of the world and secure thereby to the American Union inappreciable political and commercial advantages." "Fifty years will not elapse ere the

destinies of the human race will be in our hands," a Louisiana congressman proclaimed, as he and others looked to "mastery of the Pacific" and control over the resources on which European rivals were dependent. Polk's Secretary of Treasury reported to Congress that the conquests of the Democrats would guarantee "the command of the trade of the world."

The national poet, Walt Whitman, wrote that our conquests "take off the shackles that prevent men the even chance of being happy and good." Mexico's lands were taken over for the good of mankind: "What has miserable, inefficient Mexico...to do with the great mission of peopling the New World with a noble race?" Others recognized the difficulty of taking Mexico's resources without burdening ourselves with its "imbecile" population, "degraded" by "the amalgamation of races," though the New York press was hopeful that their fate would be "similar to that of the Indians of this country, the race, before a century rolls over us, will become extinct."

The concerns of the expansionists went beyond their fear that an independent Texas would break the U.S. resource monopoly and expand to become a rival empire. It might also abolish slavery, igniting dangerous sparks of egalitarianism. Andrew Jackson thought that an independent Texas, with a mixture of Indians and fleeing slaves, might be manipulated by Britain to "throw the whole west into flames." His earlier conquest of Florida had been justified by John Quincy Adams, with Thomas Jefferson's enthusiastic approbation, by the need to thwart British efforts to launch "mingled hordes of lawless Indians and negroes" in a "savage war" against the "peaceful inhabitants" of the United States.

It is evident without further comment that the logic of the Jacksonian Democrats was essentially that attributed to Saddam Hussein by U.S. propaganda after his conquest of Kuwait. But the comparisons should not be pressed too far. Unlike his Jacksonian precursors, Saddam Hussein is not known to have feared that slavery in Iraq would be threatened by independent states nearby or to have publicly called for their "imbecile" inhabitants to "become extinct" so that the "great mission of peopling the Middle East with a noble race" of Iraqis can be carried forward, placing "the destinies of the human race in the hands" of the conquerors. Even the wildest fantasies did not accord Saddam potential control over the major resource of the day of the kind enjoyed by the expansionists of the 1840s. Like Qaddafi, Saddam still has a few things to learn from our history, so extolled by enraptured intellec- tuals.

The U.S. was also instrumental in maintaining a high level of slaughter and terror from Mozambique to Angola, while "quiet diplomacy" helped the Administration's South African friends to cause over $60 billion in damage and 1.5 million deaths from 1980 to 1988 in the

After the successful mid-19th century conquests, New York editors proudly observed that the U.S. was "the only power which has never sought and never seeks to acquire a foot of territory by force of arms"; "Of all the vast domains of our great confederacy over which the star spangled banner waves, not one foot of it is the acquirement of force or bloodshed"; the remnants of the native population, among others, were not asked to confirm this judgment.

The U.S. is unique among nations in that "By its own merits it extends itself." That is only natural, since "all other races...must bow and fade" before "the great work of subjugation and conquest to be achieved by the Anglo-Saxon race," conquest without force. Leading contemporary historians accept this flattering self-image.

Samuel Flagg Bemis wrote in 1965 that "American expansion across a practically empty continent despoiled no nation unjustly." Arthur M. Schlesinger had earlier described Polk as "undeservedly one of the forgotten men of American history": "By carrying the flag to the Pacific he gave America her continental breadth and ensured her future significance in the world," a realistic assess-

ment, if not exactly in the intended sense. Such doctrinal fantasies could not easily survive the Vietnam War, at least outside the intellectual class, where we are regularly regaled by orations on how "for 200 years the United States has preserved almost unsullied the orig- inal ideals of the Enlightenment...and, above all, the universality of these values" (Yale Professor Michael Howard, formerly Regius Professor of Modern History at Oxford, among many others).

Writing today on "the self-image of Americans," *New York Times* correspondent Richard Bernstein observes that "many who came of age during the 1960s protest years have never regained the confidence in the essential goodness of America and the American government that prevailed in earlier periods," a matter of much concern to ideologists and a factor in the appeal of dreams of Camelot, an interesting topic that merits separate discussion. The conquest of the New World set off two vast demographic catastrophes, unparalleled in history: the virtual destruction of the indigenous population of the Western hemisphere, and the devastation of Africa as the slave trade rapidly expanded to serve the needs of the conquerors.

The basic patterns persist to the current era. As the slaughter of the indigenous population by the Guatemalan military approached virtual genocide, Ronald Reagan and his officials, while lauding the democracy-loving assassins, informed Congress that they were providing them with arms "to reinforce the improvement in the human rights situation following the 1982 coup" that installed Rios Montt, perhaps the greatest murderer of them all; although "the primary means" by which Guatemala obtained U.S. military equipment, the General Accounting Office of Congress observed, was commercial sales licensed by the Department of Commerce (putting aside the network of allies and clients that are always ready to contribute to genocide if there are profits to be made).

The U.S. was also instrumental in maintaining a high level of slaughter and terror from Mozambique to Angola, while "quiet diplomacy" helped the Administration's South African friends to cause over $60 billion in damage and 1.5 million deaths from 1980 to 1988 in the

> *We instituted civil affairs [in 1982] which provides development for 70 percent of the population, while we kill 30 percent. Before, the strategy was to kill 100 percent.*

neighboring states. The most devastating effects of the general catastrophe of capitalism through the 1980s were in the same two continents: Africa and Latin America. One of the grandest of the Guatemalan killers, General Hector Gramajo, was rewarded for his contributions to genocide in the highlands with a Mason Fellowship to Harvard's John F. Kennedy School of Government—not unreasonably, given Kennedy's decisive contributions to the vocation of counterinsurgency. Cambridge dons will be pleased to learn that Harvard is no longer a dangerous center of subversion.

While earning his degree at Harvard, Gramajo gave an interview to the *Harvard International Review* in which he offered a more nuanced view of his own role. He said that he was personally in charge of the commission that drafted the "70 percent-30 percent civil affairs program, used by the Guatemalan government during the 1980s to control people or organizations who disagreed with the government" (*Central America Report* (CAR), Guatemala City).

He outlined with some pride the doctrinal innovations he had introduced: "We have cre-

ated a more humanitarian, less costly strategy, to be more compatible with the democratic system. We instituted civil affairs [in 1982] which provides development for 70 percent of the population, while we kill 30 percent. Before, the strategy was to kill 100 percent." This is a "more sophisticated means" than the previous crude assumption that you must "kill everyone to complete the job" of controlling dissent.

It is unfair, then, for journalist Alan Nairn, who exposed the U.S. origins of the Central American death squads, to describe Gramajo as "one of the most significant mass-murderers in the Western Hemisphere," as Gramajo was sued by the Center for Constitutional Rights in New York for damages for murders, disappearances, torture, and forced exile of Guatemalan citizens. We can also understand now why former CIA director William Colby sent Gramajo a copy of his memoirs with the inscription: "To a colleague in the effort to find a strategy of counterinsurgency with decency and democracy," Kennedy-style. We can be assured that Gramajo, like Colby, understands what is "compatible with the democratic system," as envisioned by the masters.

Given his understanding of humanitarianism, and democracy, it is not surprising that Gramajo appears to be the State Department's choice for the 1995 elections, CAR reports, citing Americas Watch on the Harvard fellowship as "the State Department's way of grooming Gramajo" for the job, and quoting a U.S. Senate staffer who says: "He's definitely their boy down there." The *Washington Post* reports that many Guatemalan politicians expect Gramajo to win the elections, not an unlikely prospect if he's the State Department's boy down there. Gramajo's image is also being prettified. He offered the *Post* a sanitized version of his interview on the 70 percent-30 percent program: "The effort of the government was to be 70 percent in development and 30 percent in the war effort. I was not referring to the people, just the effort." Too bad he expressed himself so badly—or better, so honestly—before the Harvard grooming had taken effect.

It is not at all unlikely that the rulers of the world, meeting in G7 conferences, have written off large parts of Africa and much of the population of Latin America, superfluous people who have no place in the New World Order, to be joined by many others, in the home societies as well. Diplomacy has perceived Latin America and Africa in a similar light. Planning documents stress that the role of Latin America is to provide resources, markets, investment opportunities with ample repatriation of capital, and in general, a favorable climate for business.

If that can be achieved with formal elections under conditions that safeguard business interests, well and good; if it requires death squads "to destroy permanently a perceived threat to the existing structure of socioeconomic privilege by eliminating the political participation of the numerical majority..." that's too bad, but preferable to the alternative of independence; the words are those of Lars Schoultz, the leading U.S. academic specialist on human rights in Latin America, describing the National Security States that had their roots in Kennedy administration policies. As for Africa, State Department Policy Planning chief George Ken- nan, assigning to each part of the South its special function in the New World Order of the post-World War II era, recommended that it be "exploited" for the reconstruction of Europe, adding that the opportunity to exploit Africa should afford the Europeans "that tangible objective for which everyone has been rather unsuccessfully groping..." a badly needed psychological lift. Such recommendations are too uncontroversial to elicit comment, or even notice.

The genocidal episodes of the Colombian Vasco da Gama era are by no means limited to the conquered countries of the South, as is sufficiently attested by the achievements of the leading center of Western civilization 50 years ago.

Savage Conflicts

Throughout the era, there have also been regular savage conflicts among the core societies of the North, sometimes spreading far beyond, particularly in this terrible century. From the point of view of most of the world's population, these have been much like shoot-outs between rival drug gangs or mafia dons. The only question is who will gain the right to rob and kill. In the post-World War II era, the U.S. has been the global enforcer, guaranteeing the interests of the club of rich men. It has, therefore, compiled an impressive record of aggression, international terrorism, slaughter, torture, chemical and bacteriological warfare, human rights abuses of every imaginable variety. This is not surprising; it goes with the turf. Nor is it surprising that the occasional documentation of these facts far from the mainstream elicits tantrums among the commissars, as it regularly does.

This horrifying record, if noticed at all, is considered insignificant, even a proof of our nobility. Again, that goes with the turf. The most powerful mafia don is also likely to dominate the doctrinal system. One of the great advantages of being rich and powerful is that you never have to say: "I'm sorry." It is precisely here that the moral and cultural challenge arises, as we approach the end of the first 500 years.

Persistent Themes

Since its liberation from Spanish rule, Latin America has faced many problems. One of the most grave was foreseen by the Liberator, Simon Bolivar, in 1822: "There is at the head of this great continent a very powerful country, very rich, very warlike, and capable of anything." Citing this comment, Latin America scholar Piero Gleijeses observes that "In England, Bolivar saw a protector; in the United States, a menace." Naturally so, given the geopolitical realities.

The United States was ambivalent about the independence of the Spanish colonies. "In the Congressional debates of the period," Gleijeses notes, "there was much more enthusiasm for the cause of the Greeks than that of the Spanish Americans." One reason was that Latin Americans "were of dubious whiteness," at best "from degraded Spanish stock," unlike the Greeks, who were assigned a special role as the Aryan giants who created civilization, in the revision of history constructed by European racist scholarship (the topic of Martin Bernal's *Black Athena*). Yet another reason was that, unlike the Founding Fathers, Bolivar freed his slaves, thus becoming a rotten apple that might spoil the barrel, a virus that might infect others, to borrow the terminology of

> *In the 19th century, there was a problem in establishing U.S. dominance of the hemisphere: the British deterrent. But the conception of "our confederacy" as "the nest, from which all America, North and South, is to be peopled" (Thomas Jefferson) was firmly implanted*

U.S. planners in the modern period, expressing their concerns over the threat to "stability" caused by a dangerous good example.

A still more fundamental issue was brought forth by the major intellectual reviews of the day. They concluded that "South America will be to North America...what Asia and Africa are to Europe"—our Third World. This perception retains its vitality through the 20th century. Commenting on Secretary of State James Baker's efforts to enhance "regional problem-sharing" through the hemisphere, *Times* correspondent Barbara Crossette notes "the realization in the United States and throughout the hemisphere [by the sectors that matter, at least] that European and Asian trading blocs

can be best tackled by a large free-trade area in this part of the world," a resurrection of what Roosevelt's Secretary of War, Henry Stimson, called "our little region over here which never has bothered anybody" when he was explaining in May 1945 why all regional systems must be dismantled in the interests of liberal internationalism, apart from our own, which are to be extended.

The World Bank is less sanguine about the prospects. A recent report concludes that the U.S. will gain more from free trade agreements than Latin America, apart from Mexico and Brazil, and that the region would do better with a customs union on the model of the European Community, with a common external tariff, excluding the U.S., something definitely not in the cards. In the 19th century, there was a problem in establishing U.S. dominance of the hemisphere: the British deterrent. But the conception of "our confederacy" as "the nest, from which all America, North and South, is to be peopled" (Thomas Jefferson) was firmly implanted, along with the Jeffersonian corollary that it is best for Spain to rule until "our population can be sufficiently advanced to gain it from them piece by piece."

There were internal conflicts over the matter. American merchants "were eager to contribute to the cause of freedom—as long as the rebels were able to pay, preferably cash," Gleijeses notes. And the well-established tradition of piracy provided a reservoir of American ship owners and seamen (British, too) who were happy to offer their services as privateers to attack Spanish shipping, though extension of their terrorist vocation to American vessels led to much moral outrage and a government crackdown. Apart from England, liberated Haiti also provided assistance to the cause of independence, but on the condition that slaves be freed. Haiti, too, was a dangerous rotten apple, punished for independence with huge reparations to France, the former colonial power, and a half-century U.S. embargo followed by Woodrow Wilson's destructive rampage and other such benefits, until this very moment.

Monroe Doctrine

The concept of Pan Americanism advanced by Bolivar was diametrically opposed to that of the Monroe Doctrine at the same time. A British official wrote in 1916 that, while Bolivar originated the idea of Pan Americanism, he "did not contemplate the consummation of his policy under the aegis of the United States." In the end, it was "Monroe's victory and Bolivar's defeat," Gleijeses comments. The status of Cuba was of particular significance, another illustration of the resilience of traditional themes. The U.S. was firmly opposed to the independence of Cuba, "strategically situated and rich in sugar and slaves" (Gleijeses). Jefferson advised President Madison to offer Napoleon a free hand in Spanish America in return for the gift of Cuba to the United States. Secretary of State John Quincy Adams, the author of the Monroe Doctrine, described Cuba as "an object of transcendent importance to the commercial and political interests of our Union." He, too, urged Spanish sovereignty until Cuba would fall into U.S. hands by "the laws of political...gravitation," a "ripe fruit" for harvest. Support for Spanish rule was near universal in the executive and Congress; European powers, Colombia, and Mexico were approached for assistance in the endeavor of blocking the liberation of Cuba.

A prime concern was the democratic tendencies in the Cuban independence movement, which advocated abolition of slavery and equal rights for all, unlike the U.S., which, in its Constitution, designated Black slaves as less than human. There was a threat that "the rot might spread," even to our own shores.

By the end of the 19th century, the U.S. was powerful enough to ignore the British deterrent and conquer Cuba, just in time to prevent the success of the indigenous liberation struggle. Standard doctrines provided the justification for relegating Cuba to virtual colonial status. Cubans were "ignorant niggers, half-breeds, and dagoes," the New York press observed, "a lot of degenerates...no more capable of self-government than the savages of Africa," the military command added. The U.S. imposed the rule of the white propertied

> In March 1960, the Eisenhower administration formally adopted a plan to overthrow Castro in favor of a regime "more devoted to the true interests of the Cuban people and more acceptable to the U.S.," emphasizing again that this must be done "in such a manner as to avoid any appearance of U.S. intervention"

classes, who had no weird notions about democracy, freedom, and equal rights, and were thus not degenerates. The "ripe fruit" was converted to a U.S. plantation, terminating the prospects for successful independent development. In the 1930s, FDR cancelled the "good neighbor policy" to overturn a civilian government regarded as a threat to U.S. commercial interests.

The Batista dictatorship served those interests loyally, thus enjoying full support. Castro's overthrow of the dictatorship in January 1959 soon elicited U.S. hostility, and a return to the traditional path. By late 1959, the CIA and the State Department had concluded that Castro had to be overthrown. One reason, State Department liberals explained, was that "our business interests in Cuba have been seriously affected." A second was the rotten apple effect: "The United States cannot hope to encourage and support sound economic policies in other Latin American countries and promote necessary private investments in Latin America if it is or appears to be simultaneously cooperating with the Castro program," the State Department concluded in November 1959. But one condition was added: "in view of Castro's strong though diminishing support in Cuba, it is of great importance, however, that the United States government not openly take actions which would cause the United States to be blamed for his failure or downfall."

As for Castro's support, public opinion studies provided to the White House (April 1960) concluded that most Cubans were optimistic about the future and supported Castro, while only 7 percent expressed concern about communism and only 2 percent about failure to hold elections. Soviet presence was nil. "The liberals, like the conservatives, saw Castro as a threat to the hemisphere," historian Jules Benjamin observes, "but without the world communist conspiracy component."

By October 1959, planes based in Florida were carrying out strafing and bombing attacks against Cuban territory. In December, CIA subversion was stepped up, including supply of arms to guerrilla bands and sabotage of sugar mills and other economic targets. In March 1960, the Eisenhower administration formally adopted a plan to overthrow Castro in favor of a regime "more devoted to the true interests of the Cuban people and more acceptable to the U.S.," emphasizing again that this must be done "in such a manner as to avoid any appearance of U.S. intervention."

That dictate remains in force as the U.S. now advances towards the traditional goal of preventing Cuban independence. Crucially, the ideological institutions must suppress the record of aggression, campaigns of terror, economic strangulation, and the other devices employed by the lord of the hemisphere in its dedication to "the true interests of the Cuban people." Cuba's plight must be attributed to the demon Castro and "Cuban socialism" alone. Castro bears full responsibility for the "poverty, isolation, and humbling dependence" on the USSR, the *New York Times* editors inform us, concluding triumphantly that "the Cuban dictator has painted himself into his own corner," without any help from us.

That being the case, by doctrinal necessity, we should not intervene directly as some "U.S. cold warriors" propose: "Fidel Castro's reign deserves to end in home-grown failure, not martyrdom." Taking their stand at the dovish extreme, the editors advise that we should continue to stand aside, watching in silence as we have been doing for 30 years, so the naive reader would learn from this (quite typical) version of history, crafted to satisfy doctrinal requirements.

The U.S. concern for "the true interests of the Cuban people" merits no comment. The concerns over public opinion in Cuba and Latin America, and crucially the "true interests" of U.S. business, have always been real enough. The former are understandable in the light of the public opinion polls just cited, or the Latin American reaction to the Agrarian Reform Law of May 1959, acclaimed by one UN organization as "an example to follow" in all Latin America; or by the conclusion of the World Health Organization's representative in Cuba in 1980 that "there is no question that Cuba has the best health statistics in Latin America," with the health organization "of a very much developed country" despite its poverty; or by the interest in Brazil and other Latin American countries in Cuban biotechnology, unusual if not unique for a small and poor country.

It is not Castro's crimes that disturb the rulers of the hemisphere, who cheerfully support the Suhartos and Saddam Hussein's and Gramajos, however grotesque their crimes, as long as they perform their service role. Rather, it is the elements of success that arouse fear and anger and the call for vengeance, a fact that must also be suppressed by ideologists, not an easy task, given the overwhelming evidence confirming this primary principle of world order. Sabotage, terror, and aggression were escalated further by the Kennedy administration, along with the kind of economic warfare that no small country can long endure. Cuban reliance on the U.S. as an export market and for imports had, of course, been overwhelming and could hardly be replaced without great cost. In February 1962, the Kennedy administration imposed an embargo.

In the 1980s, the U.S. barred from the U.S. industrial products containing any Cuban nickel, an effort to block a major Cuban export. It prohibited a Swedish medical supply company from providing equipment to Cuba because one component is manufactured in the U.S. Aid to the former Soviet Union is conditioned on suspension of commercial relations with Cuba. In early 1991, the U.S. resumed Caribbean military maneuvers, including rehearsal of a Cuba invasion, a standard technique of intimidation. In mid-1991, the embargo was tightened further, cutting remittances that Cuban- Americans are permitted to send to relatives, among other measures. Legislation now under consideration calls for extending the embargo to U.S. subsidiaries abroad and the barring of ships from U.S. ports for six months after any landing in Cuba, as well as seizure of cargo if they enter U.S. territorial waters. The ferocity of the hatred for Cuban independence is extreme, and scarcely wavers across the narrow mainstream spectrum.

Currently, there is no effort to conceal the fact that the disappearance of the Soviet deterrent and the decline of East bloc economic relations with Cuba offers an opportunity to achieve U.S. aims through economic warfare or other means. In a typical reaction, the editors of the *Washington Post* urge that the U.S. seize the opportunity to crush Castro: "For his great antagonist, the United States, to give relief and legitimacy to this used-up relic at this late hour would be to break faith with the Cuban people—and with all the other democrats in the hemisphere."

Pursuing the same logic, the editors, through the 1980s, called on the U.S. to co-

erce Nicaragua until it was restored to the "Central American mode" of the Guatemalan and Salvadoran death squad "democracies," observing their admirable "regional standards"; and scoffed at Gorbachev's "New Thinking" because he had not yet offered the U.S. a free hand to achieve its objectives by force.

The *Post* speaks for the people of Cuba just as State Department liberals did in the Eisenhower and Kennedy years; as William McKinley spoke for "the vast majority of the population" of the Philippines who "welcome our sovereignty" and whom he was "protecting... against the designing minority"; and as his proconsul Leonard Wood spoke for the de-

> *Pursuing the same logic, the editors, through the 1980s, called on the U.S. to coerce Nicaragua until it was restored to the "Central American mode" of the Guatemalan and Salvadoran death squad "democracies"*

cent (i.e., wealthy European) people of Cuba who favored U.S. domination or annexation and had to be protected from the "degenerates." The U.S. has never been short of good will for the suffering people of the world who have to be protected from the machinations of evil-doers. As for the *Post's* love of democracy, charity dictates silence.

The Cuban record demonstrates clearly, once again, that the Cold War framework was scarcely more than a pretext to conceal the standard U.S. refusal to tolerate Third World independence, whatever its political coloration. Traditional policies remain beyond serious challenge within the economic, commercial, and financial relations. Theoretically, medicines and some food were exempt, but food and medical aid were denied after Cyclone Flora caused death and destruction in October 1963. Standard procedure, incidentally. Consider Carter's refusal to allow aid to any West Indian country struck by the August 1980 hurricane unless Grenada was excluded (they refused and received no aid); or the U.S. reaction when Nicaragua was fortuitously devastated by a hurricane in 1988; any weapon is permissible against the perpetrators of the crime of independence.

The Kennedy administration also sought to impose a cultural quarantine to block the free flow of ideas and information to the Latin American countries whose unwillingness to emulate U.S. controls on travel and cultural interchange always greatly troubled the Kennedy liberals, as did their legal systems, requiring evidence for crimes by alleged "subversives," as well as their excessive liberalism generally.

After the Bay of Pigs failure, the Kennedy terrorist attacks escalated further, reaching quite remarkable dimensions ("Operation Mongoose"). They are largely dismissed in the West, apart from some notice of the assassination attempts, one of them implemented on the very day of the Kennedy assassination. The operations were formally called off by Lyndon Johnson, who is reported by aides to have condemned the Kennedy programs as "a damned Murder Inc." The terrorist operations continued, however, and were escalated by Nixon. Subsequent terrorist operations are attributed to renegades beyond CIA control, whether accurately or not, we do not know; one high Pentagon official of the Kennedy-Johnson administrations, Roswell Gilpatric, has expressed his doubts.

The Carter administration, with the support of U.S. courts, condoned hijacking of Cuban ships in violation of the anti-hijacking convention that Castro was respecting. The Reaganites rejected Cuban initiatives for diplomatic settlement and imposed new sanctions on the most outlandish pretexts, often lying outright. We can anticipate, then, efforts of the usual kind to ensure that the "ripe fruit" drops into the hands of its rightful owners or is pulled more vigorously from the tree. A cautious policy would be to tighten the stranglehold, resorting to economic and ideological warfare (and perhaps more) to punish the population

while intimidating others to refrain from interfering. As suffering increases, it is assumed, so will protest, repression, more unrest, in the predictable cycle.

At some stage, internal collapse will reach the point where the Marines can be sent in cost-free to "liberate" the island once again, restoring the old order while the commissars chant odes to our grand leaders and their righteousness. Inability to manufacture a pre-election economic recovery, even if only on paper, might accelerate the process with the hope of deflecting popular attention by a foreign policy triumph. But it is unlikely that the Bush administration will veer far from the policies outlined in its early National Security Policy Review, which concluded that the U.S. must avoid combat when confronting "much weaker enemies," defeating them "decisively and rapidly," because domestic "political support" is so thin.

"Natural Boundaries" Of the South

Rounding out the natural boundaries was the task of the colonists in their home territory, but the "natural boundaries" of the South also have to be defended. Hence, the unremitting dedication to the task of ensuring that no sector of the South goes a separate way and the near hysteria, evident even in the internal record, if some tiny deviation is detected.

All must be properly integrated into the global economy dominated by the core state capitalist industrial societies. They must "fulfill their major function" as sources of raw materials and markets, as the State Department put it years ago, they must be protected from "communism," the technical term for social transformation "in ways that reduce their willingness and ability to complement the industrial economies of the West," in the words of an important scholarly study of the 1950s.

In this broader framework, the Cold War can be understood, in large measure, as an in-

terlude in the North-South conflict of the Colombian era, unique in scale, but similar in
character to other episodes. The Third World
historian Leften Stavrianos observes, "made
its first appearance in Eastern Europe," which
began to provide raw ma-
terials for the growing tex-
tile and metal industries of
England and Holland as
far back as the 14th cen-
tury, then following the
(now familiar) path to-
wards underdevelopment
as trade and investment patterns took their
natural course.

Russia itself was so vast and militarily powerful that its subordination to the economy of
the West was delayed, but by the 19th century
it was well on the way towards the fate of the
South, with deep and widespread impoverish-
ment and foreign control of key sectors of the
economy. The Bolshevik takeover in October
1917, which quickly aborted the incipient socialist tendencies and destroyed any sem-
blance of working class or other popular organizations, extricated the USSR from the
Western dominated periphery, setting off the
inevitable reaction, beginning with immediate
military intervention. These were, from the
outset, the basic contours of the Cold War.

The logic was not fundamentally different
from the case of Grenada or Guatemala, but
the scale of the problem was. It was enhanced
after Russia's leading role in defeating Hitler
left it in control of Eastern—and parts of Central Europe, separating these regions, too,
from Western control. A tiny departure from
subordination is intolerable, a huge one far
less so, particularly when it threatens "stability" through the rotten apple effect.

Still more ominous was the fact that the in-
subordinate deviant was able to lend support
to those targeted for subversion or destruction
by the global enforcer, while its military capacity was so enormous as to deter U.S. intervention elsewhere. Under such circumstances,

"coexistence" is even more out of the question
than in the case of Guatemala, Chile, Grenada, Nicaragua, Laos, and so on. "Detente"
could be entertained as an option only if it en-
tailed Soviet withdrawal from the world scene.

*In the Western doctrinal system, democratic forms are accept-
able as long as they do not challenge business control. But they
are secondary: the real priority is integration into the global
economy with the opportunities this provides for exploitation
and plunder.*

As noted earlier, even as the Soviet Union
collapsed through the 1980s, the test of
Gorbachev's "New Thinking" was his willingness to allow the U.S. to have its way everywhere, without impediment. Failing that
criterion, his gestures are meaningless.

For such reasons, the U.S. rejected out of
hand Stalin's proposals for a unified and de-
militarized Germany with free elections in
1952, Khrushchev's call for reciprocal moves
after his radical cutbacks in Soviet military
forces and armaments in 1961-1963, Gorbachev's proposals for dismantling Cold War confrontation in the 1980s, indeed any possibility
of reduction of tension short of the return of
the miscreants to their service role.

The Soviet Union reached the peak of its
power by the late 1950s, always far behind the
West. The Cuban missile crisis, revealing extreme Soviet vulnerability, led to a huge increase in military spending, leveling off by the
late 1970s. The economy was then stagnating
and the autocracy unable to control internal
dissidence. By the 1980s, the system collapsed
and the core countries, always far richer and
more powerful, "won the Cold War."

Much of the Soviet empire was likely to return to its traditional Third World status, following something like the Latin American
model. A 1990 World Bank report describes
the outcome in these terms: "The Soviet Union and the People's Republic of China have
until recently been among the most prominent

examples of relatively successful countries that deliberately turned from the global economy," relying on their "vast size" to make "inward-looking development more feasible than it would be for most countries," but "they eventually decided to shift policies and take a more active part in the global economy."

A more accurate rendition would be that their "vast size" made it possible for them to withstand the refusal of the West to allow them to take part in the global economy on

> *Conforming to the general practice of the leading industrial societies, the EC refuses to lower the barriers erected to protect its own industry and agriculture, thus blocking exports from the East bloc that would enable them to reconstruct their economies*

terms other than traditional subordination. That is the "active part in the global economy" imposed on the South by the world rulers. Following the standard prescriptions, tendered in this case by Harvard economist Jeffrey Sachs, Poland has seen "the creation of many profitable private businesses," the knowledgeable analyst Abraham Brumberg observes, along with "a drop of nearly 40 percent in production, enormous hardships and social turmoil," and "the collapse of two governments."

In 1991 alone, gross domestic product (GDP) declined 8-10 percent with an 8 percent fall in investment and a near doubling of unemployment.

Russia has gone the same way. Economic and finance minister Yegor Galdar warned of a further drop of 20 percent in production in coming months, with the "worst period" still ahead. Light industrial production fell by 15-30 percent in the first 19 days of January while deliveries of meat, cereals, and milk fell by a third or more—and worse was predicted. The economies of Eastern Europe stagnated or declined through the 1980s, but went into free fall as the IMF regimen was adopted with the end of the Cold War in 1989.

By the fourth quarter of 1990, Bulgaria's industrial output (which had previously remained steady) had dropped 17 percent, Hungary's 12 percent, Poland's over 23 percent, and Romania's 30 percent. The UN Economic Commission for Europe expected a further decline of 20 percent for 1991, with the same or worse likely in 1992.

One result was a general disillusionment with the democratic opening and, in fact, growing support for the former Communist Parties.

In Russia, the economic collapse led to much suffering and deprivation, as well as "weariness, cynicism, and anger directed at all politicians, from Yeltsin down," Brumberg reports, and particularly at the ex-Nomenklatura who, not surprisingly, are taking on the role of Third World elites serving the interests of the foreign masters.

In public opinion polls, half the respondents considered the August 1991 Putsch illegal, one-fourth approved, and the rest had no opinion.

Support for democratic forces is limited, not because of opposition to democracy, but because of what it becomes under Western rules. It will either have the very special meaning dictated by Western needs or it will be the target of destabilization, subversion, strangulation, and violence until the proper "mode" and "standards" are restored. Exceptions to the pattern are rare.

Loss of faith in democracy is of small concern in the West, though the "bureaucratic capitalism" that might be introduced by the Communists-turned yuppies is considered a threat. In the Western doctrinal system, democratic forms are acceptable as long as they do not challenge business control. But they are secondary: the real priority is integration into the global economy with the opportunities this provides for exploitation and plunder.

With IMF backing, the European Community (EC) provided a clear test of good behavior for Eastern Europe: a demonstration that "economic liberalization with a view to introducing market economies" was irreversible. There could be no attempts at a "Third Way" with unacceptable social democratic features, let alone worker's control. The chief economic adviser to the EC, Richard Portes, defined acceptable "regime change" not in terms of democratic forms, but as "a definitive exit from the socialist planned economy and its irreversibility." One recent IMF report, Peter Gowan notes in *World Policy Journal*, "concentrates overwhelmingly on the Soviet Union's role as a producer of energy, raw materials, and agricultural products, giving very little scope for the republics of the former Soviet Union to play a major role as industrial powers in the world market." Transfer of ownership to employees, he notes, "has commanded strong popular support in both Poland and Czechoslovakia," but is unacceptable to the Western overseers, conflicting with the free market capitalism to which the South must be subjected.

Conforming to the general practice of the leading industrial societies, the EC refused to lower the barriers erected to protect its own industry and agriculture, thus blocking exports from the East bloc that would enable them to reconstruct their economies. When Poland removed all import barriers, Gowan notes, the EC refused to reciprocate, continuing to discriminate against half of Polish exports.

The EC steel lobby called for "restructuring" of the East European industry in a way that would incorporate it within the Western industry. The European chemical industry warned that construction of free market economies in the former Soviet empire "must not be at the expense of the long-term viability of Western Europe's own chemical industry." Of course, none of the state capitalist societies accepted the principle of free movement of la-

bor, a sine qua non of free market ideology. The errant Eastern European sectors of the Third World were to return to their service role. Their resources must be free for exploitation and they must provide cheap skilled labor for Western investors, supplying the markets of the core industrial societies.

The situation is reminiscent of Japan in the 1930s or of the Reagan-Bush Caribbean Basin Initiative, which encourages open export-oriented economies in the region while keeping U.S. protectionist barriers intact, undermining possible benefits of free trade for the targeted

> *Marchers claimed that U.S. troops had killed 3,000 people and buried many corpses in mass graves or thrown them into the sea. The economy has not recovered from the battering it received from the U.S. embargo and the destructive invasion.*

societies. As noted earlier, the patterns are as pervasive as they are understandable.

The U.S. has watched developments in Eastern Europe with some discomfort. Through the 1980s, it sought to impede the dissolution of the Soviet empire and East-West trade relations. Last August, George Bush urged Ukraine not to secede just before it proceeded to do so. One reason for this ambivalence is that after a decade of spend-and-borrow economic mismanagement, the U.S. is deeply in debt at every level: federal, state, corporate, household, and the incalculable debt of unmet social and infrastructure needs. It is not well-placed to join German-led Europe and Japan in the project of despoiling the newly opening sectors of the South.

Some Free Market Successes

It would only be fair, however, to add that the IMF/World Bank recipe now being imposed upon the former Soviet empire has its successes, at least in Latin America. Bolivia is a highly-touted triumph, its economy rescued from disaster by the harsh but necessary stabilization program prescribed by its expert advisers, now plying their craft in Eastern Europe (notably, Jeffrey Sachs). Public employment was sharply cut, the national mining company was sold off leading to massive unemployment of miners, real wages dropped, rural teachers quit in droves, regressive taxes were introduced, the economy shrank as has productive investment, and inequality increased. In the capital, economist Melvin Burke writes in *Current History,* "street vendors and beggars contrast with the fancy boutiques, posh hotels, and Mercedes-Benzes." Real per capita GNP is three-fourths what it was in 1980, and foreign debt absorbs 30 percent of export earnings. As a reward for this economic miracle, the IMF, Interamerican Development Bank, and Paris Club of creditor governments (G-7) offered Bolivia extensive financial assistance, including secret salary payments to government ministers to make up for their reduced incomes.

The successes are that prices stabilized and exports are booming. About two-thirds of the export earnings are now derived from coca production and trade, Burke estimates. Drug money explains the stabilization of currency and price levels, he concludes. About 80 percent of the $3 billion in annual drug profits is spent and banked abroad, mainly in the U.S., providing a lift to the U.S. economy as well. Drug launderers and bankers, needless to say, are not targets of the U.S.-sponsored drug war.

This profitable export business "obviously serves the interests of the new illegitimate bourgeoisie and the 'narcogenerals' of Bolivia," and "also apparently serves the U.S. national interest, inasmuch as money laundering has not only been tolerated by the United States but has, in fact, been encouraged." It is "the poor peasant coca growers" who "struggle to survive against the combined armed might of the United States and the Bolivian military," Burke writes. There are always more to ensure that the economic miracle will continue, with the applause of international economists. Achievements have also been recorded else-

where, thanks to timely U.S. intervention and expert management.

Take Grenada. After its liberation in 1983, it became the largest per capita recipient of U.S. aid (after Israel, a special case), as the Reagan administration proceeded to make it a "showcase for capitalism." The austerity programs brought with them the usual disaster, condemned even by the private sector they were designed to benefit. But there is one bright spot in a generally dismal picture, Ron Suskind reports in a front-page *Wall Street Journal* article headlined "Made Safe by Marines, Grenada Now is Haven for Offshore Banks." The economy may be "in terrible economic shape," as the head of a local investment firm and member of Parliament observed—thanks to USAID-run structural adjustment programs, the *Journal* fails to add. But the capital, St. George, "has become the Casablanca of the Caribbean, a fast-growing haven for money laundering, tax evasion, and assorted financial fraud," with 118 offshore banks, one for every 64 residents. Lawyers, accountants, and some businesspeople are doing well, as, doubtless, are the foreign bankers, money launderers, and drug lords.

The U.S. liberation of Panama recorded a similar triumph. Guillermo Endara, sworn in as president at a U.S. military base on the day of the invasion, would receive 2.4 percent of the vote if an election were held, recent polls indicate. His government designated the second anniversary of the U.S. invasion as a "national day of reflection."

Thousands of Panamanians "marked the day with a 'black march' through the streets of this capital to denounce the U.S. invasion and the Endara economic policies," the French press agency reported. Marchers claimed that U.S. troops had killed 3,000 people and buried many corpses in mass graves or thrown them into the sea. The economy had not recovered from the battering it received from the U.S. embargo and the destructive invasion. But some indicators were up. The General Accounting Office reported that drug trafficking "may have doubled" since the invasion while money laundering has "flourished," as was predicted at once by everyone who paid attention to the practices and commitments of the tiny white elite whom the U.S. restored to their traditional rule. Increased drug trafficking and the economic crisis have also contributed to "an unprecedented increase in drug consumption, especially among the poor and the young," the *Christian Science Monitor* reports. Another triumph of free market democracy was recorded in Nicaragua.

Ambassador Harry Shlaudeman had recently signed accords opening the way for the U.S. Drug Enforcement Agency (DEA) to operate in Nicaragua "in an attempt to control the growing drug trafficking problem" (*Central America Report, Guatemala*). The DEA agent in Costa Rica declared that Nicaragua is now "being used as a corridor for transferring Colombian cocaine to the United States" and a Department of Justice prosecutor added that the Nicaraguan financial system was laundering drug money. There was also a growing drug epidemic in Nicaragua, fueled by the high level of drug use by returnees from Miami, as well as the continued economic decline and the new avenues for drug trafficking after the U.S. regained control. "Since the installation of the Chamorro government and the massive return of Nicaraguans from Miami," CAR reports, "drug consumption has increased substantially in a country long free from drug usage."

Miskito leader Steadman Fagoth accused two members of the Cham- orro cabinet—his former contra associate Brooklyn Rivera and the minister of fishing for the Atlantic Coast—of working for the Colombian cartels. The Nicaraguan delegate to the Ninth International Conference on the Control of Drug trafficking in Colombia in April 1991 alleged that Nicaragua "has now become a leading

link in cocaine shipments to the U.S. and Europe."

A conference attended by government officials and nongovernmental organizations in Managua in August 1991 concluded that the country had 250,000 addicts and was becoming an international bridge for drug transport, though the rate of addiction is still below the rest of Central America (400,000 addicts in Costa Rica, 450,000 in Guatemala, 500,000 in El Salvador). Nicaraguan addiction was increasing among young people, particularly with the return of many from years in Miami. A conference organizer commented that, "In 1986 there wasn't one reported case of hard drugs consumption" while "in 1990, there were at least 12,000 cases." One hundred

> *A conference attended by government officials and non-governmental organizations in Managua in August 1991 concluded that the country had 250,000 addicts and was becoming an international bridge for drug transport*

eighteen drug dealing operations were identified in Managua alone, though it was the Atlantic Coast that had become the international transit point for hard drugs, with increasing addiction there as a consequence.

U.S. journalist Nancy Nusser reported from Managua that cocaine had become "readily available only since president Violeta Chamorro took office in April 1990," according to dealers. "There wasn't any coke during the Sandinistas' time, just marijuana," one dealer said. Carlos Hurtado, currently Minister of Government, said that "the phenomenon of cocaine trafficking existed before, but at a low level." Now it was burgeoning, primarily through the Atlantic Coast, according to "a ranking Western diplomat with knowledge of drug trafficking" (probably from the U.S. Embassy), who describes the Coast now as "a no man's land."

Drugs are becoming "the newest growth industry in Central America," CAR reported, as a result of the "severe economic conditions in which 85 percent of the Central American population live in poverty" and the lack of jobs, particularly in neoliberal Nicaragua. But the problem had not reached the level of Colombia where security forces armed and trained by the U.S. were continuing, perhaps even escalating their rampage of terror, torture, and disappearances, targeting political opposition figures, community activists, trade union leaders, human rights workers, and the peasant communities while U.S. aid "is furthering the corruption of the Colombian security forces and strengthening the alliance of blood between right-wing politicians, military officers, and ruthless narcotics traffickers," according to human rights activist Jorge Gomez Lizarazo, a former judge. The situation in Peru was still worse.

These are only symptoms of a much deeper malaise in Latin America and in the South more generally. They suggest that Year 501 and what follows will be a classic case of Old Wines, New Bottles: traditional policies adapted to new contingencies.

A change of lasting importance was recognized officially in August 1971 when Richard Nixon announced his "New Economic Policy," dismantling the international economic order established after World War II (the Breton Woods system), in which the U.S. served, in effect, as international banker. By the time "the affluent alliance had come to the end of the road" and "the disorder was getting too serious for aspirins," international economist Susan Strange observed. German-led Europe and Japan had recovered from wartime destruction, thanks in no small part to U.S. international military Keynesian measures from the early 1950s. The U.S. economy was facing the unanticipated economic costs of the Vietnam War. The world economy was entering an era of "tripolarity"—and also, crucially, of stagnation and declining profitability of capital.

The End of the Affluent Alliance

The predictable reaction was a rapid intensification of the bitter class war that is waged with unremitting dedication by the corporate sector, its political agents, and ideological servants. The years that followed saw an attack on real wages, social services, and unions—indeed any kind of functioning democratic structure—so as to overcome the troublesome "crisis of democracy" brought about by the "illegitimate" efforts of the public to bring their interests to the arena of democratic politics. These moves were accompanied by an intensified ideological offensive to strengthen authority and habits of obedience, to diminish social consciousness and such human frailties as concern for others, and to instruct young people that they partake in a "culture of narcissism."

Another objective was to establish a de facto government insulated from popular awareness or interference, devoted to the task of ensuring that the world's human and material resources were freely available to the Transnational Corporations (TNCs) and international banks that are to control the global system. The U.S. remains the largest single economy, though declining relative to its major rivals, which are not without their own problems.

Nixon's response to the decline of U.S. economic hegemony was to suspend the convertibility of the dollar to gold, to impose temporary wage-price controls and a general import surcharge and to initiate fiscal measures that direct state power, beyond the previous norm, to welfare for the rich: reduction of federal taxes and domestic expenditures, apart from the required subsidies to the corporate sector.

These have been the guiding policies since. They were accelerated during the Reagan years, largely following the Carter administration prescriptions that were reshaped to bring about a huge growth in debt at every level (federal, state, local, household, corporate), with little to show in the way of productive investment. One crucial element is the incalculable debt of unmet social needs, a mounting burden imposed on the large majority of the population and future generations.

Nixon's initiatives constituted "a sort of mercantilist revolution in domestic and foreign policy," political economist David Calleo observed a few years later. The international system grew more disorderly, less regulated, "with rules eroded and power more significant." There was less "rational control over national economic life," hence great advantages to internationalist business and banking, freed from capital controls and official restraint and secure in the knowledge that there would be a state-organized public bail-out if something went wrong. International capital markets rapidly expanded as a consequence of the decline of regulation and control, the huge flow of petrodollars after the 1973-1974 oil price rise, and the information/telecommunications revolution, which greatly facilitated capital transfers.

Vigorous bank initiatives to stimulate new borrowing contributed to the Third World debt crisis and the instability of the banks themselves. The outcome has been described as "a system of world economic governance with parameters defined by the unregulated market and rules administered by supranational banks and corporations" (Howard Wachtel), a system of "corporate mercantilism (Peter Phillips), with managed commercial interactions within and among huge corporate groupings and regular state intervention in the three major Northern blocs to subsidize and protect domestically-based international corporations and financial institutions.

The rise in oil prices (preceded by comparable increases in price of coal, uranium, and U.S. agricultural exports) yielded temporary advantages for the U.S. and British economies, providing windfall profits for the energy corporations, primarily U.S. and British, and inducing them to bring into production high-cost oil (Alaska, North Sea) that had been withheld from the market. For the U.S., rising energy costs were substantially compen-

> *Vigorous bank initiatives to stimulate new borrowing contributed to the Third World debt crisis and the instability of the banks themselves. The outcome has been described as "a system of world economic governance with parameters defined by the unregulated market and rules administered by supranational banks and corporations..."*

sated by military and other exports to the Middle East oil producers and construction projects for them.

Their profits also flowed to Treasury securities and investment and support for the economies of the U.S. and its British lieutenant had long been the primary responsibility of the family dictatorships that served as local managers in the Middle East.

The same years saw the stagnation and collapse of the Soviet Empire, which had interfered with the planned global order in several crucial ways. It excluded a vast region of the traditional Third World from Western exploitation and control. Its very existence as a counterforce provided space for non-alignment and limited forms of independent initiatives in the regions still bound to the traditional service function of the South—providing resources, markets, cheap labor, opportunities for investment, and, more recently, export of pollution.

With the Soviet collapse, both problems were overcome. The power of the state capitalist industrial societies was enhanced further by the economic catastrophe that swept through most of their domains in the 1980s. The sense of foreboding throughout the Third World was readily understandable.

In earlier years, the nonaligned countries had sought to gain some control over their fate. Initiatives were developed through UNCTAD (the Conference on Trade and Development) to create a "new international economic order" with support and stabilization programs for primary commodities, in the hope of stemming the deterioration in terms of trade and controlling the sharp price fluctuations that have a devastating impact on economies that rely on few primary exports. UNESCO undertook parallel efforts to provide Third World countries with access to international communications, a virtual monopoly of the advanced industrial societies.

Both initiatives naturally elicited enormous hostility from world rulers; both were turned back decisively in the 1980s. The U.S. led a fierce attack on the United Nations that effectively eliminated it as an independent force in world affairs. UNESCO inspired particular hatred because of its Third World orientation and its threat to U.S. ideological domination. The demolition operation and the return of the UN to U.S. control has been lauded here as a restoration of the ideals of the founders.

The extraordinary levels of deceit that accompanied the government-media campaign to extirpate the UNESCO heresies are documented in an important book, which, needless to say, had no effect whatsoever on the flow of

> The UN Economic Commission for Africa found that countries pursuing the recommended IMF programs had lower growth rates than those that relied on the public sector for basic human needs.

necessary lies (William Preston, Edward Herman, Herbert Schiller, *Hope & Folly*, University of Minnesota press, 1989). The current hysteria about "political correctness" is a domestic analog; to the totalitarian mentality, even the slightest loss of control is an unimaginable catastrophe and evokes the most impressive frenzy.

Some of the realities are described in a study of the South Commission, which brings together economists, government planners, religious leaders, and other Third World elites (*The Challenge to the South*). The study observes that gestures to Third World concerns in the 1970s were "undoubtedly spurred" by concern over "the newly found assertiveness of the South after the rise in oil prices in 1973." As the threat abated, the rich lost interest and turned to "a new form of neo-colonialism," monopolizing their control over the world economy, undermining the more democratic elements of the United Nations, and, in general, proceeding to institutionalize "the South's second class status."

Vile Maxim of the Masters

The world economy has not returned to the growth rates of the Bretton Woods era. The decline of the South was particularly severe in Africa and Latin America where it was accompanied by rampant state terror. The catastrophe was accelerated by the neoliberal economic doctrines dictated by the world rulers. The UN Economic Commission for Africa found that countries pursuing the recommended IMF programs had lower growth rates than those that relied on the public sector for basic human needs. The disastrous impact of neoliberal policies in Latin America was striking, heightened by the openness of their economies which allow no such frivolity.

There is a technical term for the predictable effects of the dictates of the powerful. They are called "economic miracles"—meaning, improvement of the investment climate and the prospects for domestic elites associated with the foreign beneficiaries, along with rapid increase in poverty, starvation, and general misery for the undeserving public. Another concomitant is great satisfaction and self-adulation in the commissar culture.

Meanwhile, the same state authorities and their minions preach ruinous economic doctrines and block the way to independent development in the South, and in numerous other ways ensure that wealth and power centralize among the truly deserving in the corporate board rooms. It is not their business that the doctrines they preach have regularly been evaded when necessary by the visitors in the game while punishing those subjected to these dogmas, once again through the 1980s.

Approved doctrine holds that the "trickle down" and "export promotion" policies that have always led to disaster in the past will succeed today. And they will, for the usual beneficiaries who run the process and understand it well enough. The basic truth is captured in the headline of a lead article in the *Wall Street Journal* on the initial social costs" of the "shock therapy" administered by their benefactors: "People Say the New Wealth Is Slow to Trickle Down; Leaders: Stay the Course."

On the occasion, developed societies, too, take the rhetoric seriously and fail to protect themselves from the destructive impact of unregulated markets. The consequences are the same, though not so lethal as in the traditional colonial domains. Australia in the 1980s is a case in point. Deregulation and other free market experiments (carried out by a labor government that adopted the prescriptions of the right) created what one leading economic commentator calls a "capital disaster" (journalist Tom Fitzgerald).

The approved policies succeeded in reducing national income by over 5 percent a year by the end of the decade. Real wages declined. Australian enterprises fell under foreign control and the country advanced towards the status of a resource base for the Japan-centered state capitalist region, which maintained its dynamic growth, thanks to radical departures from neoliberal dogma.

Fitzgerald observed that nothing different should be expected from selective obeisance to Adam Smith, ignoring his warnings about "the vile maxim of the masters: All for themselves and nothing for other people."

The rich industrial societies themselves are taking on something of a Third World cast, with islands of extreme wealth and privilege amidst a rising sea of poverty and despair. This is particularly true of the U.S. and Britain, subjected to Reagan-Thatcher discipline. Continental Europe is not too far behind, despite the residual power of labor and the social contract it had defended, and Europe's ability to export its slums through the device of "guestworkers." The distribution of privilege and despair in a society with the enormous advantages of ours is not, of course, what one finds in Brazil or Mexico. But the tendencies are not hard to see.

The collapse of the Soviet empire offers new means to establish the North-South divide more firmly within the rich societies. During the May 1992 strike of public workers in Germany, the chair of Daimler-Benz warned that the corporation might respond to strikes of production workers by transferring manufacturing facilities for its Mercedes cars elsewhere, perhaps to Russia with its ample supply of trained, educated, healthy, and (it is hoped) docile workers. The chair of General Motors can wield similar threats with regard to Mexico and other sectors of the Third World that remain economic colonies of the West and, thus, do not offer as favorable a work force. Capital can readily move; people cannot, or are not permitted to.

It is not that Daimler-Benz is greatly suffering from the labor costs that management deplores. Two weeks after issuing the threat to move Mercedes production to Russia, the same chief executive, Edzard Reuter, announced the "excellent result" of an exceptionally strong first quarter performance for 1992, with a profit rise of a 14 and 16 percent increase in sales, largely abroad. German workers are not quite the intended market for the Mercedes division, the chief profit earner for this huge conglomerates.

Such facts, however, do not impress the U.S. press where the news columns bitterly assailed the strikers for the "soft life," long vacations, and general lack of understanding of their proper place as tools of production for the rich and powerful. They should learn the lessons taught to American workers by the Caterpillar Corporation—profits and productivity up, wages down, the right to strike effectively eliminated by the free resort to "permanent replacement workers."

Class Warfare Ideology

These are the fruits of the fierce corporate campaign undertaken as soon as American workers finally won the right to organize in the mid-1930s, after long years of bitter struggle and violent repression unmatched in the industrial world. Perhaps we may even return to the days when the admired philanthropist Andrew Carnegie could preach the virtues of "honest, industrious, self-denying poverty" to the victims of the great depression of 1896, shortly after he had brutally crushed the Homestead steel strike to great media applause, while announcing that the defeated workers had sent him a wire saying "Kind master, tell us what you wish us to do and we will do it for you." It was because he knew "how sweet and happy and pure the home of honest poverty is" that Carnegie sympathized with the poor, he explained, meanwhile sharing their grim fate in his lavishly appointed mansions. So a well-ordered society should run, according to the "vile maxim of the masters."

It is, therefore, only natural that when the battered unions finally recognized the reality of the ceaseless class war waged against them by the highly class-conscious corporate sector, the business press should react with wonder at the fact that some unions still cling to outdated "class warfare ideology" and the "battered Marxist view" that "workers form a class of citizens with shared interests separate from those who own and control business"—not to speak of such "quirks" as low pay for executives who are treated like other members (*New York Times*). The masters, in contrast, keep firmly to this "battered Marxist view," often expressing it in vulgar Marxist rhetoric—with values reversed, of course.

Under existing conditions of social organization and concentration of power, selective free trade is hardly likely to increase the general welfare, as it might under other social arrangements. The two-year experience of the U.S.-Canada free trade agreement illustrates the process. Canada lost hundreds of thousands of jobs, many to industrialized regions of the U.S. where government regulations virtually bar labor organizing (the Orwellian term is "right to work," meaning "effectively illegal to organize"). These state policies, natural in a business-run society with the public largely marginalized, leave workers unprotected and much easier to exploit than Canada, with its more vigorous union movement and its cultural climate of solidarity.

The agreement has also been used to require Canada to sell water to the U.S. even in times of local water scarcity; to abandon measures to protect the threatened Pacific salmon; to bring pesticide regulations in line with laxer U.S. standards; to ban the sale of irradiated food and steps to reduce emissions from lead, zinc, and copper smelters; and to end subsidies for replanting forests after logging. All such practices have been judged illegal barriers to free trade. By similar reasoning, the U.S. objects to a GATT provision that allows countries to restrict food exports in times of need, demanding that U.S. agribusiness must control raw materials no matter what the human cost.

At the same time, Canada, an asbestos exporter, is bringing charges against the U.S. for imposing EPA standards on asbestos use in violation of trade commitments and the "international scientific evidence" about health risks of asbestos. The EPA has improperly gone beyond the "least burdensome requirements" for the corporations, Canada claims. At the

GATT negotiations, the U.S. backed corporate proposals to restrict environmental and consumer protection to cases supported by "scientific evidence" to be judged by an agency made up of government officials and executives from chemical and food corporations.

Perhaps the most dramatic current examples of the cynical pursuit of the "vile maxim" in international trade are the U.S. government and GATT actions to force Third World countries to accept U.S. exports and advertising for lethal narcotics—the world champion being tobacco, by a huge margin. The Bush administration launched its hypocritical "drug war" (timed nicely to produce the proper mood for the invasion of Panama) simultaneously with steps to force Third World countries to import this leading killer, with advertising aimed at women and children particularly. GATT backed these murderous efforts.

> *Current social policy in the U.S. is to coop them up in urban centers where they can prey on one another; or to lock them in jail, often for such crimes as possession of hard drugs, another useful concomitant of the drug war*

The media, while climbing aboard the "drug war" bandwagon with appropriate fanfare, obliged the Administration further by suppressing the major drug story of the day. There were no headlines reading "U.S. Demands to be World's Leading Narcotrafficker"—or even a line in the back pages. The discipline was impressive.

With Eastern Europe returning to its approved Third World status, drug pushers led the way in investment. "Cigarette makers flock to E. Europe," an upbeat front-page story was headlined in the *Boston Globe*: "While many American companies have been criticized for not being aggressive in investing in Eastern Europe, American cigarette companies have been trailblazers." Doubtless reveling in the applause for aggressively responding to U.S. government efforts to encourage investment in Western Europe, a tobacco executive explains. "There is little awareness of health and environmental problems in Hungary. We have about ten years of an open playing field. We have ten years of profits before the PC left fascists impose conditions on lucrative mass murder. Of 30 developed countries," the news report reads, "life expectancy is shortest in Eastern Europe." Guided by the vile maxim, U.S. corporations will try to improve the statistics further—trailblazers for capitalism, free from criticism. In the same issue of the *Boston Globe*, another story illustrates how supple an instrument economic doctrine can be. It celebrates the achievements of New Hampshire in dealing with its fiscal problems. Their method was to encourage a successful enterprise that became "the largest retail volume outlet for wine and liquor in the world, according to state officials," with $62 million in profits from sales of over $200 million in 1991, a $5 million increase in profit in a year. The increase is attributed in part to doubling the advertising budget for alcohol, which ranks just below tobacco as a killer.

The enterprise is a state monopoly. Hence, its profits allow the most conservative state in the union to keep to the free market doctrines its leaders revere and to avoid taxes that would rob the wealthy to "enrich welfare mothers." Another free market triumph, unnoticed.

In theory, free trade arrangements should lower wages in high-wage countries and raise them in the poorer areas to which capital shifts, increasing global equity. But in prevailing conditions, a different outcome is likely. The senior economist at the Environment Department of the World Bank, Herman Daly, points out that the vast and growing supply of underemployed people in the Third World will "keep the supply of labor very large and will make it impossible for wages worldwide to be raised up very much." The effect will be huge profits and elimination of high wages and social gains, including laws against child labor, limits on working hours, and protection of the environment. "Anything that raises costs [is] going to tend to be competed down to the lowest common denominator in free international trade"—precisely the intended outcome.

Under the prevailing conditions of power and control, free trade will tend to drive the level of existence to the lowest grade for people who are spectators, not participants in the decisions that affect their lives.

Overall, the 1980s accelerated a global rift between a small sector enjoying great privilege and a growing mass of people suffering deprivation and misery. Though superfluous for wealth production or consumption, the only human functions recognized in the dominant institutions and their ideology, they must be dealt with somehow. Current social policy in the U.S. is to coop them up in urban centers where they can prey on one another; or to lock them in jail, often for such crimes as possession of hard drugs, another useful concomitant of the drug war. The latter policies have the further merit of providing a Keynesian stimulation to the economy through booming prison construction and employment for security guards, the fastest growing white collar profession.

The maxim "All for themselves and nothing for other people" requires a slight amendment: "all for themselves now." The longer term is as irrelevant as other people. Thus, in a lead news story, the *Wall Street Journal* hails Bush's "extraordinary coup" in compelling the entire world to abandon plans for a meaningful agreement on greenhouse gases at the June Rio conference (the official reason for the U.S. demand for empty verbiage is that a treaty would impede "growth"—like "jobs," a code word meaning "profits").

The internationalization of capital has accelerated since 1971, giving a somewhat new character to competition among national states. To cite one indication, while the U.S. share in world manufactured exports declined 3.5 percent from 1966 to 1984, the share of U.S.-based TNCs slightly increased. International trade patterns yield a very different picture if imports from overseas subsidiaries are counted as domestic production.

Commercial products reflect these tendencies. For example, almost a third of the market price of a GM Pontiac Le Mans goes to producers in South Korea, over a sixth to Japan, about the same to a combination of Germany, Singapore, Britain, Barbados, and others. As a geographical entity, the country and most of its population may decline, but the corporate empires are playing a different game. With between one-fourth and one-half of world trade already conducted within North-based TNCs, these are factors of growing importance as we look towards Year 501.

From Z Magazine, *March 1992 (Part 1)*
Volume 5, Number 3;
July/August 1992 (Part 2)
Volume 5, Number 7/8

2.

The Global Empire

By Edward S. Herman

DURING THE YEARS of disintegration of the Soviet bloc, numerous articles in the mainstream media referred to the ongoing collapse of the Soviet "empire." The same media never apply the word empire to the U.S. (or other western dominated) client

> *...the New World Order (NWO) gives daily manifestations that a new, more centralized, sophisticated, but blatantly hypocritical phase of imperialism has evolved in which trade, aid, loans, debt management, proxy armies, techno-wars, and international "law" are deployed to keep Third World countries in a dependent status*

states. By ideological premise these are free and, at most, temporarily advised, aided, threatened, and occupied until the natives are ready for self-rule and responsible leaders are in place.

This word avoidance is actually quite comic, as the New World Order (NWO) gives daily manifestations that a new, more centralized, sophisticated, but blatantly hypocritical phase of imperialism has evolved in which trade, aid, loans, debt management, proxy armies, techno-wars, and international "law" are deployed to keep Third World countries in a dependent status. Free World imperialism has been extended to a virtually global regime with the dismantlement of the Soviet Union and "Yeltsinization" of Russia; i.e., the deliberate rendering of Russia into an economic basket case by radical and unworkable "reforms," which are enforced as the condition of aid by the IMF and imperial powers, and which, in effect, ensures the planned return of Russia to a dependency status.

With the collapse of the former Soviet Union, the principal obstacle to the First World's use of force against the Third World has disappeared and the UN system has once again become serviceable in the cause of freedom. In short, a higher stage of "the highest stage" of capitalism has been reached. The new system is now working very well to quash or prevent the emergence of Third World leaders and movements that might embark on an independent course of development.

Michael Manley, recently retired from office in Jamaica, points out that social reform has become impracticable, with Jamaica desperate for foreign exchange and "strapped up to its eyeballs, totally dependent on an IMF that's more powerful than ever." His own earlier experiment in reform was undermined by Reagan policies, as well as normal market forces, and the more mature Manley, returning to office in 1989, opted to accept the constraints of the NWO and eschew any attempt at progressive politics. He now not only regards these constraints as inescapable, he has surrendered spiritually, as well as in practice, to the new realism. He contends that, "The market is the guarantee that you will attain the necessary level of competitive efficiency to be able to survive in a world market," (Jack Heyman, "Jamaica's Manley converts to 'free marketeer'," *Guardian*, February 12, 1992).

The Imperialism of Free Trade

A notable article by John Gallagher and Ronald Robinson entitled, "The Imperialism of Free Trade" (*Economic History Review*, 1953), stressed the importance of "economic dependence and mutual good-feeling" as the basis for domination of less developed countries (LDCs) by imperial powers. Trade, loans, dependence on ports and markets, investment in and control over railroads and other forms of communication, produced an "informal paramountcy" over LDCs. This was frequently confirmed by a "treaty of free trade and friendship made or imposed on a weaker state," which was perhaps "the most common political technique of British empire." Technical, marketing, and financial dependency were supplemented by the political influence of local comprador elements. Once the LDC's economy became dependent on foreign trade, "the classes whose prosperity was drawn from the trade normally worked themselves in local politics to preserve the local political conditions needed for it." Gallagher and Robinson emphasized that intervention was only a supplement to a dominant influence that normally flowed from free market forces. Force by the imperial power would be required only when local polities "fail to provide satisfactory conditions for commercial or strategic integration." Subsequent analyses have added the consideration that economic penetration and marketing has brought LDC elites into a new social nexus, including acculturation to the advanced consumerism of the First World. "Denationalization" of elites in Latin America thus took the two-fold form of working for foreigners and representing their interests, and absorption in the foreigner's culture and repudiation of one's own.

The so-called "international demonstration effect" followed from the latter and was characterized by a gradual shift of elite purchases to high style foreign imports. This weakened domestic industry and, via enlarging imports, made for balance of payments difficulties, enlarged debt, and increased dependency. Some analysts have pointed to the contrast between the Latin American and Japanese elites in this respect. For many decades the latter rejected denationalization in both its aspects. This helped preserve Japanese economic and cultural autonomy and contributed to their ability to take off into sustained economic growth.

The United States and other great powers also "manage" trade via tariffs, quotas, subsidies, harassment, and seizure of imports, threats of retaliation, and boycotts. Much of this management is done under the guise of combating somebody else's "unfair trade." Thus, beyond the power stemming from the dependency relations of normal trade flows, the great powers manipulate the trade environment with "bilateral initiatives based on bullying smaller trading partners" (Robert Hudec, in Bhagwati and Patrick, *Aggressive Unilateralism*).

The Aid System

Government aid has long been deployed to supplement private trade and financing. In the post-World War II era this was improved and given international sanction by the creation of major international lending institutions, including the World Bank, International Monetary Fund (IMF), and Inter-American Development Bank, all dominated by the United States. Given U.S. power, U.S. hostility to a small country has traditionally resulted not only in the cutoff of direct U.S. aid, but defunding on the part of "international" institutions and then by private finance. When added to "managed trade" attacks, the pressures on small countries through these economic channels can be very severe.

On the other hand, states meeting U.S.-IMF-World Bank standards are treated generously. The criteria of acceptability are a suitable degree of political subservience and policy choices that, as Gallagher and Robinson described in connection with imperial policy in general, "provide satisfactory conditions for commercial or strategic integration." Such policies: namely, establishment of an open economy, privatization, a stress on raw materials exports, protection of the rights of foreign investors, cutbacks in social budgets, and devotion to inflation control, are the elements of Structural Adjustment Programs (SAPs), implemented by IMF enforcers and missionaries. James Morgan, an economics correspondent for BBC World Services compares

SAP to the "word of God" dispensed by missionaries going out from Western Europe to visit the barbarians in the Middle Ages.

SAPs have often been implemented by terror states that were the ultimate in non-democracy. But aid and bank funding flowed their way. Nicaragua, pursuing the "logic of the majority" in the early 1980s, was quickly defunded and even put on a Free World hit list. Argentina under the generals after 1976 murdered thousands, but received lots of Free World money. Marcos, Pinochet, and the Brazilian generals after the 1964 coup met the twofold criteria of freedom noted above: economic freedom and adherence to the proper rules of behavior in Third World countries

> *When added to "managed trade" attacks, the pressures on small countries through these economic channels can be very severe. On the other hand, states meeting U.S.-IMF-World Bank standards are treated generously.*

(which would coincidentally make them serviceable to the needs of the First World). The needs and demands of the local majority are irrelevant in this system and, in fact, a willingness to resist demands for change in the face of mass pain and suffering is an important part of the obligations of qualified leaders. In this framework, we can see that Yeltsin is now the IMF "hit man," who inflicts pain on the general population as virtual agent of the West—as Pinochet and Marcos did before him—with much of his power now resulting from the fact that the aid is conditioned on Yeltsin's retaining authority and preserving the "confidence" of the West.

Structural "reform" funded by "aid" can move only in one direction. If it were designed to advance social democracy, confidence would sag, funding would dry up, and the leaders pursuing such outlandish ends would become demagogues and perhaps even qualify for destabilization.

The Subversion System

Subversion is an invidious word which the mainstream media and intelligentsia rarely, if ever, apply to their own government about acts by the United States that would be gross subversion if done by others, but which are normalized in the U.S. media. Most notable was the arming, training and brainwashing of Latin American police and military from the 1950s onward, to reorient them to U.S. needs and provide a counterweight to populist and radical movements at home. This was followed by the rapid proliferation of military dictatorships, death squads, torture, and disappearances on a continent-wide basis in our most closely watched sphere of influence. Brazil in the early 1960s is a classic case (see Jan Black's *United States Penetration of Brazil*), where the United States operated as a quasi-occupying power in this supposedly sovereign country, the largest in Latin America.

The U.S. Embassy expected to be consulted on major decisions. The United States subsidized hundreds of politicians, intellectuals, and journalists, organized think tanks, bought space in newspapers, and established close relations with a significant segment of the military establishment and other security forces. It was a virtual partner in the 1964 coup and the generals expressed their deepest appreciation and loyalty to the Godfather in the years that followed. In lesser client states, U.S. intervention in policy-making and manipulation of the political environment was equally or more blatant,

> *In lesser client states, U.S. intervention in policy-making and manipulation of the political environment is equally or more blatant, but it is treated in low key and as "natural" in the mainstream media*

tant, but it was treated as "natural" in the mainstream media. For example, while U.S. law prohibits foreigners from funding and organizing our elections, U.S. intrusions in the Nicaraguan elections of 1984 and 1990 were treated as perfectly legitimate in what we must call the "journalism of imperialism."

The Proxy Army System

In addition to subversion by the provision of "military aid and training," proxy forces may be organized and funded to attack a target country whose military forces are not easily weaned to counterrevolution. This was the case in Nicaragua after July 19, 1979, where the United States had to make do with Somoza National Guard remnants in Honduras, supplemented by mercenary recruitment, just as it used the Chinese Nationalist Army remnants in Burma after 1949 to harass China, and the Khmer Rouge and its allies in Thailand to attack Cambodia after 1979.

As is well known, U.S. support automatically makes these proxies "freedom fighters," as opposed to terrorists. It is also clear that any ruling by the World Court declaring the proxy army system illegal in a particular case (unlikely in the new NWO) would render the Court momentarily a "hostile forum" that could be reasonably ignored.

The Techno-War Option

Panama in 1989 and Iraq in 1991 demonstrated the efficacy of a short, capital intensive assault as a useful imperial option for displacing a disobedient leader (Panama) or reducing to the stone age the society of a disobedient and threatening one (Iraq). The option has been made more viable by the disappearance of the Soviet Threat (i.e., Soviet constraint), the associated return of the UN system from demagoguery to reasonableness and utility, and mastery of the art of the short war that minimizes U.S. casualties while providing the media and public with a modern version of the Roman circus (with bombs dropped on "mere gooks," Arabs, etc., instead of barbarians/Christians being fed to lions).

The New Imperial System

A crowning touch to the new imperial system has been its refurbished base and legitimation in imperial law. First, there was the reconquest of the Security Council, with the demise of the Soviet Union eliminating the threat of a veto and the virtual dependency status of the members assuring a majority vote in favor of proposals by the United States and its eager British Tory ally. Iraq can be devastated and starved by the United States under UN auspices. At the same time, the United States can protect its Israeli client from enforcement of a long-standing Security Council Resolution (242) condemning Israel's illegal occupation of territory, and can veto or simply ignore a Security Council vote condemning its invasion and occupation of Panama.

In a further development of imperialist legality, the World Court, which challenged U.S. direct and sponsored terrorism against Nicaragua in 1986 (albeit without effect), dismissed Libya's appeal to international law which, according to the Montreal Convention of 1971, appeared to give Libya certain options in handling the case of its two citizens accused of involvement in the Pan Am 103 bombing. The World Court now declares that a Security Council resolution supersedes international law. This rounds out the legal system of the NWO nicely.

The centralization of the new imperial order, which dates from 1945, has been strengthened by the Soviet collapse and Chinese counterrevolution. It has been weakened somewhat by the economic disabilities of the United States and the rise in economic strength of Japan and Germany. But the United States is still far and away the largest and most diversified economy, has the largest aid budget, and dominates the international lending institutions. Its huge investment in military power, and the relatively small Japanese and German military establishments, continue to give the United States preeminent power and considerable discretion in dealing with Third World countries. The Gulf War displayed the structure of power as Germany and Japan were compelled to support and even help fund U.S. actions damaging to their own interests.

It is likely that imperialist rivalries will intensify and that Germany and Japan will have a larger imperial role in the future, along with other countries of increasing economic importance. At present, however, the centralization of imperial power and the ability of the United States to push small countries around are as great as ever. Taking into account the entire arsenal of instruments of empire, the forces constraining and threatening Third World governments are at a new peak of efficiency and imperialism has moved beyond the "highest stage."

From Z **Magazine,** *July/August 1992*
Volume 5, Number 7/8

3.

Suppression of Indigenous Sovereignty in 20th Century U.S.

By Ward Churchill

A
S THE 20TH CENTURY prepared to take its rightful place in the dustbin of history, the last vestiges of sovereignty among the more than 300 indigenous nations trapped inside the claimed boundaries of the United States are rapidly sliding into a kind of final oblivion. In one of official America's supreme gestures of cynicism,

> *American representatives at the United Nations and elsewhere have long been aggressively peddling their government's Indian policy to other countries as the "most enlightened, progressive, and humanitarian model for the actualization of indigenous self-determination in the modern world"*

American representatives at the United Nations and elsewhere have long been aggressively peddling their government's Indian policy to other countries as the "most enlightened, progressive, and humanitarian model for the actualization of indigenous self-determination in the modern world." It would do well to consider this policy carefully, with an eye towards separating fact and implication from the fantasies induced by Washington's propaganda mills. In such clarity reside the analytical tools with which any effective (re)assertion of native sovereignty must be forged.

Towards the end of the 19th century, with the wrap-up of the protracted series of military campaigns known as the "Indian Wars"—through which it had, after 1790, invaded and occupied most of its land base west of the Appalachian Mountains—the U.S. set out to simultaneously absorb the remaining 150 million acres of native-held territory inside its borders and to digest the residue of about a quarter-million indigenous people residing on these treaty-reserved tracts. The stated federal agenda devolved on bringing about a comprehensive forced culture dissolution and eventual physical dispersal of every surviving American Indian society. It was the stated objective of this formally articulated "Assimilation Policy" that no Indians, culturally identifiable as such, remained within the U.S. by 1935.

Although there were a range of antecedent experiments, the real opening round of Washington's assimilation program came with the 1885 Major Crimes Act, under which U.S. jurisdiction was unilaterally asserted over every reservation in the country (each of which, it had previously been conceded in American law, constituted a distinct and separate national sovereignty). This was followed, in 1887, by passage of the General Allotment Act, described by Indian Commissioner Francis Leupp as a "great engine for grinding down the tribal mass," through which the U.S. effected another sweeping and uninvited intervention in the internal affairs of indigenous nations, this time by supplanting their traditional modes of collective landholding with the Anglo-American system of individuated property ownership.

In compiling the lists—"tribal rolls"—of those eligible to receive title to land parcels averaging a mere 160 acres each, federal agents typically relied on eugenicist "blood quantum" methods, thus converting native peoples from their prior status as national/cultural entities into "racial" groups for purposes of U.S. legal and bureaucratic administration. The "standard" was set very high, usually at one-half or more "degree of blood," in order to minimize the number of individuals entitled to retain any property at all. Once all those meeting the racial criteria had received their allotments of land, the balance of the territory belonging to each indigenous nation was declared "surplus" and handed over to non-Indians.

In this manner, some 100 million acres—about two-thirds of the 1880 reservation land base—was stripped away by the early 1930s, the bulk of it acquired not by average American citizens, but by various corporate and governmental interests. What was left was managed in perpetual "trust" under a "plenary power" relationship imposed by Congress, exercised by the Interior Department's Bureau

of Indian Affairs (BIA), and not only upheld, but amplified by the Supreme Court in its 1903 Lonewolf decision. In the latter, the "justices" opined, in a manner grossly contrary to even the most elementary principles of international law, that the United States possesses an "absolute and unchangeable right" to abrogate the provisions of any treaty into which it had entered with any indigenous nation, but that the latter remains legally bound to comply with whatever provisions the U.S. found useful.

Meanwhile, the campaign to achieve total destruction of native cultures was proceeding apace. The main vehicle for this was a massive and prolonged forced transfer of indigenous children to government-run boarding schools situated in locations quite distant from their families, friends, and societies. The purpose of this, according to Colonel Richard Pratt, a prominent "educator" of the period, was to "kill the Indian" in each youngster by systematically deculturating them.

Kept at the institutions for years on end, the children were forbidden under penalty of corporal punishment to speak—and in many cases ever to know—their own languages, practice their own religions, dress or wear their hair in the accustomed manner, learn their own histories, or to be otherwise raised as who they were. Instead, they were indoctrinated from the earliest possible age to embrace Christianity, compelled to speak only English, to accept Anglo-America's self-serving intellectual constructions, and to adopt its values and socio-cultural mores. All the while, they were trained to perform menial labor in service of their conquerors.

To enhance the effects of the boarding school system, through which perhaps 80 percent of successive generations of native youth were processed between 1875 and 1965, the BIA proclaimed a series of draconian regulations on the reservations. In 1897, for example, it was decreed that the practice of traditional spiritual ceremonies was an offense punishable by fines, imprisonment, and impoundment of property. Local agents also increasingly utilized their "delegated trust authority" to lease whatever productive land remained on the reservations to non-Indian ranching and agricultural concerns, always at a pittance and often for periods of 99 years. Under this combination of conditions, the U.S. portion of Native North America was in utter disarray by 1930—politically, economically, and militarily prostrate, socio-culturally destabilized to an extreme degree, and literally verging on the very sort of ultimate extinction federal policymakers had so confidently predicted.

Reorganization and "Reform"

The basis on which U.S. assimilation policy was reversed embodies one of history's more sublime ironies. During the period of allotment, the few remaining American Indians were largely consigned to die off, comfortably out of sight and mind of the immigrant society, which had annihilated and usurped them, in remote and barren locales thought to be essentially valueless by federal planners. By the early 1920s, however, it was increasingly apparent that there had been something of a miscalculation in this respect. What remained of the reservations was some of the most mineral-rich territory in the world, containing about two-thirds of what the U.S. now claims as its own domestic uranium reserves, a quarter of the readily accessible low sulfur coal, a fifth of the oil and natural gas, as well as substantial deposits of copper, iron, zeolite, molybdenum, and several other ores.

This presented an interesting dilemma for U.S. elites, not because of any regard for the obvious native interest in the resources at issue or other humanitarian concerns, but because of the predictable results of allowing America's vaunted and entirely mythical "free market" system to hold sway over them. Previous experience in this respect, notably in the Indian-owned oil fields of Oklahoma, had demonstrated that pursuing such a course led to chaotic production inefficiencies and a considerable squandering of potential wealth. It was perceived as vital that native assets be kept out of the public domain and placed instead under a sort of centralized governmental management, which could not control royalty rates and other overhead costs—thus channeling highly inflated profits to officialdom's preferred corporate partners—and also coordinate overall timetables of reservation resource extraction in conformity with America's broader economic and strategic interests.

The already well-advanced liquidation of indigenous nations had to be abandoned in favor of a program preserving most of them as demographic/geographic entities. Equally essential, a structure had to be created to oversee this archipelago of permanent internal colonies. Both requirements were accommodated by passage of the Indian Reorganization Act (IRA) in 1934.

The basic thrust of the IRA, while canceling such assimilationist initiatives as allotment, was to follow closely on the models of

> *By the early 1920s, however, it was increasingly apparent that there had been something of a miscalculation in this respect. What remained of the reservations was some of the most mineral-rich territory in the world, containing about two-thirds of what the U.S. now claims as its own domestic uranium reserves....*

colonial governance perfected by the European imperial powers. In essence, this involved supplanting whatever remained of the traditional organic forms of indigenous government entities. Over the years, the U.S. had entered into more than 370 ratified treaties and a host of other international agreements—with federally designed and sponsored local/territorial councils, each of which derived its exceedingly limited authority, its operational funding—its very existence—to Congress rather than to its ostensible constituency. While such bodies were meant, under strict BIA supervision, to handle many of the day-to-day details of U.S. policy implementation on the reservations, their larger purpose was to foster the illusion of native consent to and participation in their own exploitation.

To this end, the IRA's "tribal councils" were formed behind a carefully crafted facade of "democracy." Much was made of the fact that council functions were to be anchored on formal tribal constitutions. Unmentioned was the reality that these were boilerplate instruments written by BIA bureaucrats, containing provisions concerning council powers, the racial criteria of tribal membership, and so forth, which were flatly antithetical to the traditions of the people whose values they supposedly reflected. The procedures through which indigenous nations "voluntarily accepted" these constitutions were similarly rigged. Probably the most glaring example is that of the Hopi, where 85 percent of eligible voters actively boycotted the entire referendum process. In the aftermath, U.S. Indian Commissioner John Collier decreed that all abstentions should be counted as "aye" votes, instantly transforming an overwhelming and unequivocal refusal by the Indians into an apparently near-unanimous endorsement of the IRA.

Such official fraud was hardly unique. In the 1936 referendum conducted by the BIA among the Lakotas, for example, it was later discovered that a sufficient number of ballots had been cast on behalf of dead people to change the outcome from rejection to an appearance of acceptance. It has also been well-documented that throughout California federal officials engaged in a systematic pattern of deception, fundamentally misrepresenting the nature of the IRA during pre-referendum "educational workshops" conducted in 1936 and 1937. Many native people in that state were thus led to believe that by casting ballots to affirm the IRA they were actually voting the exact opposite. In each instance—and many more—such transparently fraudulent results were not only allowed to stand, but promoted as evidence of the enthusiasm with which indigenous peoples embraced reorganization.

While the IRA structure was being set in place between 1934 and 1939, the federal school system "serving" Native America, which had been geared to delivering "education for extinction," was largely retooled to train and indoctrinate the petty functionaries and technicians needed to make the system work. With the spawning of this comprador elite among Indians, a direct counterpart to the "talented tenth" identified by W.E.B. DuBois as having been selected and groomed to fill a similar management role within the African-American population, federal overseers could increasingly rely on a strata within virtually every indigenous nation to carry out their instructions. Moreover, they could rely on this "broker class" to cast an aura of legitimacy over its own domination by claiming—as Indians—that it comprised the very foundation of any genuine exercise in native self-governance.

Termination and Relocation

By the early 1950s, the U.S. internal colonial system was functioning rather well. The mining of reservation resources, particularly uranium and copper, had commenced on a relatively massive scale. Although the royalty rates assigned to these minerals by the BIA rarely exceeded 10 percent of what they might have generated on the open market—and despite the fact that most of the arrangements included no requirement that mining companies perform even minimal cleanup of the mess they'd made—the once profitably extractable ores had been exhausted, all leases allowing for corporate development had been duly approved by the relevant tribal "governments." The shallow pretense of indigenous self-determination embodied by the IRA was even sufficient to prevent the United Nations from requiring, in accordance with its charter, that the reservations be inscribed on a list of "non-self-governing territories" scheduled for timely decolonization.

It was at this point that congressional conservatives decided the time was ripe for a "trimming of fat" from federal budget allocations to underwrite the administration of Indian affairs. Pursuant to House Resolution 108, effected in 1953, a lengthy series of "termination acts" were passed, each of them withdrawing U.S. recognition of the existence of one or more indigenous nations.

By the time this throwback to assimilationism had run its course a decade later—the policy was for the most part implemented by Indian Commissioner Dillon S. Myer, a man whose qualifications for the job seem to have consisted mainly of having presided over the mass internment of Japanese Americans during World War II—some 108 native peoples had been arbitrarily declared "extinct," their reserved land bases officially dissolved. While the victims ranged from the tiny, impoverished "mission" bands of southern California to the much larger and more prosperous Klamaths of Oregon and Menominees of Wisconsin, their common denominator was that their reservations had no mineral wealth substantial enough to warrant the government's paying the costs of continuing to hold it in trust.

Simultaneously, emphasis was placed on "relocation," a program designed to remove a substantial portion of the population from non-terminated reservations, dispersing them in major urban areas. While funding was deliberately withheld from initiatives which might have improved living conditions in Indian Country—according to federal census data, American Indians comprised the poorest identifiable population sector in the U.S. from 1935-1995, with gross unemployment running well over 60 percent for the entire period— the government displayed a peculiar willingness to engage in relatively lavish spending to convince native people to "voluntarily" aban-

don their homelands and melt into the vastly larger "main stream" society.

The results of this rather crude carrot-and-stick routine are striking. In 1900, 99.6 percent of all federally recognized American Indians were land based. By 1930, as a steady rebound in the size of the indigenous population—from a little over 237,000 in 1890 to more than 333,000 a generation later—began to push against the territorial constraints imposed by allotment, the proportion had declined to 90.1 percent.

In 1950, 86.6 percent of all recognized native people in the U.S. still lived on reservations. By 1960, the federal relocation program had abruptly brought the proportion down to 72.1 percent, nearly as great a drop in just 7

> *Simultaneously, emphasis was placed on "relocation," a program designed to remove a substantial portion of the population from non-terminated reservations, dispersing them in major urban areas*

years as had occurred in the preceding 60. By 1970, 44.5 percent of all recognized Indians had been removed from the reservations. By 1980, the figure had climbed to 49 percent; today, it stands somewhere around 55 percent.

The sorts of governmental/corporate benefits of this process are readily discernible, beginning with the fact that keeping huge tracts of certain reservations effectively depopulated makes it far easier to engage in wholesale strip mining and related activities. The conditions of stark destitution imposed on most reservation residents also tends to render them more malleable, less resistant to any kind of activity, no matter how destructive, which might generate income, no matter how meager, than might otherwise be expected. At another level, termination and relocation have served to make indigenous societies unstable in a cultural sense, fracturing the close knit kinship relations which made them extraordinarily cohesive, eroding the abilities of many peoples to perpetuate their languages, and so on. This, in turn, has left the majority of Indians in the U.S. steadily more "adaptable" to and dependent on the Euro-American settler society which dominates and exploits them.

At yet another level, the proportionately massive population dispersal brought on by a calculated governmental relocation pattern of manipulating native identity criteria resulted in a pronounced undercounting of indigenous people during the past quarter-century. Analyst Jack Forbes estimated that federal census data admitted just under two million Indians in the U.S. by 1980. The real number should have been closer to 15 million.

As might be expected, federal methods of circumscribing native demography have been avidly embraced and promoted by the IRA's "Vichy" governments and their adherents, a matter that radically undercut the numerical basis on which Native America as a whole might force some favorable alteration in its collective circumstance. Worse, such posturing has unleashed a recurrent cycle of bitter infighting among indigenous peoples, as "certified" Indians endeavor to protect their tiny shares of each year's pitifully small congressional appropriation against the prospect of their federally negated cousins joining the queue. At this point, the bestowal of formal recognition on several long neglected peoples—the Abenakis of Vermont, Miamis of Ohio, and Lumbees of North Carolina among them—is resisted fiercely by the leaders of several "federally recognized tribes."

Rebellion and Repression

During the 1960s, the final dissolution of Europe's colonial empires and Third World efforts to prevent their replacement by neocolonial modes of exploitation became a primary international agenda. By the end of the decade, the important segments among the internally colonized "minorities" of the United States—most especially blacks, Chicanos, and Puertorriquenos (both on the mainland and in their externally colonized island homeland), but also other groups, including Appalachian whites—inspired by the tangible short-term successes of this global struggle, had embarked on decolonization initiatives of their own.

In this environment of generalized sociopolitical ferment and instability, a new spirit of militancy began to congeal among native peoples, not only in the lower 48 states, but in Alaska and Hawai'i as well. Beginning in the mid-1960s, increasingly substantial confrontations occurred in the Pacific Northwest between state and federal authorities, and several indigenous nations intent on exercising their treaty-guaranteed fishing rights. In 1969, a multi-tribal group of relocatees in the San Francisco Bay Area seized Alcatraz Island, site of an infamous but, by then, abandoned federal prison, in order to establish a landbase for the area's displaced Indians.

Before the Alcatraz occupation ended a year-and-a-half later, others had begun in Fort Lawton, near Seattle, a Nike missile base in Chicago, the Mayflower replica at Plymouth, Massachusetts, and Mt. Rushmore National Monument in South Dakota.

By late 1972, a coalition of native groups calling themselves the Trail of Broken Treaties took over the BIA headquarters in Washington, DC, on the eve of the U.S. presidential election, holding it until the incumbent administration of Richard M. Nixon agreed to review a 20-Point Program redefining U.S./Indian relations. Among the program's more significant features were demands that the government meet its existing treaty obligations to indigenous nations, reinstate terminated peoples, repudiate blood quantum criteria and other such impositions on native identity, and resume the nation-to-nation relationship with indigenous peoples required by the first article of its own constitution. Instructively, the strongest outcry against any such changes came from the National Tribal Chairman's Association (NTCA), a federally-funded consortium of IRA council heads.

Buffered by these "representative tribal leaders," federal officials not only dismissed the Trail of Broken Treaties' 20 points out-of-hand (once the militants had withdrawn from the BIA building), but launched a major campaign of repression against them. Marked as a priority for neutralization was the American Indian Movement (AIM), a group described at the time as being comprised of the "shock troops of Indian sovereignty." Most sensationally, this involved a force of several hundred federal paramilitaries—advised, equipped, and supplied by army counterinsurgency specialists—laying siege to virtually the entire organization at the hamlet of Wounded Knee, on the Pine Ridge Reservation, in South Dakota.

In the aftermath of the 71-day standoff at Wounded Knee, several key AIM leaders were assassinated. The rest were targeted for multiple prosecutions—Russell Means, to name a prime example, was charged with 37 felonies and several other offenses carrying a combined potential sentence of triple life plus 113 years imprisonment—a process which, although it resulted in almost no convictions, tied them up in U.S. courts for several years. The demands of meeting their usually high bails and underwriting their various legal defenses also effectively bankrupted the organization, while diverting considerable time, energy, and atten- tion away from other sorts of political organizing.

While this was going on, more than 60 grassroots AIM members and supporters were killed on Pine Ridge, victims of death squads assembled by Richard Wilson, head of the reservation's IRA government, and funded by the BIA. As has now been confirmed by at least one leader of the "goons," as Wilson's gunmen called themselves, they were composed mostly of off-duty BIA police personnel, armed, coordinated, and essentially immunized from prosecution by the politically repressive Federal Bureau of Investigation (FBI). The arrangement was remarkably similar to those engineered by the Central Intelligence Agency (CIA) in roughly the same period as a means of maintaining "order" in U.S. client states throughout Latin America.

The orgy of state violence culminated on June 26, 1975, when a large body of FBI agents and BIA police surrounded and attacked a small AIM encampment on Pine Ridge. In the resulting firefight, one AIM member and two agents were killed, a circumstance used by the government as a pretext to assault the entire reservation with overwhelming force. Using armored personnel carriers and helicopters loaned by the military, and brandishing automatic weapons, several hundred FBI men swept Pine Ridge and the adjoining Rosebud Reservation for nearly two months. It was not until late September when open resistance on both reservations had been thoroughly suppressed, that the last of these occupation troops were finally withdrawn.

Shortly thereafter, the government was able, on what it now concedes was a fraudulent basis, to obtain the extradition from Canada of Leonard Peltier, head of the group which had fought off the FBI in June. Subjected to a travesty of a trial for "murdering" the two FBI agents—two codefendants in the case had already been found by a jury to have acted in self-defense and federal prosecutors now admit they have "no idea" who fired the lethal shots—Peltier was sentenced in 1977 to serve two consecutive life sentences in prison. Twenty years later and in failing health, he remains incarcerated in a maximum security facility, a symbol of the high price which can be extracted by federal authorities from anyone bold enough to seriously assert native rights to sovereignty in the United States.

Decimated, exhausted, heavily infiltrated, and completely outgunned, AIM disintegrated during the late 1970s. Although there have been occasional flashes of life, as with the Yellow Thunder Camp occupation in the Black Hills during the early 1980s, and a series of successful demonstrations to prevent public celebrations of the Columbian Quincentenniary in Denver a decade later, the movement's overall decline could not be reversed. Today, while chapters continue to exist in Denver and a few other localities, references to AIM are associated mainly with a governmentally/corporately funded Minneapolis corporation run by the brothers Clyde and Vernon Bellecourt, apparently subsidized to subvert the reputation and rhetoric of the movement's past radicalism into a blanket endorsement of the colonial status quo.

Subterfuge and Self Determination

Even as the repression of AIM crested in the wake of Wounded Knee, the movement sought to broaden its latitude of action. In response to requests by elders like Frank Fools Crow, who had proclaimed the continuing existence of an Independent Oglala [Lakota] Nation during the siege, a meeting on the Standing Rock Reservation, North Dakota,

Decimated, exhausted, heavily infiltrated, and completely outgunned, AIM disintegrated during the late 1970s

was convened during the summer of 1974. Its purpose was to consider ways of placing the question of American Indian treaty rights before the community of nations as a whole. The result was the formation of the International Indian Treaty Council (IITC), an AIM subpart specifically to establish an indigenous presence at the United Nations. Under direction of Cherokee activist Jimmie Durham, an organizational office was opened at New York's UN Plaza and a lobbying effort begun.

Durham's initial strategy was straightforward. Article I, Section 10, of the U.S. Constitution both reserves American treaty-making prerogatives to the level of federal authority and disallows the government from entering into a treaty relationship with any lesser entity. Hence, each time the Senate ratified a treaty between the U.S. and one or more native peo-

ples— as it did more than 370 times between 1778 and 1871—it simultaneously conveyed formal recognition of the full national sovereignty inhering in the other party or parties.

Since no nation possesses a right in international law to unilaterally extinguish the sovereignty of another and, since the indigenous nations formally recognized as such by the U.S. have never willingly relinquished their sovereignty, it follows that they still retain it in a legal sense.

Since all nations are expressly prohibited under provision of the United Nations Charter, the 1960 Declaration on the Granting of Independence to Colonial Countries and Peoples and other international legal instruments from preempting the exercise of sovereignty by any other, it was/is quite reasonable to conclude that, when presented with the facts, the UN would have no valid alternative but to enter a resolution requiring the decolonization of Native North America.

Well aware of what was afoot, the Nixon administration moved decisively to co-opt IITC's initiative. The vehicle for this was the American Indian Self-Determination and Educational Assistance Act, passed in 1975, long after Nixon had been driven from office. Although the statute had absolutely nothing to do with the concept of self-determination articulated in international law (it offers a hiring preference to American Indians in implementing federal policies, thus incorporating them even more directly into the matrix of U.S. colonial domination) the government's use of the term greatly confused the situation.

This was all the more true in that the NTCA and comparable organizations offered themselves as what amounted to a cheering section for the measure, lauding it as "the final confirmation of American Indian sovereignty in the modern era."

Thus, when Durham was finally able to arrange for IITC's participation in an unprecedented UN conference on discrimination against indigenous peoples during the summer of 1977, the U.S. announced—falsely, but with the apparent agreement of most native people within its domain—that, in its case, many of the matters raised had already been resolved. Only the fact that Durham had cannily solicited representation of 98 indigenous nations, including a number from South and Central America, averted a probability of the process stalling right there. As it was, since a U.S. domestic statute could hardly be argued as bearing on the circumstances of native peoples elsewhere, the Human Rights Commission's parent body, the Economic and Social Council (ECOSOC), determined that matters would have to be considered in more depth.

This led, after much maneuvering, to creation of the United Nations Working Group on Indigenous Populations in 1981. Although much-heralded as a major breakthrough in the cause of native rights worldwide, this entity carried within it the seeds of a fundamentally different outcome. To begin with, its very title consigned it to considering the circumstances of certain "populations" rather than "peoples." The wording, insisted on by the U.S. and Canada, is legally significant. Under international law, all peoples are guaranteed the right of true self-determination—as opposed to the grotesque parody embodied in American law—while populations, defined as demographic subsets of a given country's polity, are not. It was not until 1989 that the two North American super states abandoned their terminological objections and then only with the caveat that they were doing so with the specific understanding that use of the term "peoples" would not be construed as con- veying legal connotations.

Secondly, rather than being charged with responsibility for exploring the applicability of existing international legal instruments to the situations of various indigenous peoples, the Working Group was assigned to first conduct a comprehensive global survey of the condi-

tions which had been imposed upon them; then, after 1984, to draft an entirely new element of law to address their needs. It, in reality, set the stage for a formal codification of their collective demotion from the status of either nations or peoples to that of "domestic minorities" within assorted UN member-states.

In 1979, Durham resigned in disgust when, among other things, the Treaty Council board of trustees decided the organization should push for the drafting of the new international instrument. His replacement, closely associated with those who engineered the chartering of "National AIM, Inc." in Minneapolis, pi-

> *It, in reality, set the stage for a formal codification of their collective demotion from the status of either nations or peoples to that of "domestic minorities" within assorted UN member-states*

loted the organization, first into alignments with a welter of nation-state governments considered hostile to the United States—regardless of their own records on indigenous rights —and finally into "cooperative" relations with any government, including that of the U.S., willing to subsidize it. By 1987, the tiny clique who had assumed control was prepared to drop all but the most shallow pretense of complying with the wishes of the grassroots people whose interests they ostensibly served, reforming IITC as a San Francisco-based corporation accountable only to a handpicked board of directors.

This course of action resulted in an almost complete erosion in the base of support which had propelled IITC to its early prominence. Although it has never abandoned its grossly misleading claim to represent them—it actually increased the putative number to over 100 during the early 1990s—virtually all of the indigenous nations which participated in Durham's 1977 delegation had carefully separated themselves from "AIM's international diplomatic arm" by 1985. Some, like the Hawaiians, the Haudenosaunee (Six Nations Iroquois Confederacy), the Treaty 6 Chiefs of Canada, the Hopi, and the Lakotas, elected to represent themselves in international fora. Others, including virtually all the indigenous peoples of South and Central America, founded far more representative organizations of their own.

The capstone to the whole charade came in November 1996, when, prior to its submission to ECOSOC, and thence the General Assembly, a subgroup of the Commission on Human Rights convened to consider a Draft Declaration on the Rights of Indigenous Peoples, which had been approved by native delegates in 1993 and subsequently adopted by both the Working Group and its parent body, the Sub-Commission on Prevention of Discrimination and Protection of Minorities. When the Commission's panel of nation-state "reviewers" set out to alter the draft in a manner intended quite literally to gut it, a unified body of indigenous delegates demanded that it go forward unchanged. U.S. representatives, who

> *The sheer audacity with which the U.S. had moved to convert a supposed universal declaration of indigenous rights into little more than an extrapolation of its own posture in foreclosing on the most meaningful of these, clearly, describes one direction in which things are moving*

had for the most part remained much more circumspect in their approach over the preceding 20 years, at last openly responded that no draft instrument would be approved which "conflicts with the principles of American legal doctrine."

While this affront precipitated a mass walkout by native delegates, the Treaty Council delegation was conspicuous in breaking ranks. Not only did its members refuse to join their ostensible colleagues in a separate strategy session, they opted instead to engage in a sequence of informal caucuses with offending American officials before launching a margin-

ally successful campaign to convince individuals from other organizations to return to the session and endorse the draft document. Meanwhile, back in the U.S., a concerted effort was mounted to discredit those in opposition on the rather bizarre grounds that they were suspected "FBI provocateurs, CIA agents, or both." Instructively, the "representative group of Indian leaders" issuing these increasingly bitter communiqués were not to be found in the ranks of the NTCA. Instead, they were located in the IITC-affiliated offices of National AIM, Inc.

Prospects and Potentials

The recent events in Geneva represented something of a crossroads in the struggle for native sovereignty and self-determination, not only within the United States, but globally. The sheer audacity with which the U.S. had moved to convert a supposed universal declaration of indigenous rights into little more than an extrapolation of its own posture in foreclosing on the most meaningful of these, clearly, describes one direction in which things are moving. Should the American initiative prove successful— and it was strongly supported by the governments of Canada, Australia, and a number of other UN member states—the ever more refined and sophisticated model of internal colonialism developed by the U.S. for world replication would be formally legitimated, enshrined as international law. At that point, the only legally sanctioned option available to native people would be incorporation into the governing structures of their colonizers, a status amounting to permanent subjugation within their own homelands.

The craven performance of the National AIM/IITC amalgam reveals the utter bankruptcy of these twin husks of 1970s radicalism ever mounting even token resistance to such an outcome. While their irrevocably supine posture in the face of U.S. power may provide valuable lessons on how repression, subversion, and co-optation can be used to deform genuine national liberation movements, it furnishes nothing by way of an alternative to capitulation. The "something" they now offer in seeking to facilitate an indigenous ratification of the Draft Declaration is no better than nothing at all. On the contrary, it would present for the first time an appearance of native consent to the denial of its sovereignty and self-determining rights.

This is the point taken by the delegates who walked out of the November Working Group session. In their collective refusal of any formulation which might legally consolidate the notion of an intrinsic right of states to wield hegemony over our peoples and homelands, they have paved the way for an indefinite stalemate or even cancellation of the drafting process.

Salient in this respect are Chapters XI and XII of the United Nations Charter, which require, among other things, that all non-self-governing territories (colonies) be inscribed on a list of entities placed under UN supervision and within which the self-assigned trust authority of colonizing powers is strictly limited in terms of both scope and duration, exercised only in such manner as may be required to ensure the resumption of genuine "self-governance or independence as may be appropriate to each territory and the freely expressed wishes of the peoples concerned" in the most timely possible fashion. Amplification and clarification of what is intended by these chapters of the Charter is found in the Declaration on the Granting of Independence to Colonial Countries and Peoples (General Assembly Resolution 1514 (XV), 1960), which states that:

> The subjection of peoples to alien subjugation, domination, and exploitation constitutes a denial of human rights, is contrary to the Charter of the United Nations, and is an impediment to the promotion of world peace and cooperation

> All peoples have the right to self-determination; by virtue of that right they freely determine their political status and freely pursue their economic, social, and cultural development

>Inadequacy of political, economic, social, or educational preparedness should never serve to delay independence

> All armed action or repressive measures directed against dependent peoples shall cease in order to enable them to exercise peacefully and freely their right to complete independence, and the integrity of their national territory shall be respected

> Immediate steps shall be taken, in Trust and Non-Self-Governing Territories or all other territories which have not yet attained independence, to transfer all powers to the peoples of those territories, without any conditions or reservations, in accordance with their freely-expressed will or desire, without any distinction as to race, creed or color, in order to enable them to enjoy complete independence and freedom

> Any attempt aimed at the partial or total disruption of the national unity and territorial integrity of a country is incompatible with the purposes and principles of the Charter of the United Nations

Reinforcement of such principles obtains from the Universal Declaration of Human Rights (General Assembly Resolution 217 A (III), 1948), the International Covenant on Economic, Social and Cultural Rights (General Assembly Resolution 2200 (XXI), 1966), the International Covenant on Civil and Political Rights (General Assembly Resolution 2200 (XXI), 1966) and other instruments. Possible impingements on the applicability of this stream of international to indigenous internal colonies—notably General Assembly Resolution 1541(XV; 1966), which posits that the decolonization procedures required by the

UN Charter and Resolution 1514 pertain only territories which are "geographically separate and...distinct ethnically and/ or culturally from the country administering it"—are hardly insurmountable.

Although Resolution 1541 has typically been construed as meaning that, to be eligible for inscription as non-self-governing territories, colonies must be separated from colonizing powers by at least 30 miles of open ocean, strict adherence to this so-called "Blue Water Thesis" is indefensible insofar as it would not even admit to the fact that Germany colonized contiguous Poland during the Second World War or that the Poles possessed a legal right to decolonization.

Ultimately, the issue can be resolved only on the basis of a logically/legally consistent determination of whether indigenous peoples actually constitute "peoples" in the legal sense. While the deliberately obfuscatory arguments entered on this matter by the U.S. and other nation-states have thoroughly muddled the situation with respect to a host of untreatied peo-

> *Any such progression serves to disempower nation-states, even as it re-empowers those on whose subordination statism depends heavily for its very existence*

ples throughout the world, the same cannot be said concerning the treated peoples of North America, most especially those within the United States.

As was noted above, we have long since been recognized not only as peoples, but as nations, and are thereby entitled in existing law to enjoy the rights of such regardless of our geographic disposition vis-a-vis our colonizers. The route leading to an alternative destiny for native people is just as clear as that prescribed for us in the newly-revised Draft Convention. By relentless and undeviating assertion of the basic rights of treated peoples—at all levels, through every available venue, and excluding no conceivable means of doing so—we can be-

gin to (re)secure them, restoring to ourselves and to our posterity our/their rightful status as sovereign and coequal members of the community of nations, free of such pretense as IRA-style "self-governance" and subterfuges like the 1975 "Indian Self-Determination" Act.

Only by achieving success in this enterprise can we eventually position ourselves to tangibly assist our relatives in other quarters of the globe, untreatied and thus unrecognized as being imbued with the same self-determining rights as we, to overcome the juridical/diplomatic quandary in which this circumstance places them.

Any such progression, of course, serves to incrementally disempower nation-states, even as it steadily (re)empowers those on whose subordination statism depends heavily for its very existence. This, for its part, undermines a cornerstone on which that rapidly metastasizing malignancy described by U.S. President George Bush in 1991 as constituting a "New World Order" is designed to rest. The inestimable benefit to all humanity deriving from a trajectory of this sort should be readily evident to anyone not already vested in the perpetuation of planetary business as usual and may serve to explain why the agenda of indigenous liberation deserves the broadest imaginable prioritization and support among those who profess commitment to constructive sociopolitical and economic change.

Fittingly, the contours of the liberatory strategy which has begun to congeal among the dissidents who walked out of the Working Group session last November may be readily discerned in the charge delivered by the elders to those assembled at the first International Treaty Council gathering 23 years ago. Theirs was a vision from which, as Jimmie Durham rightly insisted, we should never have departed.

Whether we can recover the sense of cohesion, purpose, and momentum they so generously bestowed on us—and which we so frivolously squandered in the arrogance of our belief that we might somehow dance with the devil and win—remains to be seen.

Our struggle will be longer and harder than it might have been had we heeded our old people during the late 1970s. It is likely also to be much harsher, given that we have by now wasted most of the moral authority gained through the sacrifices of AIM warriors at Wounded Knee and elsewhere. We may have to undergo the whole grim process once again, or many times, in order to recoup what has been lost. We are nonetheless obliged to regain our stride, however painfully and belatedly. We are obliged because if our histories have taught us anything at all, it is that whatever the future may hold for our peoples, it must be something we collectively forge or it will be too dreadful to contemplate. Our coming generations surely deserve far better.

From Z Magazine, *May 1997*
Volume 10, Number 5

4.

U.S. Savage Imperialism

By Noam Chomsky

IT'S TEMPTING TO GO back to the beginning. The beginning goes pretty far back, but it is useful to think about some aspects of American history that bear directly on current U.S. policy in the Middle East. The U.S. is a pretty unusual country in many ways. It's maybe the only coun-

> *The U.S. is a pretty unusual country in many ways. It's maybe the only country in the world that was founded as an empire. It was an infant empire—as George Washington called it—and the founding fathers had broad aspirations.*

try in the world that was founded as an empire. It was an infant empire—as George Washington called it—and the founding fathers had broad aspirations. The most libertarian of them, Thomas Jefferson, thought that this infant empire should spread and become what he called the "nest" from which the entire continent would be colonized. That would get rid of the "Red," the Indians as they'd be driven away or exterminated. The Blacks would be sent back to Africa when we don't need them anymore and the Latins will be eliminated by a superior race.

It was a very racist country all the way through its history, not just anti-black. That was Jefferson's image and the others more or less agreed with it. So it's a settler colonialist society. Settler colonialism is far and away the worst kind of imperialism, the most savage kind because it requires eliminating the indigenous population. That's not unrelated, I think, to the kind of reflexive U.S. support for Israel—which is also a settler colonial society. Its policies resonate with a sense of American history. It's kind of reliving it. It goes beyond that because the early settlers in the U.S. were religious fundamentalists who regarded themselves as the children of Israel, following the divine commandment to settle the promised land and slaughter the Amalekites and so on and so forth.

All this was done with the utmost benevolence. So, for example, Massachusetts (the Mayflower and all that business) was given its Charter by the King of England in 1629. The Charter commissioned the settlers to save the native population from the misery of paganism. In fact, if you look at the great seal of the Bay Colony of Massachusetts, it depicts an Indian holding an arrow pointed down in a sign of peace. And out of his mouth is a scroll on which is written: "Come over and help us." That's one of the first examples of what's called humanitarian intervention. And it's typical of other cases up to the present. The Indians were pleading with the colonists to come over and help them and the colonists were benevolently following the divine command to come over and help them. It turned out we were helping by exterminating them.

That was considered rather puzzling. Around the 1820s, one Supreme Court justice wrote about it. He says it was kind of strange that, despite all our benevolence and love for the Indians, they are withering and dispersing like the "leaves of autumn." And how could this be? The divine will of providence is "beyond human comprehension." It's just God's will. We can't hope to understand it. This conception—it's called Providentialism. Whatever we're doing, we're following God's will. It's an extremely religious country, off the spectrum in religious belief. A very large percentage of the population—I don't remember the numbers, but it's quite high—believes in the literal word of the Bible and part of that means supporting everything that Israel does because God promised the promised land to Israel. So we have to support them.

These same people—a substantial core of solid support for anything Israel does—also happen to be the most extreme anti-Semites in the world. They make Hitler look pretty mild. They are looking forward to the near total annihilation of the Jews after Armageddon. There's a whole long story about this, which is believed, literally, in high places—probably people like Reagan, George W. Bush, and others. It ties in with the kind of settler colonial history of Christian Zionism—which long preceded Jewish Zionism and is much stronger. It provides a solid base of reflexive support for whatever Israel happens to be doing.

The conquest of the national territory was a pretty ugly affair. It was recognized by some of the more honest figures like John Quincy Adams who was the great grand strategist of expansionism—the theorist of Manifest Destiny and so on. In his later years, long after his own horrifying crimes were in the past, he did lament what he called the fate of that "hapless race of native Americans, which we are exterminating with such merciless and perfidious cruelty." He said that's one of the sins that the Lord is going to punish us for—still waiting for that.

His doctrines are highly praised right to the present. There's a major scholarly book by John Lewis Gaddis, a leading American historian, on the roots of the Bush doctrine. Gaddis correctly, plausibly, describes the Bush doctrine as a direct descendent of John Quincy Adams's grand strategy. He says, it's a concept that runs right through American history. He praises it; thinks it's the right conception that we have to protect our security, that expansion is the path to security and that you can't really have security until you control everything. So we have to expand, not just over the hemisphere, but over the world. That's the Bush doctrine.

By WWII, without going into the details, though the U.S. had long been by far the richest country in the world, it was playing a kind of secondary role in world affairs. The main actor in world affairs was the British—even the French had a more global reach than the U.S. WWII changed all that. American planners during WWII, Roosevelt's planners, understood very well from the beginning of the war that it was going to end with the U.S. in a position of overwhelming power.

As the war went on and the Russians ground down the Germans and pretty much won the European war, it was understood that the U.S. would be even more dominant. And they laid careful plans for what the post-war world would look like. The United States would have total control over a region that would include the Western Hemisphere, the Far East, the former British Empire, and as much of Eurasia as possible, including, crucially, its commercial and industrial core—Western Europe. That's the minimum. The maximum was the whole world and, of course, we need that for security. Within this region, the U.S. would have unquestioned control and would limit any effort at sovereignty by others.

The U.S. ended the war in a position of dominance and security that had no remote counterpart in history. It had half the world's wealth, it controlled the whole hemisphere, the opposite sides of both oceans. But It wasn't total. The Russians were there and some things were still not under control, but it was remarkably expansive. At the center of it was the Middle East.

One of President Roosevelt's long-time, high-level advisers, Adolf A. Berle, a leading liberal, pointed out that control of Middle East oil would yield substantial control of the world—and that doctrine remains operative and a leading theme of policy.

After World War II

For a long time during the Cold War years, policies were invariably justified by the threat of the Russians. It was mostly an invented threat. The Russians ran their own smaller empire with a similar pretext, threat of the Americans. These clouds were lifted after the collapse of the Soviet Union. For those who want to understand American foreign policy, an obvious place to look is what happened after the Soviet Union disappeared.

> *And they laid careful plans for what the post-war world would look like. The United States would have total control over a region that would include the Western Hemisphere, the Far East, the former British Empire, and as much of Eurasia as possible, including, crucially, its commercial and industrial core—Western Europe. That's the minimum.*

That's the natural place to look and it follows almost automatically that nobody looks at it. It's scarcely discussed in the scholarly literature though it's obviously where you'd look to find out what the Cold War was about. In fact, if you do look, you get very clear answers.

The president at the time was George Bush I. Immediately after the collapse of the Berlin Wall, there was a new National Security Strategy, a defense budget, and so on. They make very interesting reading. The basic message is: nothing is going to change except pretexts. So we still need, they said, a huge military force, not to defend ourselves against the Russian hordes because they're gone, but because of what they called the "technological sophistication" of third world powers.

Now, if you're a well-trained, educated person who came from Harvard and so on, you're not supposed to laugh when you hear that. And nobody laughed. In fact, I don't think anybody ever reported it. So, they said, we have to protect ourselves from the technological sophistication of third world powers and we have to maintain what they called the "defense industrial base"—a euphemism for high tech industry, which mostly came out of the state sector (computers, the Internet, and so on), under the pretext of defense.

With regard to the Middle East, they said, we must maintain our intervention forces, most of them aimed at the Middle East. Then comes an interesting phrase. We have to maintain the intervention forces aimed at the Middle East where the major threats to our interests "could not be laid at the Kremlin's door." In other words, sorry folks, we've been lying to you for 50 years, but now that pretext is gone, we'll tell you the truth. The problem in the Middle East is and has been what's called radical nationalism. Radical just means independent. It's a term that means "doesn't follow orders." The radical nationalism can be of any kind. Iran's a good case.

The Threat of Radical Nationalism

So in 1953, the Iranian threat was secular nationalism. After 1978, it's religious nationalism. In 1953, it was taken care of by overthrowing the parliamentary regime and installing a dictator who was highly praised. It wasn't a secret. The *New York Times,* for example, had an editorial praising the overthrow of the government as an "object lesson" to small countries that "go berserk" with radical nationalism and seek to control their own resources. This will be an object lesson to them: don't try any of that nonsense, certainly not in an area we need for control of the world. That was 1953.

Since the overthrow of the U.S.-imposed tyrant in 1979, Iran has been constantly under U.S. attack—without a stop. First, Carter tried to reverse the overthrow of the Shah immediately by trying to instigate a military coup. That didn't work. The Israelis—in effect the ambassador, as there'd been close relations between Israel and Iran under the Shah, although theoretically no formal relations—advised that if we could find military officers who were willing to shoot down 10,000 people in the streets, we could restore the Shah. Zbigniew Brzezinski, Carter's National Security advisor, had pretty much the same advice. That didn't quite work.

Right away, the U.S. turned for support to Saddam Hussein in his invasion of Iran—which was no small affair. Hundreds of thousands of Iranians were slaughtered. The people who are now running the country are veterans of that war and deep in their consciousness is the understanding that the whole world is against them—the Russians, the Americans were all supporting Saddam Hussein and the effort to overthrow the new Islamic state.

It was no small thing. The U.S. support for Saddam Hussein was extreme. Saddam's crimes—like the Anfal genocide, the massacre of the Kurds—were just denied. The Reagan administration denied them or blamed them on Iran. Iraq was even given a very rare privilege. It's the only country other than Israel which has been granted the privilege of attacking a U.S. naval vessel and getting away with complete impunity. In the Israeli case, it was the *Liberty* in 1967. In Iraq's case it was the *USS Stark* in 1987—a naval vessel which was part of the U.S. fleet protecting Iraqi shipments from Iran during the war. They attacked the ship using French missiles, killed a few dozen sailors, and got a slight tap on the wrist, but nothing beyond that.

U.S. support was so strong that they basically won the war for Iraq. After the war was over, U.S. support for Iraq continued. In 1989, George Bush I invited Iraqi nuclear engineers to the U.S. for advanced training in nuclear weapons development. It's one of those little things that gets hushed up because a couple of months later Saddam became a bad boy. He disobeyed orders. Right after that came harsh sanctions and so on, right up till today.

Transcribed from a talk at Z Media Institute, printed in Z Magazine, *December 2010 Volume 23, Number 12*

5.

Protecting Americans Abroad: Pretext For Intervention

By Stephen R. Shalom

WITH THE END of the Cold War, the most commonly used rationale for U.S. interventionism evaporated. No longer would anyone believe that Washington has to send in the Marines or subvert governments in order to combat So-

With the end of the Cold War, the most commonly used rationale for U.S. interventionism has evaporated. No longer will anyone believe that Washington has to send in the Marines or subvert governments in order to combat Soviet expansionism.

viet expansionism. Accordingly, U.S. policymakers need to devise new justifications for their intervention policies. One rationale that we are likely to hear with increasing frequency in coming years is that of "humanitarian intervention." Its persuasiveness lies in the fact that even for those who hold the principle of nonintervention to be extremely important, there is a competing principle that is also important, namely, that when possible one ought to try to prevent massive human suffering. Sometimes, these two principles may be in conflict. For example, imagine if a government were to start massacring its population. Should foreign nations intervene to put a halt to the killing? To make the example specific, what if the government of South Africa were to methodically set up gas chambers and proceed to exterminate the black population of the country? Would foreign intervention be justified?

The risk in granting blanket endorsement to humanitarian intervention is that governments are not typically motivated by humanitarian concerns. If they intervene somewhere, they will be doing it for their own reasons and in such a way that humanitarianism will probably be ill-served.

Indeed, there is the danger that if the doctrine of humanitarian intervention became widely adopted, there would be no end to wars and their attendant human misery.

Humanitarian intervention comes in two varieties: intervention to protect one's own citizens and intervention to protect the citizens of a foreign nation. When one looks at the actual occasions on which claims of humanitarian intervention in either version have been put forward, the record is not reassuring. Hitler justified his occupation of Bohemia and Moravia in

Not surprisingly, such accounts make no mention of the Platt Amendment (which forced Cuba to include in its constitution a provision allowing the U.S. to intervene) or the U.S. domination of the island for the next half century

1939 as humanitarian intervention to protect minorities. To this day, some scholars cite the Spanish American War as another example of humanitarian intervention because the U.S. freed Cuba from the Spanish yoke. Not surprisingly, such accounts make no mention of the Platt Amendment (which forced Cuba to include in its constitution a provision allowing the U.S. to intervene) or the U.S. domination of the island for the next half century.

One leading authority asserts that there was at most a single genuine case of humanitarian intervention in the century and a half before World War II: the French occupation of Lebanon/Syria in 1860-61 to prevent the massacre of the Maronite Christians at the hands of the Druses. But a British government report on these events leaves doubts even in this instance. "It is an admitted fact that the original provocation proceeded from the Christians, who had been for months beforehand preparing an onslaught on the Druses, which their leaders confidently expected would terminate, if not in the extermination, in all events in the expulsion of that race."

Moreover, the Christian clergy attempted "to animate the courage of their flocks, by tell-

ing them that their endeavor to attain undisputed possession of Lebanon would be warmly countenanced by the Powers of Christendom." The British, of course, were not neutral observers, but there is certainly the possibility that Maronite hopes of foreign intervention on their behalf helped to precipitate the violence.

The record with respect to protecting one's nationals is scarcely better. As the president of the American Society of International Law noted some years ago: "The claimed right to intervene to protect one's own citizens was the most cited rationalization for the episodic acts of interventionary imperialism all the way to the Boxer Rebellion and on down the line." The concept was the "international legal rationalization for the most important intrusions of great powers into the lives and social structures of small and weak powers in recent history." One can imagine imperial policymakers suggesting this rationale to their colleagues, as Richard Nixon did in urging the overthrow of Castro in 1961: "I would find a proper legal cover and go in. There are several legal justifications that could be used, like protecting American citizens living in Cuba...." One reason we must be extremely cautious before endorsing a right of humanitarian intervention is that this right is, as Richard Falk has noted, an asymmetrical claim in international law. That is, it is a claim advanced only by the strong against the weak.

No one bothers debating whether Cuba has the right to land Marines in Los Angeles to protect the population there from undoubted police brutality. Likewise, people haven't stayed up nights arguing about whether the Philippines had the right to deploy troops in Tienanmen Square to protect the democracy movement from cruel repression.

Because humanitarian intervention is this sort of privileged claim of the powerful, we would want to impose the strictest constraints on its use to prevent abuse—if we were going to endorse it at all. Surely one would want minimally to insist that any humanitarian intervention meet a number of standards: that the intervener be able to credibly prove genuine concern about the humanitarian issue. For example, China was outraged at Vietnam's treatment of its Chinese minority in the late 1970s. But given Beijing's utter silence while its Kampuchean ally butchered 200,000 ethnic Chinese in the same period, a Chinese claim of humanitarian intervention against Vietnam would be highly suspect. And one ought to be particularly wary of cases where the intervener has blocked the possibility of more peaceful solutions. It might seem that the issue of protecting foreign nationals abroad could not be a very significant matter in U.S. foreign policy. After all, as Thomas Franck once remarked, "The actual number of Americans killed abroad by events in foreign countries that are intentionally directed at Americans would come somewhere in the list between Category 17 of deaths, which would be a surfeit of claret, and Category 19, which would be a paucity of green vegetables." In addition, in 1936 the United States signed a convention in Buenos Aires under which it gave up the right to intervene in Latin America "for whatever reason." Nevertheless, the protecting-Americans-abroad justification for intervention has been used quite a number of times by Washington since World War II. Three of the major such instances are worth looking at for they tell us a great deal about how this rationale might be used in the future.

The Dominican Republic

In 1963 the elected government of Juan Bosch was overthrown in a military coup. On April 24, 1965, Bosch supporters in the armed forces led an effort to restore the constitutionally elected president to office. Key Dominican military officers vacillated and it briefly seemed as if the victory of the constitutionalist rebels would be almost bloodless.

Had it been so, of course, the danger to American citizens would have been precisely nil. But it was not to be. According to Jerome Slater, whose account is not unsympathetic to the U.S. government, U.S. military attaches "urged the military to resist and told them they had U.S. 'support' if they did." Concludes Slater: "Undoubtedly, this U.S. intervention proved decisive with those commanders who were still wavering." The ranking official in the U.S. Embassy endorsed an attack by the military on the rebels, "even though it could mean more bloodshed." The Dominican Air Force proceeded to strafe the palace and other sites held by the rebels. The latter urgently asked the U.S. Embassy to try to prevent these air strikes, but the Embassy rejected the plea.

The military onslaught was stopped, however, by civilians who had been armed by the rebels and, starting on April 26, military leaders called on the United States to support them with troops. Still confident that the military would prevail, Washington turned down the request for the time being. With their abiding commitment to nonintervention, U.S. policymakers took the position that, "We don't want to intervene unless the outcome is in doubt." As civil war spread, the U.S. Embassy informed those American citizens who wanted to leave to gather at the Embajador Hotel in Santo Domingo. A right-wing radio announcer had tried to hide among the evacuees and armed rebels came to the hotel looking for him. Some shots were fired in the air, frightening the assembled Americans. No one was hurt and there had been no attempt to terrorize the Americans. Shortly thereafter, rebel officers agreed to cooperate fully in the evacuation of the U.S. citizens. Washington expected the military to soon be in firm control and no U.S. official thought U.S. troops were needed to protect the Americans.

The military offensive ran aground the next day and at 3:00 PM the head of the military junta, Colonel Benoit, telephoned the U.S.

Embassy to ask for U.S. troops. The request was passed on to the State Department, but neither the U.S. Ambassador nor officials in Washington believed troops should be sent unless the outcome was in doubt. At 4:00 PM, Benoit submitted a formal written request for U.S. troops. The request warned of the dangers of "another Cuba," claiming that the rebels were controlled by Communists and committing widespread atrocities. No mention was made of any danger to Americans. Washington was still not persuaded that troops were needed.

An hour later, the U.S. Ambassador became convinced that the military could not prevail on its own and he cabled Washington, urging the dispatch of U.S. Marines. He asserted that U.S. citizens were now at risk, but emphasized the reverses suffered by the military (their officers were dejected, several of them were weeping). "If Washington wished," the Ambassador suggested, the Marines could be landed for the mission of protecting the evacuation of Americans.

Lyndon Johnson approved the landing of the Marines and the Ambassador was instructed to get a written request from Benoit asking for U.S. troops specifically to protect American lives. The Marines landed several hours before the revised request arrived. Johnson's speech announcing the intervention justified it exclusively in terms of protecting U.S. citizens. Secretary of State Dean Rusk and Lyndon Johnson later spoke of the Embajador Hotel episode as though it had been the incident precipitating the decision to land the Marines. As noted, however, it had occurred the day before. The actual danger to American citizens is indicated by the fact that (to quote Slater) "not a single American" was attacked. Moreover, there were "remarkably few" rebel

"atrocities of any sort. What few attacks did occur were highly selective, aimed almost exclusively at a few extreme rightists and then mainly at their property." To be sure, there

> *The real bloodbath was yet to come. Initially, 500 U.S. Marines landed, but the number was quickly increased to more than 20,000. Within 48 hours, U.S. troops were deployed so as to block a rebel victory. "Your announced mission," the commander of U.S. forces was told on April 30, "is to save American lives. Your unstated mission is to prevent the Dominican Republic from going Communist."*

were many civilian casualties in the civil war, but "many more innocent civilians died as a result of the Air Force bombing and strafing" than at the hands of the rebels. U.S. officials repeated stories of hundreds of people being lined up against the wall and shot, of hacked off heads being carried around as trophies, of embassies being torn up. In fact, there had been no mass killings, no disembodied heads, no torn-up embassies, not even widespread looting in rebel zones.

The real bloodbath was yet to come. Initially, 500 U.S. Marines landed, but the number was quickly increased to more than 20,000. Within 48 hours, U.S. troops were deployed so as to block a rebel victory. "Your announced mission," the commander of U.S. forces was told on April 30, "is to save American lives. Your unstated mission is to prevent the Dominican Republic from going Communist." (The claim that the rebels were controlled by Communists was nonsensical. Administration officials explained that, although they could only identify a few Communists among rebel forces, Castro had begun with just 12 men and Hitler at one time had only 7 supporters.)

U.S. troops interposed themselves between rebel and military units. After the military had regrouped and been resupplied with U.S. assistance, they were then allowed, if not encouraged, to move through the U.S. lines to attack rebel forces who had been cut off from their rural base by U.S. troops. Hundreds of rebel fighters and innocent civilians were butchered. To quote Jerome Slater again: "Although the Johnson administration had proclaimed as one of the main purposes of the intervention the need to save Dominican lives in a bloody civil war, in fact most of the estimated 3,000 Dominican deaths occurred after the intervention, some of them in clashes between the constitutionalists and U.S. troops, and the rest at the hands of a Dominican military that the United States had rescued from probable annihilation in April and thereafter had helped protect and rebuild."

In closed hearings, Secretary of State Rusk had declared that the decision to send troops was "99 percent the problem of protecting American and other foreign nationals." The U.S. troops remained in the Dominican Republic for 17 months. Before they left, they organized elections in which an associate of former dictator Rafael Trujillo defeated Bosch for the presidency. The elections were stage-managed in a variety of ways by the U.S. and its local allies, though this did not stop commentators like Slater from praising the workings of Dominican democracy.

Slater does acknowledge, however, that the United States probably would not have let Bosch undertake such radical measures as placing supporters of the constitution in military command positions. In subsequent years, death squads appeared in the Dominican Republic, corruption grew rampant, living standards for the majority of the population declined, and the labor movement was repressed to ensure large profits for foreign companies. As a reporter for the *Wall Street Journal* put it in 1971, "The terrorism, corruption and misery that marked Rafael Trujillo's 31-year dictatorship...are even more widespread today...." Such are the fruits of 'humanitarian' intervention.

Cambodia

Ten years after the Marines landed in Santo Domingo, innocent American lives were once again said to be in danger, requiring military action. A U.S. merchant ship, the Mayaguez, and its crew of 40 had been seized by the new revolutionary government of Cambodia. Cambodia had been the victim of years of U.S. subversion, bombardment, and direct invasion. This U.S. intervention and the parallel interventions in Vietnam and Laos resulted

> *In closed hearings, Secretary of State Rusk had declared that the decision to send troops was "99 percent the problem of protecting American and other foreign nationals." The U.S. troops remained in the Dominican Republic for 17 months.*

in a devastating defeat for the aspirations of the people of Indochina as millions of people lay dead, economic life was shattered, and the massive devastation would take decades to overcome. But the wars on Vietnam, Laos, and Cambodia were also viewed in Washington as defeats for the United States; despite the application of unprecedented violence. The U.S. had been unable to subdue the peasant armies that ultimately took power in April 1975. On May 10, Secretary of State Henry Kissinger urged his boss, President Gerald Ford, to respond to the defeat in Vietnam with "a tough, even abrasive foreign policy." *Time Magazine* reported that Ford "had been searching" for a means to show that the U.S. was now conducting this "abrasive" foreign policy when the *Mayaguez* was seized. Even before the seizure, one U.S. official had told *Time*, "There's quite a bit of agreement around here that it wouldn't be a bad thing if the other side goes a step or two too far in trying to kick us while we're down. It would give us a chance to kick them back—hard."

Perhaps the Ford administration decided to help things along. That the Cambodians claimed a 12-mile limit to their territorial waters was known; that they were battling with Vietnam over claims to islands off the coast was also known; that they had in the previous few days fired on at least one ship and detained another for sailing within 12 miles of islands they claimed was known as well. Nevertheless, the State Department issued no warning to vessels in the area. Kissinger later asserted that, though no advisory to ships was issued, maritime insurance companies were informed of the danger. The president of the American Institute of Marine Underwriters, however, denied that any such warning had been received.

In his memoirs, presidential press secretary Ron Nessen wrote: "News accounts told of a Panamanian freighter and a South Korean vessel being harassed by Cambodian patrol boats a few days before the *Mayaguez* was seized. Actually there were a number of similar incidents, beginning much earlier, which were never revealed. In addition, the United States had picked up intelligence that Cambodia intended to extend its territorial claims around the offshore islands, including Poulo Wai, and to enforce its claim by seizing ships that strayed too close."

Nessen goes on to ask the obvious question: If the United States knew this, why wasn't a warning to merchant shipping issued? "It could have been simply a bureaucratic screw-up, one agency not knowing what another agency knew." He then adds: "I never saw a shred of evidence that the *Mayaguez* was deliberately allowed to sail into a Cambodian trap in order to provoke an international incident."

On May 12, the *Mayaguez* sailed, according to its captain, within seven miles of Poulo Wai. Given Cambodia's response to other ships in its waters and given the well-documented xenophobia and paranoia of Khmer Rouge officials—traits not discouraged by two decades of U.S. interventionism—it is not surprising that the Cambodians reacted by seizing the ship. The captain of the *Mayaguez* later guessed that the Cambodians "thought I was making a survey of the island to find out just how much military force they had there."

In Washington, a National Security Council meeting was promptly convened and Kissinger argued that what was at stake was far more than the capture of an American cargo ship. As Nessen recalls, Kissinger said "the capture of the *Mayaguez* gave Ford the chance to assert strongly that there was a point beyond which the United States would not be pushed." The immediate use of force was impossible. As Kissinger's assistant Brent Scowcroft put it, U.S. naval vessels were "heartbreakingly" far away, at least two days' steaming time. Ford ordered military forces to be moved into place. He knew that the Thai government wouldn't be happy about the U.S. using its bases in Thailand for this purpose, "but until *Mayaguez* and her crew were safe, I didn't give a damn about offending their sensibilities." Bangkok sent Washington a note explicitly telling the United States not to use bases in Thailand for any military operations relating to the *Mayaguez*, but Ford ignored the note.

Nessen announced that the President "considers the seizure an act of piracy." But even by the U.S. account, the ship was within Cambodia's territorial waters. The co-chair designate of the American Bar Association's committee on international law thought that Cambodia at least had a viable claim that it was arresting violators of traditional international law. Ship seizures were not unusual in international practice (for example, the U.S. seized and detained a Polish fishing vessel off the San Francisco coast that same week). Though there are legal differences between fishing vessels and other ships, and though one can argue the legal merits of the case, there was no justification for characterizing the Cambodian action as an "act of piracy"—and State Department lawyers admitted as much.

Nessen further announced that the president had "instructed the State Department to demand the immediate release of the ship. Failure to do so would have the most serious consequences." Kissinger later asserted that the U.S. rejected the idea of sending an ultimatum to Cambodia because it was feared that this might harden Cambodia's attitude even more. A number of sources claimed that in a private message sent to Phnom Penh the U.S. gave the Cambodians 24 hours to surrender the ship and crew. When the General Accounting Office (GAO) of Congress later tried to confirm or deny this story, they were blocked by the State Department's refusal to declassify the message. Even if there were no deadline set, the threat of force was evident in Nessen's statement and subsequent U.S. statements. As Kissinger put it, "We felt we had, in effect, given an ultimatum without giving a specific time." The Cambodians docked the *Mayaguez* at Koh Tang island and transferred the crew to a fishing boat, which, along with some gunboats, set out for Kompong Som (formerly Sihanoukville) on the mainland. The U.S. Air Force tried to get the boats to turn back by dropping bombs in front of them. When this failed, U.S. aircraft sank three of the gunboats and immobilized four others. The Deputy Assistant Secretary of Defense testified that he "can't be sure" that there were no Americans aboard the vessels that were sunk. The fishing boat was bombed and strafed 100 times, the captain of the *Mayaguez* later recalled, and three of the *Mayaguez* crew were wounded by shrapnel. When U.S. pilots confirmed that Caucasians were aboard the boat, the bombing gave way to gas attacks. In the *Mayaguez* captain's words, "Everybody on the ship vomited. Their skin was burning." The fishing boat finally made it to Kompong Som.

Blowing The Hell Out Of 'Em

The National Security Council met again that afternoon. Kissinger and Ford "felt that we had to do more" than rescue the ship and crew. As Ford acknowledges, they were "eager to use *Mayaguez* as an example for

Asia and the world." Diplomacy was never seriously considered. Early that morning a report had been received indicating that a foreign government was using its influence to seek the ship's early release and expected the release to come soon. According to the GAO, the report was basically ignored and the U.S. made its first approach to the United Nations at about 1:00 PM that day, more than 48 hours since the beginning of the crisis.

> *When this failed, U.S. aircraft sank three of the gunboats and immobilized four others. The Deputy Assistant Secretary of Defense testified that he "can't be sure" that there were no Americans aboard the vessels that were sunk.*

The Secretary General appealed to the United States and Cambodia to refrain from further acts of force to facilitate a peaceful settlement, whereupon President Ford gave the order for a military operation.

Ford's battle plan called for the Marines to attack Koh Tang island and recover the *Mayaguez*, while bombing raids were conducted on an airport, a naval base, and an oil refinery on the mainland. Kissinger, Vice-President Nelson Rockefeller, and Scowcroft favored using B-52s for the air strikes; Ford, however, opposed using these incredibly inaccurate planes when he was advised that a U.S. aircraft carrier with tactical bombers was then in the area. "Even so," noted *Time* magazine's correspondent, "the B-52s were kept gassed-up, their bomb bays loaded, and their crews on the line ready for take-off."

Reporters were excluded from the air base on Guam so they wouldn't be able to see the planes being loaded with 1,000-pound bombs. Once the military operation was set in motion, Ford called in congressional leaders for a briefing which characteristically began with a standing ovation for the President. Ford explained: "We gave the Cambodians clear orders. They disregarded them. They were not to try to take the ships from the island to the mainland." For this act of disobedience to the ruler of the universe, Cambodian ships were blown out of the water. Ford then described the military action that had been ordered and the congressional leaders asked a few bland questions. The president pro tempore of the Senate, James Eastland, sat slumped down in his chair throughout the session, mumbling several times, "Blow the hell out of 'em."

Just minutes before the Marines arrived at Koh Tang and several hours before the first bombs were dropped on the mainland, Radio Phnom Penh began a 19-minute broadcast by Hu Nim, Cambodia's Minister for Information and Propaganda. After criticizing U.S. interference in Cambodia, Hu Nim declared: "Regarding the *Mayaguez,* we have no intention of detaining it permanently and we have no desire to stage provocations. We only wanted to know why it came and to warn it against violating our waters again." This was the same warning, said Hu Nim, given to "the ship flying the Panamanian flag which we released on 9 May 1975." The broadcast continued: "Wishing to provoke no one or to make trouble, adhering to the stand of peace and neutrality, we will release this ship, but we will not allow the U.S. imperialists to violate our territorial waters, conduct espionage in our territorial waters, provoke accidents in our territorial waters, or force us to release their ships whenever they want by applying threats."

It took just under an hour for the U.S. government monitoring agency in Bangkok to translate the broadcast and transmit it to Washington. Kissinger and Ford were determined to go ahead with their military plans, ignoring the conciliatory nature of the broadcast. Ford told one journalist, "I said to the secretary, 'They don't mention the crew,' and apparently the information Henry had, he had not been told or the announcement didn't include the crew. So I said to him, 'Proceed as we had agreed, with the air strikes and the full operation'." It is true that the announcement did not specifically mention the crew, but Ford did not

know this for sure—Kissinger had received only a preliminary translation of the broadcast.

Any reasonable reading of the Cambodian message would assume that the release of the crew was intended. Hadn't the message spoken of the release of the Panamanian "ship" as a way to refer to the release of that vessel and its crew? In fact, wasn't this very same shorthand of using the word "ship" to refer to vessel and crew employed by the United States in its initial public statement on the crisis (the President "instructed the State Department to demand the immediate release of the ship").

No pause was ordered in the Marine assault. The air strikes on the mainland were put on hold, but then ordered resumed just 20 minutes later when no further word was received from Cambodia. It is not surprising that no further word was received in these 20 minutes, given that the United States did not issue its message saying it wanted to hear specific word on the crew until an hour later. The operative principle for U.S. policymakers seemed clear—when in doubt, use force.

In fact, at the very same time as the Phnom Penh radio broadcast, the Cambodians had put the *Mayaguez* crew on a fishing boat and sent them, unaccompanied, back towards the *Mayaguez* and Koh Tang island. About three hours later they were spotted by a U.S. plane. Nevertheless, air strikes were carried out against the mainland air and naval base; aircraft, hangars, fuel storage facilities, runways, and anti-aircraft sites were hit at the airfield and barracks and fuel storage facilities at the naval base. Within half an hour, the entire *Mayaguez* crew was reported picked up, all hands safe, by a U.S. destroyer.

Ford announced that offensive operations would now cease, but 30 minutes later air strikes were ordered and carried out against an oil refinery, warehouses, and a railroad marshalling yard building at Kompong Som. The U.S. defended these last raids as necessary to protect the Marines trying to extricate themselves from Koh Tang—a rather preposterous claim, given that these targets were hardly going to enable the Cambodians to project military power 35 miles across waters controlled by the U.S. Navy and Air Force—particularly not an oil refinery that the U.S. knew to have been inoperative. According to the GAO, the Defense Department was unable to cite any indications that Cambodia—which had few boats or planes remaining after the previous air strikes—were preparing to attack the U.S. forces still on Koh Tang. Kissinger is said to have put the matter a little differently in private. Asked by Scowcroft whether there was any reason for the Pentagon not to disengage, Kissinger told him: "No, but tell them to bomb the mainland. Let's look ferocious. Otherwise they will attack us as the ship leaves." Ford makes no mention in his memoirs of the post-release air strike, though he does complain that still another wave of air attacks that he authorized somehow never got carried out.

There was more ferocity. The U.S. dropped the BLU-82 bomb, the largest non- nuclear weapon in its arsenal, on Cambodian positions on Koh Tang. Again the claim was made that this measure was necessary to extract the Marines from the island, but there are reasons for doubt. The head of the Marine Task Group had originally asked that the bomb be used only when requested by the officer in charge of the Koh Tang assault. But, according to the GAO, the "assault commander had not requested the use of the BLU-82 and stated that he was not informed that a decision had been made to drop the weapon." The GAO was "told that the decision to use the weapon was probably made in Washington."

To "save" 40 crew members who were being released anyway, the *Mayaguez* "rescue" mission led to the deaths of 41 Americans and the wounding of 50 more: 15 Marines died in the assault on Koh Tang and 23 Air Force personnel were lost in a helicopter crash as troops were being moved into position in Thailand. (The Pentagon tried to exclude the latter 23 from the death toll on the grounds that these Air Force units ultimately were not assigned to combat, but clearly the 23 died as a result of the Mayaguez operation.)

Despite these losses, Secretary of Defense James Schlesinger was correct when he remarked that "the outcome was fortunate." It was only good fortune that prevented crew members from being killed by U.S. bombs or by Cambodians enraged at U.S. duplicity. Had the Cambodians had the evil intent that, ac-

> *The U.S. dropped the BLU-82 bomb, the largest non-nuclear weapon in its arsenal, on Cambodian positions on Koh Tang. Again the claim was made that this measure was necessary to extract the Marines from the island, but there are reasons for doubt.*

cording to U.S. policymakers, justified the operation, it is hard to see how any of the crew would have survived the rescue mission.

The captain later asserted that he and the entire crew were grateful for the rescue operation, but one wonders. Some of the crew suffered permanent damage from the gas attacks. The Cambodians were rather more solicitous of the crew's well-being. One member commented later that the Cambodians "were so nice, really kind. They fed us first and everything. I hope everybody gets hijacked by them." More typical was the reaction of chief engineer Cliff Harrington, who commented as he boarded the U.S. destroyer: "That's a damn shame they're bombing Kompong Som. Those people didn't do us any harm."

The costs of the "rescue" mission to the Cambodians were far heavier, though the final toll will probably never be known. As William Shawcross has noted, one can do no more than "speculate on the effects the attacks must have had on Khmer Rouge paranoia about their enemies."

The reaction in the United States to the *Mayaguez* affair was general enthusiasm. Said Senator Barry Goldwater: "It shows we still got some balls in this country." "Let no one mistake the unity and strength of an America under attack," declared Democratic Senator Adlai Stevenson III. "The President's firm and successful action," effused Senator Ted Kennedy, "gave an undeniable and needed lift to the nation's spirit and he deserves our genuine support." There were a few voices of dissent, among them Representative Pat Schroeder: "We have won no 'victory.' We have proved nothing to the world, except that this President is willing—as were his predecessors—to make hasty and ill-considered use of American military force against tiny countries regardless of the law."

Grenada

Cambodia was huge compared to the tiny country of Grenada. In October 1983, U.S. troops invaded this Caribbean island, claiming that they were protecting more than 1,000 American citizens, the majority of them students at St. George's University Medical School. A country of just 100,000 people, Grenada had been ruled since 1979 by a left-wing government headed by Maurice Bishop. In early October 1983, the ruling New Jewel Movement was torn by internal discord and, on October 15, Bishop was ordered arrested by the party's central committee. On October 19, a huge crowd of Bishop's supporters freed him; a clash with army units ensued and, in the aftermath, Bishop and some of his key associates were executed.

There was widespread international condemnation of the killings. Cuba declared that "No doctrine, no principle or proclaimed revolutionary position and no internal division can justify atrocious acts such as the physical elimination of Bishop and the prominent group of honest and worthy leaders who died yesterday."

Michael Manley, the leftish former Jamaican prime minister, called the killings a "squalid betrayal of the hopes of the ordinary people of our region." Neighboring Caribbean states imposed harsh economic sanctions.

The U.S., too, expressed its concern over developments in Grenada, but it obviously wasn't very concerned about Bishop. From the time he first came to power in 1979—overthrowing Eric Gairy, a corrupt and repressive leader with a rather bizarre belief in UFOs—the U.S. had been hostile to Bishop, who was no democrat, but he was genuinely popular and committed to improving the social welfare of the population.

According to the *Washington Post*, the National Security Council considered a proposal to blockade Grenada just after Bishop took over. Relations worsened when Ronald Reagan became president in 1981. Under the new Administration, any government in Central America or the Caribbean not wholly subservient to Washington was a target for destabilization. The CIA developed a plan to undermine Bishop by causing economic difficulty in the country. The plan was said to be aborted because of Senate opposition, but the U.S. did offer the Caribbean Development Bank a loan on condition that Grenada be excluded, and, in general, Grenada was barred from receiving U.S. aid.

In October 1981, the United States conducted military exercises in the Caribbean called "Amber and the Amberines" (a none too subtle reference to Grenada and the Grenadines), which involved the hypothetical freeing of Americans held hostage on "Amber" and installing a government "favorable to the way of life we espouse." Reagan refused to accept the credentials of Grenada's ambassador to Washington and he ordered the U.S. ambassador in Barbados not to present his letters of credence in Grenada, as was the usual practice.

In early 1983, a U.S. official warned that Grenada might provide missile bases for the Soviet Union. Other officials claimed Grenada was preparing a submarine base for Moscow, until a *Washington Post* reporter bothered to look at the alleged site and found that it was too shallow for any such facility. The biggest U.S. government propaganda campaign, however, was to suggest that the new airport being built at Point Salinas was to be a Cuban or Soviet military base. It is "difficult, if not impossible, to identify any economic justification" for building an airport, a Deputy Assistant Secretary of State testified in June 1982. But, as the World Bank had noted in 1980, the lack of a decent-sized airport was a major obstacle to developing Grenada's tourism industry. The length of the runway was said by U.S. officials to prove its military character, but eight other Caribbean countries had even longer runways. "Grenada does not even have an air force," blustered Ronald Reagan. "Who is it intended for?" he asked, neglecting to point out that commercial airlines use airports too.

A base at Point Salinas, Deputy Secretary Kenneth Dam charged, would allow Cuban aircraft to strike Puerto Rico, among other targets. But Puerto Rico is closer to Cuba than to Grenada. The Cubans, of course, were playing a prominent role in the construction of the airport, but so was the British firm Plessey, and even an American dredging company was taking part. Presumably, there would have been greater Western participation in the project if the U.S. had not gone to such great lengths to dissuade other nations from becoming involved.

After Bishop was killed, General Hudson Austin, head of the armed forces, announced the formation of a Revolutionary Military Command (RMC) and declared a round-the-clock, shoot-on-sight 96-hour curfew. U.S. officials subsequently claimed that the draconian curfew endangered U.S. citizens and that Americans could not leave the island. Neither of these claims was true. In later congressional testimony, Deputy Secretary Dam acknowledged that he was unaware of anyone —American or Grenadian—shot pursuant to the curfew. There is no evidence of any action taken or threatened against any foreign citizen during this period.

Reagan administration officials announced on October 27 that they had found evidence that the Grenadian government, together with Cuban advisers, was planning to take American hostages, but this claim was retracted a short while later. (Of course, this didn't stop noted legal scholars like John Norton Moore —writing after the retraction—from citing the false claim.) Not only was there no such plan, but both Grenadian authorities and Cuban officials in Havana gave explicit assurances that U.S. citizens were safe. U.S. officials did not bother to disclose these assurances publicly. When they later came to light, the White House explained that the pledges were not trusted.

The Grenadian government was particularly solicitous of the welfare of the medical students whose presence on the island was crucial to the country's economy. Austin visited the vice-chancellor of the medical school to assure him that there was no danger to the students and to offer any assistance to help the school cope with the curfew. Water was specially provided and school officials were given passes to go out despite the curfew. Students who went outside during the curfew reported that they were not stopped or threatened.

For the country as a whole, the curfew was temporarily lifted on the third day to give people a chance to buy food. The government provided the medical students with vehicles and escorts to get from one campus to the other. The medical school took a poll of its students and only 10 percent wanted to leave Grenada. On the evening of Sunday, October 23, 500 parents of the medical students met in New York City to discuss the situation. Many had been in touch with their children. They sent a telegram to President Reagan urging him not to "take any precipitous actions at this time."

In the meantime, the Reagan administration was hard at work to make the students' situation look precarious. Just before the Sunday night meeting, the chancellor of the medical school was called by various U.S. officials trying to get him to say that the students were in danger. He did not believe this to be the case and refused to make such a statement. Medical school trustees were also contacted in an effort to elicit similar statements. Over that weekend, U.S. diplomats flew into Grenada (with the permission of the Austin government) to talk with U.S. citizens. Instead of trying to ascertain the students' views, however, the diplomats tried to convince them of their danger. Late Sunday night a radio broadcast from outside Grenada announced that an invasion of the island was imminent. This caused many of the students to get worried, as well it might, for, more than anything else, it was an invasion that would put them at risk—and now perhaps half of them wanted to leave. Fear of invasion, however, is hardly a rationale for an invasion, particularly because there was no obstacle to orderly evacuation if it were desired. British and Canadian diplomats present on the island did not believe an invasion was necessary to protect their nationals. Administrators of the medical school supported this assessment, though one of them, vice-chancellor Geoffrey Bourne, later changed his view on the basis of some peculiar reasoning, and who knows what pressure.

According to Bourne, Austin had mistakenly thought that all the U.S. students were being taken out of the country and came to him very upset. Bourne explained that this was not the intention, but concluded from this that there were grave doubts whether they could have gotten out. The Grenadian government sent a diplomatic note to the United States that night and broadcast the text over Radio Free Grenada. It condemned any planned invasion and offered to hold talks to ensure good relations. "We reiterate that the lives, well-being, and property of every American and other foreign citizens residing in Grenada are fully protected and guaranteed by our government." However, the note went on, "any American or foreign citizen in our country who desires to leave Grenada for whatever reasons can fully do so using the normal procedures through our airports on commercial aircraft. As far as we are concerned, these aircraft can be regular flights or chartered flights and we will facilitate them in every way we can."

Of course, these were just promises and Deputy Secretary of State Dam asserted that, "Although the RMC gave assurances that the airport would be opened on October 24 and foreigners allowed to depart, they then failed to fulfill that assurance." This assertion is simply false. The curfew was lifted at 6:00 AM Monday morning and the airport was opened. Four small planes flew in, picked up passengers—among them the former director of Reagan's national commission on social security—and flew out. Caught in their lie, U.S. officials later argued that, though a few planes got in and out, "the airport was not open for normal traffic." This, too, was a lie. There was no normal traffic, not because the airport was closed, but rather because neighboring Caribbean states had prohibited regional airlines from traveling to Grenada as part of the sanctions they had imposed against the Austin government. The attention that U.S. officials devoted to the question of an orderly evacuation was revealed when Repre- sentative Stephen Solarz asked Deputy Secretary Dam whether, after the four small planes had landed, the U.S. tried to arrange for other, larger planes to land and pick up Americans.

Dam replied: "I cannot answer that question. First of all, I am not clear as to what extent we were aware. We were certainly aware planes were not getting in. To what extent we were aware the small planes had been able to get out, I do not know." Even without the regular regional carrier, alternative evacuation plans could be made. On the evening of October 24, the Foreign Minister of Trinidad and Tobago announced that arrangements had been made to evacuate Trinidadian and Canadian nationals by air the next day. But the next day the U.S. invaded.

"I think," commented Robert Pastor, a member of Jimmy Carter's National Security Council, "there is reason to believe that the Marines may have got there just in time before the new Grenadian government could prove publicly the private assurances that it had given to the medical school and the U.S. government that they were going to assure the safety of U.S. citizens." Perhaps it was this sense of urgency that led the Pentagon to name the invasion Operation Urgent Fury.

If there was any scheme to hold Americans hostage, the invasion provided the ideal opportunity. The Grenadians knew of the impending invasion many hours before it began. Then it took U.S. troops more than a day and a half from their first landing to reach the Grand Anse campus of the medical school—more than enough time for the Grenadians to carry out any nefarious deeds, were they so inclined. (The time lag was attributable to the students' "liberators" never having been told there was a second campus.) According to Bourne, the Grenadian army did not use school property for offensive or defensive purposes, though it would have been a perfect site from which to shoot down U.S. helicopters. (One might compare this Grena- dian concern to avoid "collateral damage" to civilian sites with the U.S.'s accidental bombing of a mental hospital, killing dozens.)

There is no doubt that the students were finally in danger. They told "of bullets crashing through their dormitory rooms during the invasion and of wading through surf to board rescue helicopters amid raging gunfire and booming explosions," but it was the invasion that endangered them.

Polls showed the American public enthusiastic about the invasion, but most did not believe that the U.S. citizens in Grenada had been in any great danger. And, in any event, the U.S. troops had done far more than evacuate Americans. They had overthrown the Austin government, so the Reagan adminis-

tration needed some other rationalizations. One claim advanced was that the intervention had been requested and authorized by the Organization of Eastern Caribbean States as a measure of collective security. This claim, however, was a transparent fig leaf.

While most OECS members did support the invasion, they had no legal authority to authorize force. The OECS treaty clearly required unanimity for its decisions, but, even aside from the abstentions, the Grenadian government—a member nation—obviously did not concur. The treaty further specifies that collective security measures are permit-

> *Polls showed the American public enthusiastic about the invasion, but most did not believe that the U.S. citizens in Grenada had been in any great danger. And, in any event, the U.S. troops had done far more than evacuate.*

ted only in cases of outside aggression, which was not relevant to the Grenada situation. U.S. officials were privately discussing intervention with OECS nations prior to the latter organization's meeting at which the secret decision to support an invasion was reached. The formal request for U.S. intervention from the OECS was drafted in Washington. The 300 Caribbean "troops" that participated in the invasion were actually police forces who saw no combat. The largest of these contingents came from Barbados and Jamaica, neither of which is a member of OECS. They are both part of another, larger regional grouping, CARICOM, which did not endorse the use of force. In any event, one might consider, for example, whether the Soviet invasion of Czechoslovakia in 1968 would have been justified even if the other Warsaw Pact members had begged Moscow to intervene.

Another U.S. claim was that the invasion had been invited by Paul Scoon, the Governor-General of Grenada. Scoon, according to the U.S., secretly transmitted a request for intervention that the U.S. could not reveal until after the invasion, out of concern for his well-being. But Scoon's position was entirely a ceremonial one.

According to People's Law Number 3 of March 1979, the Governor-General "shall perform such functions as the People's Revolutionary Government may from time to time advise." A report from the British House of Commons (recall that the Governor-General is supposed to be the representative of the British Queen) stated that "the timing and nature" of Scoon's request "remain shrouded in some mystery and it is evidently the intention of the parties directly involved that the mystery should not be dispelled." The British magazine the *Economist* (which supported the invasion) was more direct: the "Scoon request was almost certainly a fabrication concocted between the OECS and Washington to calm the post-invasion diplomatic storm." Later, Scoon told the BBC that what he had asked for "was not an invasion but help from outside." And he

> *With the pre-invasion danger to the students not credible and the legal arguments unconvincing, the White House resorted to its old standby: U.S. troops got to Grenada "just in time," Reagan declared, to prevent a Cuban takeover*

also informed reporters that he had not been aware of the possible involvement of U.S. forces until they landed in his front garden.

With the pre-invasion danger to the students not credible and the legal arguments unconvincing, the White House resorted to its old standby: U.S. troops got to Grenada "just in time," Reagan declared, to prevent a Cuban takeover. This claim was preposterous on its face—Cuba had been outraged at the killing of Bishop. But when U.S. forces captured some 25,000 documents in Grenada detailing such things as weapons deals with the Soviet Union and North Korea, the Administration proclaimed that its case had been proven. But the documents—in the words of one right-wing study—"provide no conclusive evidence that

Grenada had become a depot of Soviet arms for future use in the region, nor were there any Soviet or Cuban military bases or facilities at the time of the U.S./OECS intervention, aside from the controversial airport, which also had clear-cut civilian purposes." Moreover, the documents "do not provide evidence" that the New Jewel Movement "intended to allow Grenada to be used as a military or political base for the Cubans or Soviets to expand their influence in the region."

The arms deals revealed in the documents do not suggest plans for aggression in the Caribbean. The militia that was to receive these weapons seems to have been intended as a means of building political cadre and for internal security and self-defense. U.S. officials charged that the Grenadian armed forces were larger than any legitimate defense need, but, given the successful U.S. invasion, they evidently weren't large enough. Of course, nothing the Grenadians could have done would have prevented a U.S. military victory, but a large militia might have faced the White House with the prospect of a messy conquest, something that doesn't play as well with the U.S. public as a quick and costless intervention. As it was, the Austin government had disarmed many in the militia before the invasion for being pro-Bishop. World opinion regarding the U.S. invasion was almost uniformly hostile. In the United Nations, only EI Salvador, Israel, and a few of the east Caribbean states voted with Washington against a resolution of condemnation. (The UN, said Jeane Kirkpatrick afterwards, was "an outdated institution.")

In Britain, Reagan's close ally Margaret Thatcher was politely critical of the invasion, but a Labour MP was less restrained, noting that U.S. policy was "conducted by a bunch of ignorant businessmen led by a president who is a dangerous cretin."

Several analysts (though not the U.S. government) argued that despite worldwide censure, the Grenadian invasion should be viewed as a humanitarian intervention, not because it saved the medical students, but because it saved all Grenadians from a repressive dictatorship. In this view, the intervention promoted self-determination. Given the widespread support among the Grenadian population for the U.S. intervention, this argument has to be seriously addressed.

One can dispute particular poll results documenting this support (asking, for example, whether responses weren't colored by the hope of U.S. dollars flowing into the country), but every observer came back from Grenada reporting strong popular support for the invasion. Grenadian opinion alone, however, is not sufficient to justify one country's invading another. You might be glad that the local tough beat up a malicious neighbor, but vigilantism ultimately makes us all worse off, since once vigilantes are unleashed they are hard to control and the likelihood that their "interventions" will only be for just cause is small. When the vigilante has a record of supporting all sorts of atrocities and committing many of them, then the dangers of vigilantism are even more pronounced. The argument that foreign intervention is justified when it is the only way to promote democracy doesn't apply, however, in the Grenada case.

The evidence is clear that the Austin government almost immediately realized it had gone too far. As Michael Manley put it, "The military group that had taken over knew very well they were isolated from the Grena- dian population, isolated from the Caribbean, isolated from Cuba.... From the very start, they sent out feelers. They called in the private sector, they issued a statement saying they wanted good relations with the United States, they sent word to the Eastern Caribbean Caricom meeting in Trinidad to say, 'We're willing to talk, we're in a hopeless situation'."

On October 22, Austin had asked Scoon to help set up a broad-based civilian government. The economic sanctions imposed by the Caribbean nations had been in effect only four days when the U.S. invaded. There was, noted the leader of Trinidad's House of As-

> *There was, noted the leader of Trinidad's House of Assembly (no radical), "a great deal of room for diplomacy." But it was never tried. The use of outside force was embarked on, as the government of Trinidad and Tobago put it, "as a first resort."*

sembly (no radical), "a great deal of room for diplomacy." But it was never tried. The use of outside force was embarked on, as the government of Trinidad and Tobago put it, "as a first resort."

Was Austin bluffing? Was a peaceful solution possible? Did the Marines arrive, as Robert Pastor has suggested, "just in time before negotiations between CARICOM and the Austin regime might have produced a peaceful, negotiated outcome?" One doesn't know. But the matter was never tested and, as British correspondent Hugh O'Shaughnessy has commented, had Austin and his supporters "not given up their narrowly dictatorial aspirations it is difficult to see what force they could have relied on to maintain them against the popular anger at the massacre they were responsible for." Specifically, "the militia was demoralized and virtually disarmed," the army's morale "was unreliable and any blockade of supplies to the island would...have caused chaos in Grenada."

By mounting the invasion, the U.S. robbed them of that opportunity." Why was this opportunity important for Grenadians themselves? The first reason follows from a basic notion of not only radical, but even liberal thought. As John Stuart Mill argued more than a century ago, the internal freedom of a political community can be achieved only by members of that community, for only in the "arduous struggle for freedom" do people develop the capacities and qualities they need to live in freedom.

Polls in Grenada after the U.S. invasion revealed that the prospects for self-determination were not auspicious. Many did not want elections held for years, most could not think of any local leader they supported, and 75 percent wanted Grenada to officially become part of the United States. In place of popular enthusiasm for improving their country and their collective lives, there was a growing dependency on U.S. aid.

The second reason U.S. intervention was so injurious to the Grenadian people is that if they had achieved democracy on their own, it would have been a model of democracy, drawing heavily on the populist and egalitarian aspects of the Bishop legacy. As it was, the U.S. determined who should be part of the Grenadian political community (violating the civil rights of many in the process), U.S.-government funded agencies took over the job of "educating" the population, and Washington bankrolled its favored candidate in subsequent elections.

The result was a government that proceeded to gut all the social welfare programs introduced by the New Jewel Movement, resulting in increased misery and unemployment. Ironically, what prosperity there is in the country (in the words of a study sponsored by the U.S. government) can be largely "attributed to the completion of the interna- tional airport at Point Salinas."

That the interests of the Grenadian people were not foremost in the minds of U.S. policymakers was obvious. Anonymously, they acknowledged as much. The "overriding" reason for the invasion, they admitted to the New

York Times, was so that the United States wouldn't be seen as a paper tiger. "What good are maneuvers and shows of force, if you never use it?"

The Dominican Republic, the *Mayaguez*, and Grenada, in each case, Americans were said to be in danger, but the dangers were concocted. In each case, American soldiers and a larger number of Dominicans, Cambodians, Grenadians, and Cubans died, not to save U.S. nationals who would have been far safer without U.S. intervention, but so that Washington might make clear that it ruled the Caribbean and that it was prepared to engage in a paroxysm of violence to enforce its will.

There have been some cases where American citizens were truly in danger—for example, the four churchwomen who were killed by government-sponsored death squads in EI Salvador in 1980. But there was no U.S. intervention there, no marine landings, no protective bombing raids. Instead the U.S. backed the death squad regime with military and economic aid, military training, intelligence sharing, and diplomatic support.

Is it possible that there would be a situation in the future where unilateral U.S. military intervention would be justified to protect the lives of Americans? Anything is possible. But the record of how this justification has been used in the past and the utter cynicism shown by the U.S. government when friendly regimes such as the one in San Salvador brutalize Americans, ought to make us extremely skeptical.

From Z Magazine, *June 1991*
Volume 4, Number 6

6.

Liberals In Search of a Foreign Policy

By Edward S. Herman

IT IS VERY INTERESTING watching the liberals seek a foreign policy position that will differentiate them from conservatives. After all, they can't just go along with Bush, who, as Michael Tomasky ac-

Tomasky had the solution: liberals can fight for "democracy" abroad as the basis of U.S. foreign policy

knowledges in his chapter "Between Cheney and Chomsky" in George Packer's edited volume, *The Fight Is for Democracy,* is throwing aside all international agreements and restraint and has announced "a prescription for empire." Of course, most of the liberals went along with Bush on the Afghanistan attack, but they began to splinter in the months leading up to the Iraq invasion. Some like Paul Berman favored it, others liked the idea, but only with UN sanction and collective action. Some didn't approve of it on any basis.

Tomasky had the solution: liberals can fight for "democracy" abroad as the basis for U.S. foreign policy. This is the theme of the Packer volume, as suggested by its title. Tomasky never explains why we should take on the project of fighting for democracy abroad, as opposed to leaving foreigners to work out their own destinies, concentrating on building democracy at home, and diverting resources from the military-industrial complex to pressing needs here. Tomasky advances the project as a political strategy for the Democrats, who need a foreign policy that will prevent conservatives from effectively tagging liberals and Democrats (Tomasky merges the two) as wimps and incapable of defending our "national security." So the power structure dictated an interventionary foreign policy and the problem for the liberals was to construct their own distinctive rationale for interventionism that was presumably compatible with liberal values and would not be "a prescription for empire."

This kind of idiocy arises from the inability of liberals to question the basic structures of power. They can't challenge the immense military establishment and a forward foreign policy because these are built-in to a political-economic order that they take for granted. This power structure has tightened its control over society and badly weakened democracy at home. In his introduction, Packer acknowledged that growing corporate power and inequality has caused "money and its influence [to] claim a greater and greater share of political power," so that "for thirty years or more the musculature of democracy has atrophied, culminating in 2000 with a stolen presidential election." This suggests that the big challenge for U.S. liberals should be establishing real democracy at home, rather than looking for places abroad where their own atrophied democracy can bring a supposedly good one to somebody else by military intervention.

The other absurdity here is the pretense that the Democrats are potential vehicles for this policy of intervention-for-democracy. Common sense and history tell us that the huge U.S. military apparatus was not put in place for do-gooder purposes, but rather to serve those same business and financial interests that Packer concedes have obtained "a greater and greater share of political power." The Democrats draw their campaign funding from those same interests and have become more conservative as their dependency on these funders has increased and as the corporate media has pressed them away from "populism." Can anyone but a fool or self-deceiver believe that these strengthening power interests are going to accept a policy of spending large resources to bring democracy to the benighted, as it shrivels at home?

However, we must recognize that it is always possible to rationalize attacking some tar-

get on the grounds of dedication to enhancing democracy. Most, if not all, countries have very imperfect democracies, quite a few don't even have a nominal democracy, and many countries have dissident ethnic or other sub-national groups who feel put upon and whose cause can be taken up in the alleged interest of democracy or human rights; and the dissident group can be funded and encouraged to rebel more forcibly to justify external intervention in an alleged good cause. So the "democracy" objective can easily be fitted to serve the same ends as a strictly geopolitical or economic objective, or even to play a "wag the dog" political function.

Thus, a "liberal" like Clinton can attack Yugoslavia on the alleged grounds of principle while simultaneously servicing Turkish ethnic cleansing of the Kurds and appeasing our good friends in Indonesia as they upset the UN-sponsored referendum in East Timor—and the liberals at home are pleased. They argue that it is better to have selective humanitarian intervention than none at all. They easily swallow claims of humanitarian purpose and effects that are fraudulent (as in the Balkans wars). They fail to see that the claims of humanitarian purpose in case A provide a cover for supporting inhumanitarianism in cases B, C, and D. After all, they say, we can't do everything, while they ignore the technical ease of simply terminating support for our goons of convenience.

So the democracy project will be able to serve as a cover for an imperialist projection of power in the same way as stopping communism did for the Cold War era, for Democratic and Republican leaders alike. Both have regularly engaged in foreign policy actions that served corporate and geopolitical interests, often at the expense of democracy. In their weakened, more corporate-dependent position, there is a snowball-in-hell's chance that Democrats will alter their traditional pattern.

Tomasky devotes much space in his chapter to an attempted showing that liberal leaders

(Democrats) have been better in the foreign policy arena than the conservatives (Republicans), so that, presumably, getting them into power would make the democracy project feasible. He argues at length that Lyndon Johnson didn't want to fight the Vietnam War, but was driven to it by the belief that if he withdrew, he would be vilified and suffer electoral defeat. So it was really a conservative's war as they pushed him into escalating and invading Vietnam. Tomasky supports this by a few quotations of Johnson speaking with friends in private saying the war was a losing proposition and that political considerations forced his hand.

This proof is worse than puny. Johnson made hundreds of statements that fluctuated with his mood. The crucial fact about Johnson is that he did escalate the war. It was his war and whether he was doing it because he believed in it or for political reasons is beside the point. Tomasky fails to recognize that if a liberal Democrat will go to war contrary to his/her beliefs for political reasons, this condemns him/her even more than if he/she did it based on true belief. If fear of conservative backlash dominates policy decisions, why should we want a liberal Democrat in office? But Tomasky also misses the fact that Johnson was surrounded by liberal advisers who urged him on. Joseph Califano claims, "All Kennedy's top advisers save one pressed him [Johnson] to escalate more" (*The Triumph and Tragedy of Lyndon Johnson*). This was liberals in power making these decisions. We may note also that it was Nixon who eventually withdrew from Vietnam, not Kennedy or Johnson (and that it was Eisenhower, not Truman, who ended the Korean War).

Tomasky also ignores the fact that Lyndon Johnson invaded the Dominican Republic in 1965 to prevent the return of the democratically-elected Juan Bosch; that his Administration supported the Colonels' takeover of

Greece in 1967, displacing a democratic government there with a regime of torture; and that he helped Suharto impose a military dictatorship on Indonesia in 1965, the liberals in power celebrating this takeover and massacre of perhaps a million civilians, an event described by James Reston as "a gleam of light in Asia" and by Robert McNamara as "a dividend" from our investment in military aid to Indonesia.

> *During the liberal Kennedy and Johnson administrations, there were 18 turnovers of government in Latin America, 11 of them displacing elected governments with dictatorships*

Johnson also supported the military overthrow of the elected government of Brazil in 1964, quickly expressing his "warmest good wishes" to the coup leaders and congratulating them that the matter had been settled "within the framework of constitutional democracy." U.S. Ambassador to Brazil, and later, president of Johns Hopkins University, Lincoln Gordon, described the new regime as "totally democratic" and the imposition of the military dictatorship as "the single most decisive victory for freedom in the mid-twentieth century." During the liberal Kennedy and Johnson administrations, there were 18 turnovers of government in Latin America, 11 of them displacing elected governments with dictatorships.

Tomasky puts a similar positive gloss on other Democrats from Truman onward, with comparable selectivity and bias. On Truman's murderous counterinsurgency war in Greece that killed several hundred thousand people and established a right-wing dictatorship run by important remnants of World War II Nazi collaboration, Tomasky says "it probably did save Greece from becoming a communist state, which was handy for Americans and rather more than that for the Greeks." It doesn't bother Tomasky that we didn't allow the Greeks to decide this for themselves (Stalin was honoring Yalta and not intervening in Greece at all); and as noted earlier, after the Greeks finally succeeded in ousting the U.S.-sponsored collaborationist regime in 1967, another liberal Democrat, Lyndon Johnson, supported a right-wing military coup, again on the spurious claim of saving Greece from becoming a communist state. Tomasky, of course, does not mention that it was under Truman in 1947 that the United States began to organize and subvert the new democratic regime in Guatemala, timed, as Blanche Wiesen Cook has shown, with the regime's recognition of the rights of workers to form unions.

Tomasky argues that the Cold War was righteous, although it did have bad features and its rhetoric led us into the Vietnam War. But it "contained an idea about liberal democracy that was grounded in Enlightenment principles and tried to bring those principles to life in the institutions it built." So liberals can view the late 1940s as the beginning "of a struggle on behalf of defending and spreading the values of democracy."

As in Greece and Guatemala, and Thailand —where in 1947 the Truman administration supported "the first pro-Axis dictator to regain power after the war"—as in the Kennedy-

> *Tomasky, of course, does not mention that it was under Truman in 1947 that the United States began to organize and subvert the new democratic regime in Guatemala*

Johnson era of support and underwriting the rise of the National Security State in Latin America.

This brings me to Tomasky's juxtaposition of the two extremists, with Tomasky and his allies situated "Between Cheney and Chomsky." Tomasky says that "liberals must make a clear break with Chomskyism," which represents a worldview that suggests "equivocation about America's capacity as a moral force," but also involves "a matter of adapting to the world as it now is." On these points, Tomasky is clearly much closer to Cheney than to Chomsky. Cheney doesn't equivocate on U.S. capacity as a moral force. He would certainly agree with Tomasky that bringing democracy everywhere is at least one of our objectives in force projection and the Bush government has moved further on that point, making liberation our alleged chief objective in Iraq. Tomasky is explicit that the aim of spreading democracy would have been a reasonable basis for attacking Iraq. Cheney and his associates have in the past acknowledged geopolitical and economic grounds for the attack and, in the runup to the war, constructed a series of lies in their effort to gain public and UN support. Tomasky liberals in power would have been less open and crass. While gaining support and doing what the power structure and main lobbies wanted done for their own reasons, the liberals would have focused more intently on democracy and human rights.

Tomasky, Packer, Berman, Gitlin, and company hate Chomsky for many reasons. One is that he so effectively undercuts their claims with facts and coherent analyses, which is why they always mention him only in hit-and-run attacks, never confronting his arguments. They also often lie in these attacks. Thus, in his only other mention of Chomsky, Tomasky says, "The first reaction to September 11 was easy, at least for everyone this side of Noam Chomsky. A country is not only justified in answering such an attack but has a moral obligation to do so." The implicit lie is the claim that Chomsky didn't think the attack had to be answered, he did, but against the attackers and their direct supporters and within the framework of international law. Tomasky slithers over such matters and, like many liberals, he follows the Bush party line according to which international law is for somebody else.

Chomsky has unearthed and used in his writings internal U.S. planning documents that have shown U.S. intention to control and dominate in pursuit of U.S. economic interests that fly in face of any notion of democracy. The Grand Area concept developed during World War II spoke about the need to arrange things via the use of power to serve the needs of the U.S. economy, with Latin American countries (among others) to be kept in a dependent and raw materials supplier mode. Later, National Security Council documents were quite clear on the threat of "nationalistic regimes…[seeking] immediate improvement in the low living standards of the masses, with the result that most Latin American governments are under intense domestic political pressures to increase production and diversify their economies."

These internal documents make clear that such concern for the masses and pressures from those masses are a threat and they also make clear that the vast military aid and training programs developed for Latin America, that produced such a great "dividend" in Indonesia, were designed as a political counterweight to these democratic threats.

These documents and Chomsky's analysis make Tomasky's conventional clichés about the noble ends of Cold War liberals look like the ideological baloney they really are. His documentation on the rise of the National Security State in Latin America and its regimes of torture, regularly supported by Democratic as well as Republican leaders, is also hard to swallow and impossible to confute, so Tomasky and company simply ignore these and rely on strands of compatible evidence, frequently misrepresented as well as decontextualized (as in the Truman-Greece case). But one conclusion is possible: Chomsky refuses to ignore or apologize for U.S. sponsorship of violently undemocratic states while Tomasky and his colleagues in "The Fight for Democracy" offer de facto apologetics for this sponsorship that departs a bit from the pursuit of enlightenment values.

Tomasky et al also hate Chomsky because he is a critic of Israel and of U.S. support for Israeli policy. Tomasky says that one of the great accomplishments of U.S. Cold War policy was that, "it created a democratic Jewish state." This exhausts his discussion of the issue. But that Jewish state was created in a massive process of ethnic cleansing and that

> *The occupation is not only illegal and ruthlessly racist, it violates all democratic standards. So again, the liberal "fight for democracy" turns out to be limited and politicized in accord with non-enlightenment principles.*

ethnic cleansing continues with U.S. support (opposed by virtually all the rest of the world) up to today. This is approved ethnic cleansing, supported by both major political parties in the United States and the ongoing violations of international law and morality do not bother Tomasky and company. Furthermore, Israel's democracy is very constrained within Israel and the notion of a "Jewish state," rather than a state of all its citizens, should bother believers in democracy, but Berman and company are bothered only by the notion of an "Islamic state." The occupation is not only illegal and ruthlessly racist, it violates all democratic standards. So again, the liberal "fight for democracy" turns out to be limited and politicized in accord with non-enlightenment principles.

As noted, Packer mentions the increasingly plutocratic character of the political system and its atrophy, but neither he nor his fellow liberals seemed very urgent about structural repair. They have spent far more time and energy in attacking Chomsky, Nader, the left, and protest movements than in writing about and organizing for ways to move from a plutocracy to democracy.

They are preoccupied with getting Democrats in office and give the impression that will suffice, despite the constraints now placed on who can run and what the victor can do.

Tomasky does not equivocate on the "moral force" that a Democrat would bring to his democracy-enhancing project, even under present plutocratic conditions.

He seems to believe, like Berman, that the Bush administration, despite its imperial project, is exercising a moral influence abroad, but that we need liberal Democrats in office to carry out the democracy project effectively. The "fight for democracy" is not at home, despite the atrophy. It is only a fight to get Democrats in office and fend off left critiques that might impede the pursuit of democracy elsewhere—an aim that neither Democratic or Republican leaders have ever pursued in the past.

From Z *Magazine, December 2003*
Volume 16, Number 12

7.

Cuba and the United States in the 21st Century

By Jane Franklin

SIMÓN BOLÍVAR SAW it coming. In 1829 the Great Liberator of Latin American colonies warned that the United States "appears destined by Providence to plague America with miseries in the name of Freedom." Now, in the 21st century, we witness the global spread of that plague as Washington, obsessed with being a unipolar power in a multipolar world, demands that each and every nation adhere to its dictate of "democracy" and "freedom." Powerful words have become shibboleths in the service of imperialism.

> *Now, in the 21st century, we witness the global spread of that plague as Washington, obsessed with being a unipolar power in a multipolar world, demands that each and every nation adhere to its dictate of "democracy" and "freedom." Powerful words have become shibboleths in the service of imperialism.*

In an alternate history, things could have been different after the terrorist attacks of September 11, 2001. But this is a history of imperialism, with its ineluctable imperatives. As flames, smoke, and ashes billowed from the wreckage of the Twin Towers and the Pentagon, the first country to express sympathy and offer aid was Cuba. President Fidel Castro expressed his government's profound "grief and sadness" about the "violent surprise attacks carried out this morning" and offered Cuba's medical aid.

On 9/11 the entire world seemed in sympathy with the United States. But the U.S. response was unilateral and imperial. On September 20, in a televised address before a joint session of

Congress, President George W. Bush declared a "war on terror." He simply announced war, without asking Congress to declare war as required by the U.S. Constitution. He called it "our" war because it already belonged to all U.S. citizens, like it or not: "Our war on terror begins with al Qaeda," he said, "but it does not end there."

Bush was looking beyond the war in Afghanistan, which would begin the following month. "Americans should not expect one battle but a lengthy campaign, unlike any other we have ever seen." For his international audience, he warned, "Every nation, in every region, now has a decision to make: Either you are with us or you are with the terrorists." For his domestic audience, he announced the creation of the Office of Homeland Security, kicking off an era that would leave U.S. constitutional rights crumbling amid the destruction.

A few months later Bush's commencement address to the graduating class of the U.S. Military Academy at West Point was an order to transform U.S. armed forces into a "military that must be ready to strike at a moment's notice in any dark corner of the world. We must," he commanded, "uncover terror cells in 60 or more countries."

Bush's "war on terror" created a new paradigm in which U.S. imperialism wages a forever war against "the bad guys" as if the world

> *Bush's "war on terror" created a new paradigm in which U.S. imperialism wages a forever war against "the bad guys" as if the world is a "Call of Duty" video game*

is a "Call of Duty" video game. Perhaps the first iconic manifestation of the war's nature was the creation—on occupied territory in Cuba at the Guantánamo Naval Base—of a prison that quickly became notorious around the world for torture, serving as a 21st-century model for the infamous Abu Ghraib in Iraq as well as prisons in other countries, including Afghanistan, Jordan, Poland, Romania, and Thailand.

The plan for this imperial crusade had appeared years before the 9/11 attacks as neoconservatives from the Project for the New American Century (PNAC), like Paul Wolfowitz and Dick Cheney, developed their strategy for a "global Pax Americana." In September 2000, just before the presidential election, PNAC published "Rebuilding America's Defenses: Strategies, Forces and Resources for a New Century." The report outlined a slow transformation to total global hegemony unless there were "some catalyzing and catastrophic event—like a new Pearl Harbor."

Elections, U.S. Style

How did those neoconservatives place themselves into position to take advantage of their "new Pearl Harbor" on 9/11? They did it by systematically hijacking the first presidential election of the 21st century in the key battleground state of Florida. After the Civil War, Florida (like the other former slave states) passed laws designed to criminalize ex-slaves and then disenfranchise them—because they were "criminals." The Jeb Bush Administration actually used the 1868 Florida law that disenfranchised ex-slaves to disenfranchise former felons. At the time of that crucial 2000 election, disenfranchised former felons in Florida totaled 600,000. Of those, 256,392 were African Americans. With a devious vote count, Texas Governor Bush defeated Vice-President Al Gore in Florida by only 537 votes. If those African-Americans had been allowed to vote, on 9/11 the president would have been Al Gore.

As it was, the vote was so close that it triggered an automatic recount. Legal battles between the Bush and Gore campaigns raged for weeks. When the Florida State Supreme Court ruled that recounts could continue, Miami's Radio Mambí broadcast appeals by Republicans Ileana Ros-Lehtinen and Lincoln Díaz-Balart—both Cuban-American members of

Congress—calling for Cuban-Americans to stop the vote count for Miami-Dade County taking place at the Government Center in Miami. Consequently, the rest of the country caught a glimpse of the kind of "democracy" these Cuban- Americans would like to impose in Cuba. According to the *New York Times,* "several people were trampled, punched or kicked when protesters tried to rush the doors outside the office of the Miami-Dade supervisor of elections." When it was over, the shock troops had achieved what they wanted: the Canvassing Board shut down the Miami-Dade recount.

Meanwhile, the Republican Party was operating a machine driven by higher powers than Republican protesters in the street: Republicans in high places. Florida's Republican Secretary of State certified the election results as a 537-vote victory. Florida's Republican Governor Jeb Bush signed forms to declare that all 25 of Florida's electors were pledged to his brother George, thus tipping the national electoral votes to Bush, even though Gore won the popular vote. Then, when the Florida State Supreme Court ruled for a statewide partial recount, five U.S. Supreme Court judges overruled the State Court with a 5 to 4 vote to shut down all recounts. Those five "justices"— nominated by Republican Presidents Nixon, Reagan, and H.W. Bush—decided that Bush would be president.

The battle for Florida in 2000 showed how crucial Florida's electoral votes have become. Since 1992, no president has been elected without winning Florida. This situation gives powerful leverage to about half a million Cuban-American voters in Florida. Every four years Democratic and Republican presidential candidates compete aggressively for their favor. This task, however, is more complicated than it used to be. A developing generational difference among Cuban-Americans finds many more concerned about domestic issues

like employment and health care than about Cuba. And politicians have to pay attention to the rapidly increasing number of other Hispanic voters whose interests may not coincide with prioritizing the overthrow of the Cuban government.

President Ronald Reagan had recognized the potential challenge of the changing demographic and established a hardline Cuban-American organization to serve as an arm of U.S. domestic and foreign policy, shoring up the goal of restoring U.S. control of Cuba. In 1981, his first year as president, Reagan created the Cuban American National Foundation. A major purpose of CANF was to drown out the voices of Cuban-Americans and other Americans who wanted to improve relations

> *A major purpose of CANF was to drown out the voices of Cuban-Americans and other Americans who wanted to improve relations with Cuba*

with Cuba. President Reagan and Vice President George H.W. Bush anointed Jorge Mas Canosa as chair of CANF, designating him the "liberator" who would "return democracy" to Cuba. CANF's multimillionaire board of directors and trustees in Florida and New Jersey showered congressional campaigns with money and in return Congress established the National Endowment for Democracy that granted funds to CANF's various projects, like Radio and TV Martí. CANF quickly became the most powerful of all the U.S. organizations aimed at overthrowing the Cuban government.

Mas Canosa was a sophisticated politician who worked both sides of the political aisle, financing campaigns of Democrats as well as Republicans. Moreover, CANF engineered victorious campaigns of Cuban-Americans at all levels of government in Florida and New Jersey, from town halls to State legislatures and on to the Capitol in Washington. In 1989, CANF's choice for a special election in

Florida was Ileana Ros-Lehtinen, whose campaign manager happened to be Jeb Bush, son of then-President H.W. Bush. Ros-Lehtinen became the first Cuban-American elected to the House of Representatives. Others followed her to both House and Senate, Democrats as well as Republicans, all dedicated to overthrowing the government of Cuba.

Covert Terrorism

Unlike Omega 7, Alpha 66, and other terrorists who boast of their armed infiltrations, sabotage, and even murders, CANF persisted in claiming it engaged only in nonviolent activities, giving an aura of respectability. Cuba warned that CANF had a covert military arm. Who was telling the truth? In fact, CANF's plans for getting rid of Fidel Castro included "by any means necessary." CANF's multimillionaires, eager to make more millions in Cuba, expected immediate collapse in Havana after the disintegration of the Soviet Union in 1991. In 1992, frustrated by the delay, while one hand was engineering the lawful Torricelli

> *In fact, CANF's plans for getting rid of Fidel Castro included "by any means necessary." CANF's multimillionaires, eager to make more millions in Cuba, expected immediate collapse in Havana after the disintegration of the Soviet Union in 1991.*

Act to tighten the trade embargo, the other hand was secretly creating CANF's unlawful paramilitary branch dedicated to assassinating President Fidel Castro.

In 1997, some of CANF's gang were arrested on their way to kill Castro at an Ibero-American Summit meeting on Margarita Island in Venezuela. They were acquitted in Puerto Rico in December 1999 despite the fact that one of them had bragged to the Coast Guard that they were on their way to kill Castro. One of the two .50 caliber rifles onboard La Esperanza belonged to Francisco (Pépé) Hernández, who was then and continues to be the president of CANF. The FBI visited

Hernández and obviously told him to "lay low" for a while—the message consistently delivered by the FBI to terrorists they harbor. Even as the five CANF terrorists returned to their mansions, five Cuban anti-terrorists were facing trial in Miami.

CANF was also clandestinely supporting the two most notorious terrorists in the Western Hemisphere, Orlando Bosch Avila (who died, unimprisoned, in Miami in 2011) and Luis Posada Carriles (who at this writing continues to walk free in Miami). Bosch and Posada are known worldwide as the masterminds of blowing up Cubana Airline's Flight 455 in 1976, killing all 73 passengers and crew aboard. In his autobiography, *Los caminos del guerrero* (*The Paths of the Warrior*), Posada named three major financial supporters: Jorge Mas Canosa (CANF chair until his death in 1997), Pépé Hernández, and Feliciano Foyo (CANF boardmember until he left to join the even more extremist Cuban Liberty Council). Posada again named Mas Canosa as a financier during an astonishing interview with Ann Louise Bardach and Larry Rohter that was featured on the *New York Times* front pages for two days, July 12-13, 1998. Posada stated that U.S. intelligence agents look the other way as he carries out operations such as a series of bombings in Cuba in 1997 that killed an Italian businessperson in a Havana hotel. Speaking of relations between terrorists and the CIA, Posada boasted, "The CIA taught us everything—everything.... They taught us explosives, how to kill, bomb, trained us in acts of sabotage." He called Jorge Kiszinski, an FBI agent who was supposedly investigating terrorist activities by Cuban-Americans, 'a very good friend'."

Because the CIA and the FBI failed to apprehend terrorists who were plotting attacks against Cuba, Cuban agents were forced to take on the job. In June 1998, FBI agents were invited to Havana where Cuban officials gave them reams of information gathered by Cuban agents. But in September, instead of arresting the terrorists, the FBI arrested the agents who had gathered the evidence. Gerardo Hernán- dez, Ramón Labañino, Antonio Guerrero, Fernando González, and René González, known as the Cuban Five, were tried in Miami, convicted in 2001, and incarcerated in different prisons across the United States.

Meanwhile, other Cuban agents uncovered the most potentially deadly assassination plot of all. As Fabián Escalante, former head of Cuba's State Security Department (G-2), meticulously documented in his book, *Executive Action: 634 Ways to Kill Fidel Castro*, the CIA began these assassination attempts in 1959 while the FBI started even before that, in 1958, while Castro was still in the Sierras. Most have gone unnoticed, but President Castro made sure to call attention to this one. After arriving in Panama City in November 2000 to attend an Ibero-American Summit meeting, Castro held a news conference to announce that Luis Posada Carriles and three Cuban-American co-conspirators were planning to assassinate him by bombing the auditorium at the University of Panama where he would be speaking. He even revealed where police could find the assassins. G-2 agents not only saved the life of Fidel Castro again, but also the lives of hundreds of people, mainly students, who packed the University of Panama auditorium to hear Castro. This would not have been a single assassination. It would have been a massacre.

Less than a year after that, came the terrorist attacks of September 11, 2001. Fidel Castro, in his offer of sympathy and aid to the United States that day, urged that Washington put an end to the terrorism waged from within the United States against Cuba. However, the U.S. State Department keeps Cuba on its list of "State Sponsors of Terrorism" even though it no longer cites any evidence that Cuba is engaged in any terrorism anywhere in the world. By defining Cuba as a terrorist nation, the State Department gets away with defining terrorism aimed at Cuba as anti-terrorism. Thus, there is no chance that the terror cells in Florida and New Jersey would be targeted by the "war on terror." In fact, when Posada and his co-conspirators arrived in Miami after they were pardoned in Panama (by outgoing President Mereya Moscoso who was on her way to live in Miami), they were welcomed as heroes in their capital city of terrorism.

> *In Congress, some Cuban-American members take pride in publicly representing the views of their terrorist constituents, including threats of assassination. For example, on March 22, 2004, Florida Republican Representative Lincoln Díaz-Balart promoted the assassination of Fidel Castro on Miami television.*

How are these terrorists treated by Washington? The Justice Department refuses Venezuela's requests for Posada's extradition to continue facing charges for Flight 455. In Congress, some Cuban-American members take pride in publicly representing the views of their terrorist constituents, including threats of assassination. For example, on March 22, 2004, Florida Republican Representative Lincoln Díaz-Balart promoted the assassination of Fidel Castro on Miami television and in an interview for the 2006 British documentary "638 Ways to Kill Castro," Representative Ros-Lehtinen stated, "I welcome the opportunity of having anyone assassinate Fidel Castro."

Invasion also is openly advocated. When Ros-Lehtinen was a guest on NBC's "Today" program in 1996, Bryant Gumbel said that most Americans probably don't see Cuba as a threat. Ros-Lehtinen replied: "What was the threat in the Panama invasion? Did we think that Manuel Noriega's army was going to invade us? And what about the threat in the Persian Gulf War? Were they going to send their jets and invade us? There were no threats and yet we took forceful action." In the 2010 midterm elections, right-wingers with the Tea Party's agenda shifted the majority of the House of Representatives to the Republican Party, meaning that all House committees would now be chaired by Republicans. This enabled Ros-Lehtinen to achieve her dream of becoming the chair of the House Foreign Relations Committee. With that powerful position, she continued to demand "forceful action" against Cuba. Although there has been no subsequent outright invasion like the 1961 Bay of Pigs invasion, Cuba has reported to the UN that 3,478 Cubans have died and 2,099 have been disabled by terrorist activities.

Overt Terrorism

As deadly as it is, covert terrorism has not been as devastating as the overt terrorism of the U.S. trade embargo, which has been aimed at starving the Cuban people into submission ever since the Revolution. According to a June 24, 1959, State Department memorandum, Robert Kleberg, owner of the King Ranch in Texas with a $3 million cattle investment in Cuba, told Secretary of State Christian Herter that depriving Cuba of its sugar quota privilege would cause "widespread further unemployment" and "large numbers of people thus forced out of work would begin to go hungry." Herter cautioned that such a policy would be "economic warfare" in peacetime.

Which was it to be? Warfare or peacetime? Within a year the Eisenhower administration instituted economic warfare as permanent policy toward Cuba. In the United States people hear that it is Cuba's economic system, not the trade embargo, that hurts Cuban people. Yet the genesis of the trade embargo was explicitly to starve Cubans into submission.

On April 6, 1960, Deputy Assistant Secretary of State for Inter-American Affairs Lester Mallory sent a decisive memo to Assistant Secretary of State for Inter-American Affairs R. Richard Rubot- tom, Jr. It points out that the "majority of Cubans support [Fidel] Castro" and concludes that the "only foreseeable means of alienating internal support is through disenchantment and disaffection based on economic dissatisfaction and hardship." Therefore "it follows that every possible means should be undertaken promptly to weaken the economic life of Cuba...to bring about hunger, desperation and overthrow of government."

So Washington terminated Cuba's sugar quota in July, leaving Cuba holding 700,000 tons of unsold sugar (soon purchased by the Soviet Union). A total U.S. trade embargo took effect in February 1962 as part of the secret Operation Mongoose that led to the 1962 Missile Crisis. Although negotiations to end that crisis included an agreement with the Soviet Union by the Kennedy White House that the United States would not invade Cuba again, economic warfare, along with armed infiltrations, continued. At the UN General Assembly in 2011, Cuban Foreign Minister Bruno Rodríguez Parilla reported that economic damages to Cuba from the trade embargo totaled $975 billion.

The principal ideological justification for banning trade was that Cuba had become a Soviet "proxy" spreading communism to the Western Hemisphere. The professed anti-colonialism of the 1901 Platt Amendment appeared in an updated form, with the Soviet Union rather than Spain cast in the role of the threat to Cuban independence. But if the Soviet Union were the real cause, the embargo would have ended in 1991 when the USSR disintegrated. Instead, Washington intensified the trade embargo.

First came the Torricelli Act ("Cuban Democracy Act") signed by President H.W. Bush in 1992. Its express purpose, in the words of then-Representative Robert Torricelli, was to "wreak havoc on that island." Then in 1996 came the bizarre Helms-Burton law ("Cuban Liberty and Democratic Solidarity Act") signed by President Bill Clinton.

With the Soviet Union out of the way, the Torricelli Act and the Helms-Burton Law make no pretence of trying to save Cuba from a foreign power. Under the mantra of "democracy" both claim to be saving Cuba from its own government. Although the texts ring with calls for "democracy," "freedom," and "human rights," these two omnibus laws are focused not on Cuba in reality but on Cuba in the imagination of CANF multimillionaires, fantasizing about their return to the Batista era, again assuming ownership of Cuba in alliance with Washington.

In a frenzy to restore the past, Helms-Burton's Title III concocted a unique method of acquiring the right to regain former property: property left behind by Cuban émigrés is magically converted into U.S. property because those Cubans later became U.S. citizens. In U.S. courts, Cuban-Americans could sue foreign investors who "traffic" in property Cubans owned when they were Cuban citizens. Even some of the closest U.S. allies objected vociferously to its extraterritoriality with the result that Title III, "Protection of Property Rights of United States Nationals," has never been enforced—the president suspends it every six months.

However, Title I, "Authorization of Support for Democratic and Human Rights Groups and International Observers," has become the nexus of policy toward Cuba in the 21st century. It authorizes the president to give money and goods to individuals and nongovernmental organizations (NGOs) for "democracy-building efforts." This financial and material support of "dissidents" is, of course, a blatant attempt to create a Fifth Column to implement Washington's agenda.

Cuban Law Versus U.S. Law

In 1901, U.S. law became Cuban law. That year, in order to codify control of Cuba, the U.S. Congress passed the Platt Amendment as part of an Army Appropriations bill. The amendment provided a blueprint for turning Cuba into a neocolony. Since Washington made it clear that its military occupation would not end until the amendment became part of Cuban law, Cuba included the Platt Amendment in its 1901 Constitution.

Helms-Burton aspires to be the Platt Amendment of the 21st century. But there is a key difference between Platt and Helms-Burton. Helms-Burton is U.S. law but Cuba is de-

> *In a frenzy to restore the past, Helms-Burton's Title III concocted a unique method of acquiring the right to regain former property: property left behind by Cuban émigrés is magically converted into U.S. property because those Cubans later became U.S. citizens*

termined to keep it from becoming Cuban law. In 1999, Cuba passed its own "Law for the Protection of National Independence and the Economy of Cuba" (Law 88). It points out that Helms-Burton makes financing subversive activities part of economic warfare against Cuba. Law 88 makes it a violation of Cuban law to introduce into Cuba, accept, or distribute materials from the U.S. Government that would aid in implementing Helms-Burton. Thus, when a U.S. agent (such as Alan Gross, who was working for the State Department's USAID when he was arrested in Cuba in 2009) introduces such materials and distributes them in Cuba, the agent is implementing Helms-Burton, thus violating Cuban law.

Helms-Burton also dictates precisely how Cuba must conduct "free" elections during the "transition" between the overthrow of its government and replacement with an approved government. Title II, "Assistance to a Free and Independent Cuba," specifies that neither Fidel Castro nor Raúl Castro can be president of a "free" Cuba, whether or not they are elected.

But Cuba managed its own orderly transition, without Washington's approval. In 2006 after Fidel Castro removed himself from the presidency because of illness, Raúl Castro became acting president and then was elected president in 2008. He took office as recession struck the global economy, including both Cuba and the United States. In addition, three major hurricanes hit Cuba in 2008 with devastating economic losses. Aiming to address its problems without giving up socialist principles, Cuba launched a campaign against corruption and inefficiency, including major changes in agriculture. In April 2011, the Cuban Communist Party held its first Party Congress since 1997 and approved about 300 economic, social, and political reforms, including private sales of houses and property, more self-employment, and increasing foreign investment.

The American people were also looking for change. During that 2008 to 2012 period, the key figure was Barack Obama who ran his 2008 winning presidential campaign with a promise of change as the U.S. economy was collapsing beneath the weight of the Bush administration's two major wars and reckless economic policies.

As part of his strategy for winning the crucial electoral votes of Florida, Obama aligned himself with CANF, in favor of loosening travel restrictions for Cuban-Americans with family on the island. Four years earlier, President Bush had instituted draconian travel rules that restricted visits to relatives to once in every three years and allowed scant remittances. This mobilized 500 Cuban-Americans who attended a press conference in Miami, giving birth to a new movement for family rights. Reaching for that growing bloc of voters, Obama promised in a May 2008 Miami speech, "I will immediately allow unlimited family travel and remittances." Obama won Florida. When he took office in 2009, he kept that promise.

But what about travel for other U.S. citizens? George Bush had also terminated people-to-people exchanges that allow a relatively small number of non-Cubans to visit Cuba by traveling with groups who manage to obtain special licenses from the Treasury Department's Office of Foreign Assets Control (OFAC). In 2011, President Obama restored those limited exchanges but in the election year of 2012 once again OFAC made licenses difficult or impossible to get. Moreover, even though he is a constitutional lawyer, Obama continued the travel ban for all other people, despite the fact that the Supreme Court in 1958 ruled that U.S. citizens have a constitutional right to travel.

But what do most Americans think about relations with Cuba? Some organizations—e.g., the Venceremos Brigade (since 1969) and the IFCO Caravans for Peace (since 1992)—have continued to organize large groups to visit the forbidden island without applying for licenses, taking humanitarian aid with them. Widespread support around the United States for these ventures has made it difficult for the U.S. government to crack down on their defiance of the bans on travel and trade. A CBS/*New York Times* poll taken in April 2009 showed that 60 percent favored freedom to travel to Cuba by all citizens and 67 percent favored re-establishing diplomatic and trade relations with Cuba.

Meanwhile, the political dynamic among Cuban-Americans was changing dramatically and hardline Cuban-Americans have been forced to decide how to deal with the changes. As the 21st century dawned, CANF was no longer the bulwark that Reagan had designed. Its charismatic chair, Jorge Mas Canosa, had died; several high-ranking members were exposed in a bungled attempt to assassinate Fidel Castro. One of CANF's main protégés, Luis Posada, had bragged to the *New York Times* about CANF financing his terrorism. Then suddenly, as one century turned into another, Cuban-American attention focused on the custody battle for Elián González, a motherless child being held by relatives in Miami's Little Havana to prevent his return to his father, stepmother, brother, all four grandparents, and his classmates at school. Rescued from an innertube in the Atlantic after his mother drowned in November 1999, Elián became major news in both Cuba and the United States as a great-uncle claimed custody.

The Cuban people mobilized to demand his return. It became a showdown. The issue divided Cuban-Americans, who demonstrated in Miami on both sides of the battle. The American people watched on television as Miami relatives tried to turn a six-year-old against his father by surrounding him with possessions, including gifts from Ileana Ros-Lehtinen and the promise of a life of luxury as CANF got involved in the battle. Here was a close-up look at hardline Cuban-Americans and most people did not like what they saw, deciding that the Miami relatives were nothing more than kidnappers.

When the U.S. legal system ruled in favor of the father's right to his son, Attorney General Janet Reno ordered federal agents to rescue Elián, who was reunited in April with his father, stepmother, and baby brother, who had come to Washington. But court battles continued while demonstrations raged in Miami, for and against keeping Elián. Finally, just hours after the Supreme Court refused to hear a last-minute appeal by the distant Miami relatives, Elián and his family flew home to Cuba on June 28, 2000.

What happened in Florida after that seven-month battle to keep a child from his father? As polls showed that a majority of people in the United States disagreed with CANF's position about Elián, CANF began damage control. José Cárdenas, director of CANF's Washington office, admitted in the June 15 *Miami Herald*, "There has been an assessment that, in the past few weeks, there has been damage to the image of Cuban Americans."

Hardliners complained that CANF chair Jorge Mas Santos, the son of Jorge Mas Canosa, had not shown the leadership that his father would have provided to keep Elián out of Cuba. They vowed to retaliate against the Democrats in the upcoming November 2000 elections, which they did, helping to win a dubious victory for Bush in Florida. CANF's internal divide culminated in a split in 2001 when almost two dozen board members publicly resigned, stating that CANF had softened its line. They formed the Cuban Liberty Council (CLC), which continued the hard line of no contact at all with Cuba.

The Trade Embargo

Crucially, both CANF and CLC continued full support for Helms-Burton. When Obama made that promise in Miami in May 2008 to allow "unlimited family travel and remittances," he also made a second promise: "I will maintain the embargo." On this issue of trade, Obama could play to both CLC and CANF because this promise is stamped with the approval of all of those self-professed humanitarians who want to starve the Cuban people into submission.

But it does not have the stamp of approval from most American people. In fact, despite opposition by the usual suspects, in the year 2000 agribusinesses and pharmaceutical industries were able to persuade Congress and President Clinton to enact a major change to Helms-Burton that allows exports of food, agricultural and forestry products, and medicines to Cuba.

The change has turned the United States into one of Cuba's major trading partners. However, the trade is only in one direction. Cuba can import U.S. exports, but nobody in the United States can import Cuban exports. In addition, Cuba must pay cash in advance for those imports.

But the embargo has become a boomerang. According to Helms-Burton, the president should instruct the U.S. ambassador to the United Nations to propose in the Security Council "a mandatory international embargo against the totalitarian Cuban Government."

Instead, it is Cuba who has brought the issue to a vote every year since 1992 in the General Assembly. That year, with 179 nations, the vote was 59 to 3 against the trade embargo, with 71 abstentions and 46 not voting. As the years went by, the number of votes against the embargo kept increasing. By 2011, with 193 nations, the vote was 186 to 2, with 3 abstentions and 2 not voting. Washington could find only one country—Israel—to vote for the trade embargo.

What other nations refuse to trade with Cuba? Not one. Even Israel, despite its vote at the UN, trades with Cuba. Major trading partners—including Venezuela, China, Canada, Spain, Brazil, Mexico, Vietnam, Russia, Algeria, and the European Union—are profiting from the flow of goods and services in and out of Cuba. In the globalized and multipolar world of the 21st century, the U.S. embargo becomes ever more anachronistic and self-destructive. An historical development at the turn of the century created an opening for Cuba that continues to widen and deepen. After Hugo Chávez, a socialist, was elected Venezuela's president in 1999, Cuba and Venezuela formed a trading alliance based on the barter system—Cuba, rich in health care and Venezuela, rich in oil, traded medical personnel and oil for the benefit of each population.

In 2004 Cuba and Venezuela launched the Bolivarian Alliance for the Peoples of Our America (ALBA), an alternative to the proposed Free Trade Area of the Americas (FTAA), which was promoted by the United States and would have included all countries in the Americas except Cuba. Foreign Minister Rodríguez has called FTAA "the United States' plan to economically annex Latin America." FTAA was sidelined in 2005. ALBA has continued to grow. A dramatic change in political and economic relationships is underway in the Western Hemisphere.

In 1962, as part of Operation Mongoose—a covert plan for overthrowing the Cuban government—the Kennedy Administration launched a major campaign to isolate Cuba. A crucial component was to get Cuba suspended from the Organization of American States (OAS). Since the OAS is headquartered in and dominated by Washington, 14 of the 21 members went along with the White House, barely providing the necessary two-thirds vote for suspension. In 2009, the OAS, having grown in numbers as well as political power, rescinded Cuba's suspension.

The paradigm shift was boldly manifest the following year in the creation of the Community of Latin American and Caribbean States (CELAC), which aims to strengthen economic and political ties among its members, completely independent from Washington. When the 21st century opened, OAS members included all 35 nations of the Western Hemisphere, with Cuba suspended. By the end of the first decade of the 21st century, CELAC members included all 33 Latin American and Caribbean nations of the Western Hemisphere, with the United States and Canada excluded.

As if oblivious to the consensus of Latin America and the Caribbean regarding the status of Cuba, President Obama declared in September 2011, "It's clearly time for regime change in Cuba." When it seemed that President Raúl Castro would attend the OAS Sixth Summit in 2012, Cuban-Americans in Congress demanded that President Obama boycott the meeting if Castro attended. Obama promptly agreed. Ecuadorian President Rafael Correa, in a letter to the Summit's host, Colombian President Juan Manuel Santos, explained that he would not be attending if Cuba were excluded. When the Summit met on April 14-15 in Cartagena, Cuba's exclusion became a major agenda item. Disagreement led to no Final Statement. As an Associated Press headline put it, "U.S., Canada stand alone insisting on the exclusion of Cuba from summits."

Yet in Washington and Miami there is no sign of recognition that the center has shifted both within the Hemisphere and within the United States. During the 2012 presidential campaign, the gravitational pull continued to move Republicans around CLC and Democrats around CANF, all upholding the trade embargo and disregarding the creation of Cuban-American groups like Cuban Americans For Engagement (CAFE) and the Foundation for Normalization of U.S.-Cuba Relations (FORNORM), not to mention all the polls showing that a majority of all Americans want improved relations with Cuba.

Indeed, in the heat of the 2012 presidential campaign, the candidates of the two major political parties ignored voices of dissent and predictably engaged in outdoing each other in their fervor for empire. Just as President Obama called for regime change in Cuba, Republican presidential candidate Mitt Romney promised hardliners that "we will hasten the day when the regime will come to an end."

American Exceptionalism

What ideology allows this policy toward Cuba to continue despite almost universal condemnation around the globe?

Describing his own book, *No Apology: The Case for American Greatness,* Romney stated, "I make no apology for my conviction that America's economic and military leadership is not only good for American but also critical for freedom and peace across the world." In a speech in May 2012, he explained, "We have two courses we can follow: One is to follow in the pathway of Europe, to shrink our military smaller and smaller to pay for our social needs. The other is to commit to preserve America as the strongest military in the world, second to none, with no comparable power anywhere in the world." At a campaign stop in March, he told supporters, "Our president doesn't have the same feelings about American exceptionalism that we do."

Speaking at the Air Force Academy Commencement in May, President Obama, not to be outdone as an exceptionalist, dutifully followed those neoconservatives from the Project for the New American Century with their strategy for a "global Pax Americana." He told the graduating pilots of Forever War that "the United States has been, and will always be, the one indispensable nation in world affairs" because "America is exceptional" and "the 21st will be another great American Century." Explaining these pilots' duties in this New American Century, he invoked "American Century" seven times as he promised "military superiority in all areas—air, land, sea, space and cyber." The goal is "an international order where the rights and responsibilities of all nations and peoples are upheld and where countries thrive by meeting their obligations and face consequences when they don't." In this Pax Americana, consequences will be decided by Washington. The United States with its alleged democratic ideals is free—free to do anything it wants to do, from toppling governments with massive destruction to sending drones on assignments for the assassination of anybody anywhere.

The doctrine of American exceptionalism emerged dramatically alongside U.S. policy toward Cuba, from Jefferson's vision of Cuba as part of an "empire for liberty," to the Platt Amendment's platform for domination, and on to Helms-Burton's blueprint for starving Cuba into submission in the New American Century—all under the banner of democracy, freedom, and human rights.

From **Z** **Magazine,** *December 2012*
Volume 25, Number 12

8.

Torture, Racism, & the Sovereign Presidency

By Herbert Bix

PRESIDENT GEORGE W. BUSH has embedded murder, assassination, torture, and mistreatment of prisoners into the structure of the U.S. system of global domination. Many U.S. citizens, rightly outraged, want to know why this sort of

> *Above all, they want to know how Bush has been able to avoid impeachment for committing high crimes*

barbaric, sadistic violence has become an integral part of U.S. security policy, and what the Administration's justification of torture means institutionally for the future governance of this country. Above all, they want to know how Bush has been able to avoid impeachment for committing high crimes. Here is a select list of typical tortures, abuses, and "outrages against human dignity" inflicted by U.S. forces and mercenaries on enemy captives in the course of their arrest, detention, and interrogation:

> Beating, kicking, and treading on bodies

> Sleep deprivation and forced injection of drugs

> Rape and sodomy

> Water torture, a traditional U.S. Army practice since at least the Indian wars and the Philippines insurrection at the end of the 19th century

> Hanging prisoners whose arms are bound by shackles or handcuffs until their limbs pop from their sockets—a new U.S. form of lynching

> Handcuffing, close-shackling, and blindfolding or "hooding" for extended periods; sometimes the hoods are marked in order to alert the U.S. torturer to the particular crime that the prisoner is suspected of having committed

> Forced stripping of Muslim prisoners, keeping them naked for long periods

> Religious humiliation

> Sexual humiliation, insult, and debasement, including smearing with feces, urine, and what appears to be menstrual blood

> Screaming racial insults after unleashing violence against captives

> Shocking with electrical instruments, a method of torture commonly used by U.S. troops in Vietnam

> Exposure for prolonged periods to extremes of light and dark, heat and cold, and noise so deafening as to rupture the eardrums

> Extraction of nails, burning skin with cigarettes, stabbing or cutting the bodies of prisoners

> Threatening prisoners or their relatives with death or by having them watch other victims being tortured

> Threatening with dogs or allowing dogs to actually assault prisoners during or before interrogation

> Forcing prisoners to stand or to remain in painful positions for extended periods

> Isolation in cells, cages, wooden boxes, and barbed wire-enclosed trailers

> Depriving prisoners of food, water, drink, and toilet facilities

> Extreme or enforced rendition, i.e., torture by proxy in foreign countries

These acts were performed both before and after the Bush administration had unilaterally exempted itself from legal liabilities under international and domestic law. Some members of the U.S. military abused prisoners because senior military commanders such as Lieutenant General Ricardo Sanchez had explicitly authorized them to do so; some tortured the enemy because they found it to be "fun"; but most seem to have acted in the belief that their conduct was condoned because the White House and the Department of Defense had adopted a policy of fighting terror with terror.

In the U.S. mass media, the routine, sometimes bone-shattering, beating of prisoners in U.S. custody receives relatively little attention except as a public relations problem. Moral and legal concern seems to be reserved for the less common, more secretive practice of "rendition," in which officials of the executive branch are protected because the abuse takes place outside the U.S., avoiding monitoring by the Red Cross and due process. More so than other modes of torture, this type of contract crime may be ordered mainly for reasons of deterrence—i.e., to teach an object lesson to all people who fall afoul of the U.S., regardless of their national origin. European governments rightly considered it to be a blatant violation of their local sovereignty.

A Total War Strategy

The Bush administration's increasing reliance on imprisonment, torture, and assassination as elements in its "war on terror," needs to be explained from multiple angles, as part of a total war strategy for eliminating new challenges to the U.S. global empire. Fear, racism, and colonial wars in poverty-stricken Afghanistan and Iraq are historical frames that highlight the scope and complexity of the problem. The collapse of separation of powers, the decay of democratic processes and values,

Congress's unwillingness to destroy the perception of presidential impunity, and the increasingly secret nature of government combined to constitute a fourth frame. Let me touch briefly on each.

From the earliest days of the U.S., fear and racism have been striking features of U.S. culture. Although closely related, they are distinguishable. By fear I mean the inordinate susceptibility of the U.S. public to fits of real panic, during which fear and extremism override reason. Usually fear spreads when political elites sound the alarm and rally the country to fight some unbelievably powerful force that is out to destroy the world they inhabit. The threat can come from within or from outside, from a modern or "failed state," or from a social movement. But once defined, U.S. citizens imagine that only extraordinary leaders, willing to ignore the law, can protect them from the menace. Under strong presidents, citizens fight back in self-defense against the insidious enemy, using catastrophic weapons created by their technological genius.

The enemy can be Indians, Blacks, or Chinese; it can be Britain in one period, Spain, Japan, the Soviet Union, or international terrorists in another. In almost every case, the enemy that their leaders exhorted them to hate later turns out to be whoever had something we wanted. The pattern is old and recurs throughout the history of U.S. empire. The most spectacular case of "punishing an aggressor" with an unprecedented new super weapon was President Truman's nuclear destruction of Hiroshima and Nagasaki.

By racism, I mean attitudes of hatred and contempt directed toward those who are unlike us, mainly for reasons of color. In multicultural, allegedly color-blind U.S., with its many racial minorities, racism and de facto segregation continues. When Bush declared his "war on terror," this old dynamic assumed forms suited to 21st century conditions. Racial profiling returned; civil rights for minorities and immigrants eroded; and both developments went hand in hand with war atrocities committed by U.S. forces in Afghanistan, Iraq, and Guantanamo, Cuba.

The effects of racial bias can be seen in the world's largest, expanding prison system where the percentage of Blacks, Latinos, and Hispanics remains high and racial violence and mistreatment of minority inmates occurs frequently. Not surprisingly, in the atmosphere of revenge galvanized by the 9/11 at-

> *Usually fear spreads when political elites sound the alarm and rally the country to fight some unbelievably powerful force that is out to destroy the world they inhabit*

tacks, racial violence quickly spread from the domestic prisons and police departments to U.S. military prisons abroad. Abusive jailers and police officers from the U.S. volunteered to fight and ended up torturing prisoners at camps in Kandahar, Baghram, Guantanamo Bay, Mosul, Bucca in southern Iraq, and Abu Ghraib near Baghdad.

The Pentagon also recruited patrol officers and officials from federal and state prisons for its war on terror and sent them to the U.S.-run prisons in Iraq. According to Bureau of Justice Statistics, the U.S. state prison system is far larger than the federal system and in 2003 held nearly 1.2 million inmates, most of them ethnic minorities. Local jails contained 700,000 inmates; juvenile facilities over 100,000. Racial violence and mistreatment of inmates by guards is more likely to occur in the state prisons and local jails where the level of discipline is lower, the use of force greater. But from the Brooklyn Metropolitan Detention Center, where hundreds of Muslim detainees were recently abused, to the U.S. military prisons spread throughout the world, wherever prisoners of color have been tortured by guards, racism usually lies close to the surface.

Furthermore, race rather than national origin fundamentally shapes the U.S. soldiers' image of the terrorist. The Army sent to fight in Afghanistan and Iraq was "whiter" than it had been since 2000 as a result of five straight years of declining Army recruitment of black Americans. The 17,000 U.S. soldiers in Afghanistan reportedly turned virtually the entire country into one huge secret prison in which military guards and CIA interrogators inflicted gratuitous pain on the bodies of individual Afghani captives who are held incommunicado without charge or trial, according to a March 19, 2005 report in the *Guardian*.

Whenever this happens, the likelihood is great that they are exercising "racially-informed," irrational violence against both their victims and the entire society to which they belong. The same phenomenon can be seen in Iraq where U.S. soldiers call the inhabitants "sand niggers" and "ragheads."

A third framework for understanding the torture scandal is the regressive, colonial-like character of the current U.S. wars. Nothing illustrates this better than the bloody struggle to control Fallujah, a Sunni city located west of Baghdad on the edge of the Iraq desert, which before the U.S. invasion had a population estimated at 300,000.

The Battle of Fallujah

The initial skirmish in what became the first battle of Fallujah (March and early April 2004) was fought after four U.S. military contractors were brutally murdered by young Iraqis. The killings were in revenge for the murder in Gaza of the paraplegic Sheik Ahmed Yassin, spiritual leader of Hamas, by Israelis who were flying U.S. helicopters. Marines went into Fallujah, allegedly searching for the killers of the civilian mercenaries, but were forced out by its residents. To redeem their honor, they mounted a full-scale assault. After three weeks of rebellion, the casualty figures ranged from a low of 600 combatant and non-combatants killed and over 1,200 injured to estimates ranging upward from 1,000.

The second battle to retake Fallujah from its inhabitants began five months later in November 2004, after Marines again cut off food, water, and electricity to the city in violation of the Geneva Conventions. Their illegal acts of collective retribution were designed to empty the city of its women, children, and elderly while preventing the departure of able-bodied Iraqi civilian males. When something similar happened in Srebrenica, Bosnia in 1995 it was universally condemned in Europe and the U.S. as "genocide." The main difference was that in Srebrenica the Serbs evacuated the women and children by truck while in Fallujah the U.S. bombed them out.

As U.S. ground attacks on entrances to the besieged city of Fallujah increased, aerial bombardment—torture from the air—commenced. A U.S. specialty since 1945, the bombing of cities tends to take a primary toll on civilians while seeking to force both noncombatants and combatants to sue for peace.

Iraqi popular resistance forces responded to these U.S. assaults by stepping up attacks in Baghdad, Samarra, Ramadi, and elsewhere, killing and wounding more foreign occupiers and their Iraqi collaborators. Fallujah's struggle to end the U.S. occupation spread the nationalist resistance.

The retaking of Fallujah during November and early December through ruthless air, tank, and artillery bombardment resulted in the city's complete destruction. Under rules of engagement approved in Washington, U.S. forces reportedly used banned napalm and poison gas, killed civilians holding white flags or white clothes over their heads, murdered the wounded, killed unarmed Iraqis who had been taken prisoner, and destroyed mosques, hospitals, and health centers protected under international law. One of the most amazing, well-reported scenes from this battle took place at the Fallujah General Hospital where U.S. forces kicked down doors, cut the telephone lines, molested doctors, forced patients from their beds, and manacled their hands behind their backs.

Fallujan residents were forced to live as refugees in surrounding towns and villages. To this day no one knows how many people died in the bloodbath, but a few months earlier, in September 2004, an Iraqi mortality researcher and his interviewer, working on a public health study jointly sponsored by Johns Hopkins University and Columbia University, managed to enter the city. What they discovered was such a high number of civilian deaths that they decided to exclude the Fallujah data from their final, conservative estimate of about 100,000 Iraqi civilians (mostly women and children) killed since the U.S. invaded. In a population estimated at 24 million, that is the U.S. proportional equivalent of 1.2 million deaths.

When legal restraints are removed during a war, needless death and destruction occurs. Invariably, the main victims are civilians. In World War II, the "kill ratio" was one civilian death (mostly children, women, and the elderly) for every soldier killed. The smaller wars fought after 1945 ran the civilian-soldier count up to 8:1. But in Iraq, the kill ratio is conservatively estimated to be much higher.

Why do tens of millions of Americans refuse to confront this reality? Perhaps because they never heard about the *Lancet* study, thanks to the U.S. corporate media. Or perhaps misguided patriotism and militarism, drummed into youth through film, television, and video games, led them to consider the enormous civilian loss and suffering as unavoidable "collateral damage" or a product of military necessity. Whatever the reasons, not only the Administration, but the mainstream press and many citizens profess to care only about the lives of fellow Americans and remain unconcerned about the barbaric treat-

ment their soldiers mete out to Iraqis and Afghanis.

U.S. Assertion of Dominion

The problem of widespread, individualized interrogation-by-torture is inseparable from the pain and suffering inflicted on all those who resist U.S. assertion of dominion. In late April 2004, as the initial battle for Fallujah was winding down, the first photos appeared of uniformed, grinning U.S. soldiers torturing Iraqis at Abu Ghraib prison. Since then, the illegal acts of the Bush administration, its armed forces and intelligence operatives have received relentless news media attention abroad and only desultory attention within the United States.

Earlier, there had been news reports coming out of Afghanistan about teams of U.S. Special Forces and their Northern Alliance allies committing war atrocities at Baghram,

> *What they discovered was such a high number of civilian deaths that they decided to exclude the Fallujah data from their final, conservative estimate of about 100,000 Iraqi civilians (mostly women and children) killed since the U.S. invaded*

Kandahar, and other places in Afghanistan. UN officials had documented how uniformed U.S. officers connived in the mass killing of surrendered Taliban soldiers at Dash-E Leili. NGOs in many countries, including the International Red Cross, Human Rights Watch, and Amnesty International, had compiled massive dossiers documenting, from early 2002 onward, U.S. soldiers severely beating and kicking bound, helpless prisoners, and of Army medical personnel conniving in the abuse. Often recessed into the background of such reports was mention of U.S. forces treating Afghanis mercilessly, as subhuman, denigrating them through the use of racial epithets, demeaning their national culture.

Many people in the U.S. took the news of atrocity charges in stride. During 2003, stories broke of Israeli military advisers being invited into Iraq and to Fort Bragg, North Carolina to train U.S. assassination squads as well as video pictures of U.S. helicopter pilots murdering wounded Iraqis lying on the ground. Well before the obscene photos from Abu Ghraib were broadcast on national television, the atrocities committed by U.S. forces were steadily increasing. But the U.S. chose either not to know or to passively accept the president's disregard of international law.

By the time the torture scandal broke, Iraqi resistance against the U.S. presence had intensified and public support for the war was waning. The Bush administration rushed to deny that torture was intentionally ordered or widely practiced and blamed all abuses on a few rotten apples acting on their own. Neither Bush nor Rumsfeld offered a public apology for torture or admitted that they had prior knowledge of it.

Yet the daily routine of U.S. war crimes was too widespread to be covered up. The story of the prisons staffed with racists and sadists, just as in the U.S., kept deepening and the number of prisoners kept on increasing—in Iraq, 8,000 at the time of the Abu Ghraib pictures; 10,500 as of March 2005; and in Afghanistan 500 as of January 2005.

Bush policymakers had expressed from the outset a strong desire to inflict pain on enemy captives. They had denied the occupied people proper prisoner-of-war treatment, set aside the law of occupation, and ordered military strategies of indiscriminate violence against all who resisted. Documents generated in the White House and the Departments of Justice and Defense appeared in the press after lawsuits were brought by the ACLU. They bore out that the president, by fiat, had set aside the Geneva Conventions, denied prisoner-of-war status to Taliban and Al Qaeda captives taken in Afghanistan, and sent them for indefinite detention to the naval base at Guantanamo, Cuba. This meant they would be interrogated without legal restriction.

The torture documents reveal a mindset within the White House and Pentagon intent on destroying what remained of democratic processes. Right after the World Trade Center and Pentagon attacks, Bush issued a secret directive authorizing torture by proxy in foreign jails of those suspected of having information about terrorist operations. Thereafter, he used the "war on terror" and his commander-in-chief authority to expand the little known "state-secrets privilege," for which no constitutional foundation exists, in order to prevent the courts from discovering what crimes he directed the CIA to commit.

The torture debate is about the Pentagon's and the White House's cover-up of the massive war crimes committed by members of the U.S. armed forces and CIA against Afghanis and Iraqis. But at a deeper level it is part of a larger debate in which the issues at stake are:

> Bush's attempt to elevate the myth of presidential sovereignty

> Bush's illegal attempt to exempt the U.S. from the Geneva Conventions and his Administration's invention of the false category of "unlawful combatants" as a way of legitimating confinement and torture

> The evocation of "presidential secrecy" by executive officials to prevent the federal courts from prying into matters of national security both as they concern the Pentagon's and the CIA's global prison systems and Bush's dereliction in the performance of his duties

> The federal Constitution's modeling of the presidency on monarchy and its failure to protect from periodic presidential usurpations of power, which is exactly what its chief author, James Madison, intended

Turning to government memoranda, we see the most senior-level bureaucrats, lawyers, politicians, and soldiers—all of whom had sworn oaths to uphold the Constitution—debating over a two-year period: (a) how to justify Bush's decision to use interrogation techniques that were banned by international and domestic law; (b) how to limit the president's legal exposure in the event that a federal district court tried to block him from getting around the law by issuing a writ of habeas corpus; and (c) how to prevent a court from assessing whether U.S. conduct in Afghanistan violated the norms of international law.

Another little known finding is that the U.S. may never have ratified any human rights convention without adding reservations that exempted itself—not the 1949 Geneva Conventions, not the subsequent protocols to it, and not even the 1948 Genocide Convention, which is the first of the post-World War II human rights treaties. Technically the Senate ratified the 1984 Torture Convention in 1994, but only after changing the definition of torture to make it more restrictive "than that set out in the Convention," and thus more "interrogator-friendly."

The torture documents show President Bush and Secretary of Defense Donald Rumsfeld using the legal opinions of their lawyers—including the now notorious August 1, 2002 memo written by Assistant Attorney General Jay S. Bybee—to assert a right to order the torture, maiming, and even murder of prisoners. Drawing on his commander-in-chief authority and the advice of his counsel, Alberto Gonzales, Bush suspended the Geneva Conventions, but later, in order to protect himself, issued a written directive cautioning all military interrogators to treat detainees "humanely."

At the same time, he allowed CIA interrogators to continue using cruel and unusual methods of interrogation. Bush also authorized the use of torture techniques against prisoners detained in the war on Iraq, which initially had nothing to do with the war against the Taliban or Al Qaeda. Rumsfeld took charge and turned the Pentagon into the "nerve center for directing torture and conducting secret missions."

Over the years since U.S. forces entered Afghanistan and later attacked and occupied Iraq, U.S. soldiers scoured villages, towns, and cities in both countries, searching for "insurgents." Overall, they succeeded mainly in creating chaos and lawlessness, spreading armed resistance to their presence, and generating a keen desire for future revenge against the United States. The more U.S. forces have devastated Iraq, contaminated its land, destroyed its cities, and mistreated the Iraqi people in their local communities and inside their homes, the more resistance to U.S. presence has grown.

Tens of thousands of Iraqi civilians, as well as al-Qaeda suspects and Taliban fighters, were rounded up and imprisoned under medieval conditions. U.S. soldiers, CIA agents ("case officers"), and mercenaries ("civilians") working for privatized military firms under contract to the Pentagon, are known to have sadistically tortured large numbers of them while having their deeds photographed and filmed so that they could be seen by friends back home.

The Logic of Torture

A fourth frame for understanding why torture became just another weapon in the U.S. arsenal relates to the long decline in the spirit of democratic government that preceded 9/11. The growing immunity of the military from Congressional oversight is but an aspect of this phenomenon. At its heart is the corruption of the Congress under one-party control and the connivance of Senators and House members in shielding the president and his advisers from criminal liability for waging wars of aggression in which they themselves were complicit. The U.S. was already out of step with the rest of the world and sliding into an anti-democratic mode of governance long before the rise of the religious right and the neo-cons hastened this process. When a group of fundamentally dishonest ideological extremists took control of the presidency and the Congress, the corrupt condition of the U.S. political system began to be revealed in all sorts of criminal acts.

In Europe, during the two world wars, the United States seems not to have stooped to officially ordering the torture and mistreatment of prisoners of war, though only because arrayed against it were fighting forces that held U.S. prisoners and could retaliate. But in three Asian-Pacific wars—against Japan, North Korea, and the people of Indochina—the greater capabilities of U.S. forces made the fighting far more one-sided.

In World War II, victorious U.S. troops in the Pacific confronted an enemy equipped with inferior weapons, usually took no prisoners, and often mutilated and murdered the wounded with impunity. The Japanese army, too, mistreated Allied prisoners and civilians on the battlefield and in occupied territories, but they alone were held criminally accountable for their actions. Vietnam, and later interventions, were unprovoked colonial wars against much weaker enemies. When going against the weak, the U.S. military has invariably used torture tactics on a wide scale.

Bush built on the legacy of war crimes and atrocities ordered by past presidents, including his own father and Bill Clinton, both of whom had issued presidential directives authorizing "extraordinary rendition." In 2001, Bush expanded this practice without furnishing any meaningful guidelines. He is not the first president who ever turned his back on the fundamental principles of international order, but he and his top officials were certainly the first to have shattered the torture taboo while openly and repeatedly expressing contempt for international law. They were also the first to threaten the use of nuclear weapons even against non-nuclear states.

Today in the United States no strong public pressure exists for upholding the laws against torture of persons considered "enemy." In 2002 a poll indicated "that one-third of Americans favored the use of torture on terrorist suspects." The most recent Gallup poll, released March 1, 2005, suggested that 39 percent would support torturing "known terrorists if they know details about future terrorist attacks." Clearly, a large minority, whose views the Administration represents, believes that it is acceptable, if not wholly justified, to employ the tactics of torture in the fight against terrorist suspects in order to extract information that might save innocent lives.

> *Today in the United States no strong public pressure exists for upholding the laws against torture of persons considered "enemy." In 2002 a poll indicated "that one-third of Americans favored the use of torture on terrorist suspects."*

To intentionally inflict pain and suffering on helpless detainees, whether or not they engaged in combat, is illegal and morally wrong, besides being cowardly and counterproductive. The legal prohibition on torture is absolute and unambiguous and can never be justified under any conditions. The only problem is that the U.S. government never actually ratified any humanitarian law without inserting loopholes that would allow it to make a claim of exemption.

The best available evidence suggests that torturing defenseless captives to obtain information doesn't deter terrorist attacks. The information extracted under White House and Pentagon torture policy has proven singularly ineffective in defeating a popular resistance movement that has the support of the local population. In Iraq, Bush policies have only succeeded in creating terrorists, fueling the flames of resistance to the U.S. presence, and breaking up the coalition of governments that unwisely sent troops to Iraq. Furthermore, the history of modern warfare shows that guerilla resistance movements do not depend on hierarchical chains of command that can be broken by such interrogation methods. To stop their pain, prisoners will say anything, rendering what they say unreliable.

Secretary of State Colin Powell found this out when he delivered his infamous address to the UN Security Council in February 2003, "which argued the case for a preemptive war against Iraq." In his speech, Powell drew on the testimony of an unnamed "senior terrorist operative" who had told his interrogators that Saddam Hussein had offered to train al-Qaeda operatives in the use of 'chemical or biological weapons'."

After the U.S. invasion, it turned out that the terrorist, one Ibn al-Sheikh al-Libi, had been tortured by his CIA and Egyptian interrogators. Later, at Guantanomo, Libi recanted and admitted that he had lied. So much for evidence obtained through torture and the spin master who relied on it to justify aggression.

U.S. leaders have been intent on controlling the world ever since the Truman administration ended the war with Japan in a five-month orgy of conventional bombing before destroying Hiroshima and Nagasaki with atomic bombs. Their greed, ambition, and lack of foresight have left them with no solution, but to pit themselves against the nationalism and desire for self-determination of weaker states throughout the world. Presidents and generals solved the problem of discovering who the enemy is by defining the entire population as enemy. When the "enemy" is the civilian population who won't do our bidding, not only do the kill ratios have to be high, but reliance on torture, murder, and assassination also becomes vital. This is why Afghanistan and Iraq are in the same class as Korea and Vietnam: imperialism produces the logic of torture.

From Z **Magazine,** *July/August 2005*
Volume 18, Number 7/8

Part 2

Maintaining An Empire

9.

U.S. War on Communism, Drugs, and Terrorism in Colombia

By Jenny O'Connor

O N THURSDAY, SEPTEMBER 6, the President of Colombia, Juan Manuel Santos, rejected a proposed bilateral ceasefire by FARC (Revolutionary Armed Forces of Colombia) rebels aimed at bringing an end to Colombia's armed conflict. He declared that he had asked operations to be intensified and stated that "there will be no ceasefire of any kind."

> *Today Colombia is one of the largest recipients of U.S. military training and aid in the world. Although the U.S was involved in counterinsurgency operations in Colombia during the Cold War, the continued flow of military funding and training occurred as a result of Bill Clinton's "Plan Colombia..."*

Today Colombia is one of the largest recipients of U.S. military training and aid in the world. Although the U.S was involved in counterinsurgency operations in Colombia during the Cold War, the continued flow of military funding and training occurred as a result of Bill Clinton's "Plan Colombia" (2000–2006) and George W Bush's "Andean Regional Initiative" (2008–2010), both of which were aimed at the forced eradication of coca and fighting Colombia's left-wing guerrillas. Through these initiatives billions of dollars have been spent fighting a war on drugs followed by a war on terror. Coca production in Colombia, however, has increased—as has the intensity of the internal armed conflict with both FARC and right-wing paramilitary groups growing in size and strength.

Despite numerous studies concluding that the cheapest and most effective way to deal with the drug situation is to redirect funds from law enforcement and forced eradication into treatment and prevention, the U.S. government has maintained its militaristic approach to the war on drugs both at home and abroad. Given the resounding failure to achieve the stated objectives of these initiatives, one must ask if there's an alternative objective—one that the current strategy achieves sufficiently?

The Neoliberal Effect

The U.S. has a long-held policy of pushing neoliberal economic polices in Latin America, achieved through NGO activity, strategically allocated aid, coercive interventions, conditions attached to IMF and World Bank loans, and bi-lateral and multi-lateral free trade agreements. There is substantial literature exposing the resultant social stratification these policies have caused in Latin America but there is one particular effect of neo-liberalism that has directly resulted in increased cultivation of coca for export.

The neoliberal model aims to reorient agricultural production to the export market. While neoliberal policies remove protective tariff barriers on agricultural goods, subsidized U.S. agricultural imports undermine the price received for locally produced crops. Larger farms and ranches with sufficient resources can move into growing export crops such as coffee but these crops are more labor intensive, require more land and cost more to transport. Many small farmers and peasants therefore find that the only area in which they can maintain a competitive advantage is in the cultivation of coca. This was evident in Mexico after the signing of NAFTA when U.S.-subsidized corn imports destroyed Mexico's domestic production. Those who could not afford to invest in the production of other export crops either switched to cultivating illicit drugs or

moved to the city, where a lack of employment opportunities pushed many into other elements of the drug trade.

It is clear that if the U.S. wished to reduce the cultivation of coca in Colombia, the most effective policy would be to redirect military aid into funding government subsidization of legal crops. Yet the U.S.-Colombia Trade Promotion Agreement actually prohibits such action. Under the agreement—signed in 2006 but not taking affect until May 2012—Colombia is obliged to dismantle all domestic protections while the U.S. is permitted to maintain their own agricultural subsidies, thus gaining an unfair advantage in the trade of agricultural produce. In 2010, Oxfam International commissioned a study that demonstrated that the agreement would lower the prices local farmers would receive for major crops such as corn and beans which, in turn, would reduce domestic cultivation of these crops and substantially impact the income and livelihood of hundreds of thousands of Colombia's peasant farmers.

Biological Warfare

One major part of both Plan Colombia and the Merida initiative has been the destruction of coca fields by aerial chemical fumigation, thus impacting the cocaine trade at its source. Glyphosate, the chemical substance used to fumigate illicit crops—known by its brand name Roundup—was originally patented and produced by the most notorious of U.S. agricultural corporations, Monsanto. Glyphosate is classified by Monsanto as a "mild" herbicide, but by the World Health Organization as "extremely poisonous." Roundup is sold over the counter in the U.S. as a herbicide and carries these warnings: "Roundup will kill almost any green plant that is actively growing. Roundup should not be applied to bodies of water such as ponds, lakes or streams…. After an area has been sprayed with Roundup, people and pets (such as cats and dogs) should stay out of the area until it is thoroughly dry…. If Roundup is used to control undesirable plants around fruit or nut trees, or grapevines, allow twenty-one days before eating the fruits or nuts."

In Colombia, however, two additives—Cosmo-Flux 411 and Cosmo InD—are added, increasing the toxicity four-fold and producing what is known as Roundup Ultra or, as some call it, "Colombia's Agent Orange." In addition, the concentrations in the mixtures prepared by the Colombian military (under the guidance of their U.S. colleagues) are five times higher than is recognized as safe for aerial application by the U.S. Environmental Protection Agency. This product is regularly sprayed over inhabited areas, farmland, livestock and areas of invaluable bio-diversity. The National Environmental Justice Advisory Council, a Federal Advisory Committee to the U.S. Environmental Protection Agency, issued a letter on July 19, 2001 stating that: "Aerial spraying of the herbicide has caused eye, respiratory, skin and digestive ailments; destroyed subsistence crops; sickened domestic animals; and contaminated water supplies." Even anti-drug development projects, including ones funded by USAID, the UN, the Colombian government and international NGOs, have been destroyed by fumigation. One of many examples is that of CORCUSA, an organic coffee cooperative founded to provide peasant farmers with an alternative to coca cultivation. CORCUSA was fumigated in 2005 and again in 2007 destroying the coffee crop and the project's organic certification for future crops.

As well as the clear human health, food security, and environmental risks involved in the fumigation campaign, it has also been a massive failure in achieving its stated goal: the eradication of the coca crop. Coca, unlike most other food crops, is actually quite resistant to aerial spraying of glyphosate. Many farmers who have their food crops destroyed are left with few options when coca is all that will grow on their land after the spraying of glyphosate—so the result of the fumigation campaign has been a marked increase in coca cultivation.

Militarization of the War on Drugs

The militaristic approach to fighting the drug war has intensified the conflict in Colombia. The result has been mass displacement and disenfranchisement of people which, in turn, has pushed more people into some area of the drug trade. What's more, numerous studies dating back to the 1980s have

> *What's more, numerous studies dating back to the 1980s have mutually concluded that militarizing the drug war would have little to no effect on the consumption of illicit drugs in the United States*

mutually concluded that militarizing the drug war would have little to no effect on the consumption of illicit drugs in the United States. The effect of the militarized strategy has been a marked increase in drug related violence wherever it is initiated and there is not a more clear-cut example of this than Mexico. Before Calderon militarized Mexico's drug war the violent crime rate was actually falling. Since this approach has been adopted—with avid U.S. support including the allocation of $1.4 billion over a 3-year period (2008-2010) through the Mérida Initiative—the homicide rate has more than doubled, the violent crime rate has increased by more than 200 percent, and the number of human rights abuses committed by the military in their attempts to reign in the drug cartels has increased 6-fold.

In terms of preventing the flow of drugs into the U.S., the militarized approach has one simple economic paradox at its core. By disproportionally tackling production and distribution (the supply side of the equation) without equally tackling consumption (the demand side of the equation), the price of the product is increased, thus providing a greater profit incentive for people to take the involved risks in trafficking and producing illicit drugs.

War on Narcoguerrillas?

As previously stated, Plan Colombia's original objective was the eradication of coca plantations by targeting left-wing narcoguerrillas (FARC) who, it was explicitly claimed, were directly involved in the drug trade. Evidence of a direct link between FARC and the illicit drug trade, however, did not emerge until the early 2000s after Plan Colombia had been instigated. In fact, into the late 1990s, there was little evidence to suggest that FARC's involvement in the production and distribution of drugs extended beyond the taxation of coca cultivation in the regions it controlled. In 1997, Donnie Marshall, Chief of Operations for the Drug Enforcement Administration, admitted this in a DEA congressional testimony stating that, "there is little to indicate the insurgent groups are trafficking in cocaine themselves, either by producing cocaine HCL and selling it to Mexican syndicates, or by establishing their own distribution networks in the United States."

Plan Colombia—while stating the pursuit of left-wing narcoguerrillas as an objective—did not equally target right-wing Colombian paramilitaries. While a few high profile cases of paramilitaries being tried and convicted on drug trafficking charges have occurred, on the whole, the focus remains principally on FARC.

This is despite the fact that at least as early as 1997 the DEA were aware of their involvement in narcotics trafficking. In the same congressional testimony quoted above, Marshal stated that the AUC (United Self-Defence Forces of Colombia), the largest Colombian right-wing paramilitary group, has been "closely linked" to the Henao Montoya organization—"the most powerful of the various independent trafficking groups that comprise the North Valle drug mafia"—and that the AUC's leader, Carlos Castano, is "a major cocaine trafficker in his own right." Fumigation, too, has been concentrated mainly in FARC strongholds in the South East despite the fact that right-wing paramilitaries are known to be involved in cocaine production and trafficking in the north of the country. Suspicions have thus emerged that the real aim of the fumigation campaign is to remove one of FARC's key revenue streams (the taxation of coca cultivation in areas they control) rather than coca cultivation in general.

In 2001, an investigation by Amnesty International led to a lawsuit to obtain CIA records of Los Pepes, a vigilante organization set up by Carlos Castano. Its findings revealed "an extremely suspect relationship between the U.S. government and the Castano family—at a time when the U.S. government was well aware of that family's involvement with paramilitary violence and narcotics trafficking."

War on Drugs/War on Terror

Colombia was one of the largest recipients of U.S. military aid and training throughout the Cold War. In the Cold War era the communist threat was used to justify counter-insurgency operations against FARC rebels whose communist/socialist roots posed a particular threat to U.S. economic interests, due to Colombia's extensive natural resources and strategic geographical location. Today, even if the idea of FARC gaining control over the Colombian state has diminished in credibility, the rebels regularly attack U.S. interests, including the infrastructure (railways, pipelines etc.) of U.S. energy and mining multinationals in Colombia. As Marc Grossman, former U.S. undersecretary of state for political affairs, put it: "[Colombian insurgents] represent a danger to the $4.3 billion in direct U.S. investment in Colombia…Colombia supplied three percent of U.S. oil imports in 2001, and possesses substantial potential oil and natural gas reserves."

After the Cold War and the fall of the Soviet Union, the communist threat no longer justified U.S. counterinsurgency operations in Colombia or elsewhere in Latin America. The U.S. Military's Southern Command (SOUTHCOM) therefore welcomed the drug war as a new justification for maintaining the same levels of military spending and counterinsurgency. The training of Latin American militaries and "low intensity warfare strategies employed in Central America were easily adopted to fight a war on drugs." In Colombia, FARC, previously labelled "Communist," became "narcoguerrillas" and, post-9/11, this morphed again into "terrorists." Again, the target of this campaign remained FARC despite the fact that the Colombian Army and closely linked armed right-wing paramilitary groups have been responsible for countless grave human rights abuses.

Importance to U.S. Foreign Policy

Military training and the cultivation of allied militaries whose interests and ideologies would reflect those of Washington has, historically, been one of the main methods of U.S. control in Latin America. Several Spanish language schools were established specifically for training Latin American officers including the notorious School of the Americas (SOA) which trained nearly every officer involved in the 1973 Chilean coup and where many members of the Colombian Army continue to train today. As well as training these officers in counter-insurgency, counter terrorism, and unconventional warfare (among other forms of attack), the SOA intentionally cultivates a glorified image of "privileged capitalist modernity and a strong belief in the right-wing capitalist model."

What resulted from such instruction in the past was the creation of highly politicized right-wing military entities which remained allied to the state only insofar as the government in power reflected a similar ideology. Throughout the 1970s and 1980s this resulted in military coups overthrowing left-wing governments throughout Latin American and the Caribbean. As Latin American states transitioned to democracy, the strength of these staunchly right-wing militaries (as well as fears of U.S. military intervention) led to the establishment of pacted democracies whereby elite and military support for the democratic transition was conditioned on the formation of certain economic parameters to be enshrined into the constitution.

> *Military training and the cultivation of allied militaries whose interests and ideologies would reflect those of Washington has, historically, been one of the main methods of U.S. control in Latin America*

Despite the fact that many democratic movements mobilized on the basis of wealth redistribution, these pacts generally guaranteed the continued presence of foreign multinationals in the extractive industries as well as ruling out the nationalization of resources and the socialization of land as policy options regardless of electoral outcomes. Where specific pacts did not exist, left-leaning elected governments remained very wary of their right-wing militaries when making policy decisions. In Chile, one of the more modern examples, even though the Concertación (Chile's democratic movement) opposed neoliberalism, the intimidating power of the right-wing military caused them to accept a moderately reformed version of Pinochet's 1980 constitution, which enshrined the neoliberal model as well as a number of authoritarian enclaves with a bias to the political right.

This is also the reason why very few Latin American countries—with the notable exception of Argentina—have managed to hold military personnel accountable for atrocities of the past. Indeed, in many places, army personnel who took part in grave atrocities continue to hold high ranking positions in the military. In Colombia, this is particularly so and, as military abuses continue to this day, a culture of impunity has been created, which remains a hindering factor to any potential for peace and reconciliation.

The more recent move to the left in Latin America has been a success, in part, because the new generation of left wing leaders are acutely aware of the dangers the military pose. In Bolivia one of Morales's acts as president was to raise military wages and the recent police strikes (so severe some called them a police mutiny) were partly based on the fact that police wages were roughly half those received by similar ranking military officers. In Venezuela, Chavez holds tight to his military image and many critics have used this to claim he is

> *The more recent move to the left in Latin America has been a success, in part, because the new generation of left wing leaders are acutely aware of the dangers the military pose.*

merely another "generalissimo." This criticism fails to realize, however, the great political importance in Chavez's realignment of the Venezuelan military with the democratically elected government of the state rather than outside forces an ideologies. His success in this endeavor was demonstrated when soldiers loyal to him reversed a military coup that displaced him briefly from power in 2002. Both Chavez and Morales, due to their opposition to drug war policies and the imperialist undertones they carry, have driven the DEA out of their respective countries.

The Stability Of Instability

It is clear that the war on drugs and the subsequent war on terror in Colombia have been used as fronts to justify the continued counterinsurgency war against FARC. Or, as Stan Goff—a retired U.S. Army Special Forces officer for counterinsurgency operations and former military advisor to Colombia—put it: "the 'war on drugs' is simply a propaganda ploy.... We were briefed by the Public Affairs Officers that counter-narcotics was a cover story...that our mission, in fact, was to further develop Colombians' capacity for counterinsurgency operations."

U.S. and Colombian government anti-terror and anti-drug policy, however, has actually swelled the ranks of FARC. Peasant farmers who depend on coca for their livelihoods are forced to rely on the armed guerrillas to protect their crop from planes spraying chemicals. The displacement and terrorization of people and the destruction of subsistence crops in rural areas due to fumigation and military and paramilitary activity have created a large amount of unemployed, disenfranchised, and angry young people who gravitate towards the guerrilla movement due to the impunity of the armed forces and the perceived inability of the Colombian justice and democratic political systems to hear their grievances or reflect their interests. The fact that the Colombian army and paramilitary groups continue to see coca- growing peasants as guerrilla collaborators and therefore legitimate military targets (due to the taxes they are forced to pay FARC on their coca crops), exacerbates the divide between the military and the peasantry.

Some have been led to argue that the real aim in Colombia is, in fact, to maintain a state of constant conflict. One in which there is sufficient order to protect investments and transport links but, also, sufficient disorder and terror so as to maintain a subservient and flexible workforce and an economic system which allows only a small local elite and foreign multinationals to benefit from the country's resources. The official military protect investments and transport links important to the extractive industries while paramilitaries closely linked to the official army, and revealed to be linked to the U.S. government—intimidate any move toward reform of the system. This is achieved through a policy of assassination, suppression and terrorization of the political left, human rights activists, trade unionists and peasant and indigenous movements.

Economic Imperialism

In 1996, four years before Plan Colombia was passed by Congress, the U.S.-Colombia Business Partnership—representing U.S. companies with interests in Colombia—was founded. This organization launched a well-financed lobbying effort for U.S. intervention in the resource-rich Andean state. Among the companies represented in this Business Partnership were Occidental Petroleum, Enron, Texaco, and BP. A survey released just months prior to the passage of Plan Colombia in the U.S. indicated that there were a large number of commercially viable and unexploited oil fields in the Putumayo region of Colombia, incidentally, the same area that experiences the highest intensity of paramilitary activity and aerial fumigation.

This correlation has aroused suspicion that these policies are actually aimed at displacing local people from their land in order to open it up to speculation by foreign multinationals while simultaneously clearing the dense rainforest that makes identifying and pinpointing the location of oilfields difficult.... This seems to be a recurrent theme in local impressions of the U.S. war on drugs in a number of different countries.

In Guatemala, for example, locals have criticized militarization of the resource-rich north eastern province of Petén. While it is known that this area is used to transport drugs to Mexico locals suspect the heavy military presence is more to do with oil interests in the region.... Similar complaints have emerged from the Moskitia region of eastern Honduras which has experienced increased militarization in recent years, particularly since the 2009 coup. According to Norvin Goff Salinas, president of an indigenous Miskitu federation: "More than anything else, they're militarizing because of the natural resources that are in the Moskitia, especially the strategic spots where there is oil."

Foreign Direct Investment (FDI) flows into Colombia rose from $2.4 billion at the outset of Plan Colombia to $14.4 billion by 2011. In the mid-1990s, oil and gas constituted only 10 percent of all FDI in Colombia but by 2010 this had increased to almost one-third. Colombia, however, remains the most dangerous country in the world to be a trade unionist and one of the most unequal countries in the world with the top 10 percent of the population controlling nearly half of the country's wealth.

Conclusions

It is evident that in the stated objective of eradicating coca cultivation and narcotrafficking in Colombia U.S. anti-drug strategy has been a resounding failure. From the perspective of the U.S. State Department, however, Plan Colombia was not a failure at all, but instead "allowed for the creation of an effective new model for U.S. intervention." As the U.S. Government Accountability Office's director of international affairs and trade put it, "international programs face significant challenges reducing the supply of illegal drugs but support broad U.S. foreign policy objectives." These objectives, throughout the period of U.S. hegemony, have remained the same. U.S. imperialism is not based on territorial control but on economic control. The adoption of the neoliberal capitalist model across Latin America greatly benefited U.S. companies by making resource extraction cheaper (due to reduced corporate tax), labor cheaper (due to labor flexiblization practices) and domestic markets easier to dominate (due to the removal of all state subsidies and the breakup of state owned companies).

The difficulty lies in maintaining a system in which the main beneficiaries of economic production in a country are a tiny local elite and foreign multinationals. This, historically, has been achieved through substantial repression. Throughout the Cold War such repression was justified by labelling as communist any movement or political party whose views fell outside of radical right-wing capitalism. One crucial method of ensuring the maintenance of this economic model in Latin America has always been the cultivation of allied militaries whose ideological beliefs fall exactly in line with those of Washington. The end of the Cold war necessitated a new justification for the continuation of this practice, thus the war on drugs was born. After the 9/11 attacks, this evolved into a war on terrorism.

While U.S. Colombia policy is certainly aimed at making sure FARC never gains the strength or political unity necessary to overthrow the state, FARC is also a necessary enemy, just as the continuation of the internal conflict is necessary, to justify continued U.S. military training, aid, and intrusion in the affairs of the strategically located oil and resource-rich Andean state.

From Z Magazine, December 2012
Volume 25, Number 12

10.

The UN and Empire

By Matthew Williams

WITH THE END of the Cold War and the birth of the New World Order, the United Nations was freed up to take a more active role in world affairs. This included a greater ability to engage in what is popularly called "peacekeep-

None of these UN interventions seem to be doing much to contribute to the spread of grassroots democracy, any sort of meaningful peace, or interethnic reconciliation

ing"—military intervention. Many on the left have increasingly turned to UN military intervention as a solution to some of the truly horrible regional conflicts that seem to be flaring up more and more frequently, as in East Timor or as an alternative to NATO's bombing rampage in the Kosovo conflict. It is, however, far from clear that what the UN actually does when it intervenes is peacekeeping and democracy-building. We need to pose several questions. What are the immediate consequences for countries where UN intervention has taken place? Does UN intervention lead to increased grassroots political and economic democracy, genuine peace, and reconciliation between embittered ethnic groups?

As a result of the military interventions that laid the groundwork for a UN takeover, the world body is now effectively governing Bosnia-Herzegovina, Kosovo, and East Timor. It has also been very much involved in a number of other regions, with results ranging from the ambiguous (Cambodia) to the hideously criminal (Iraq). None of these UN interventions seem to be doing much to contribute to the spread of grassroots democracy, any sort of meaningful peace, or interethnic reconciliation. Bosnia-Herzegovina is the longest running experiment in UN "peacekeeping" and governance. The results are not pretty. As a result of the 1995 Dayton Agreement, a UN-mandated, NATO-dominated military force (IFOR-Intervention Force; later SFOR-Stabilization Force) occupied Bosnia and carved the country up along ethnic lines into two semi-separate "entities"— one Bosniak-Croat, the other Serb. IFOR also helped set up the UN-controlled provisional government, which is proving to be not so provisional. The UN High Representative, backed by the U.S. and European Union, is a de facto colonial dictator, with final decision-making powers in all civilian matters, including the right to overrule decisions by the governments of both Bosnian entities.

Under the Dayton Constitution, the economy is in the hands of the international neoliberal financial institutions. The International Monetary Fund (IMF) appoints the head of the Central Bank, who isn't allowed to be a citizen of Bosnia-Herzegovina or even a neighboring country. Furthermore, for the first six years the Central Bank is not allowed to do anything as economic reconstruction was instead in the hands of the distant London-based neoliberal European Bank for Reconstruction and Development (EBRD) and the World

> *The World Bank and EBRD have transformed Bosnia into a playground for Western corporations. The World Bank, although acknowledging the need for a minimal social safety net in the aftermath of war, has put privatization at the heart of its scheme for long-term reconstruction.*

Bank (Michel Chossudovsky, "Dismantling Yugoslavia, Colonizing Bosnia," *CovertAction Quarterly*, Spring 1996).

Under this UN military occupation, the people of Bosnia-Herzegovina have been stripped of any meaningful self-governance. Although a Western-style liberal republic has been set up in Bosnia, it is an empty one, both because decisions may be overruled by an unaccountable foreign power and because it is

still plagued by ethnic chauvinism (a situation the unaccountable foreign power has done little to effectively address). While I don't wish to fetishize state sovereignty, popular control can't exactly bloom under colonialism. In the current world order, independence is a necessary prerequisite to moving towards greater democracy.

The World Bank and EBRD have transformed Bosnia into a playground for Western corporations. The World Bank, although acknowledging the need for a minimal social safety net in the aftermath of war, has put privatization at the heart of its scheme for long-term reconstruction. As long as the World Bank, IMF, and EBRD are enforcing the dogma of the "free" market, it will be impossible for Bosnians to create even a reasonably humane Keynesian capitalist economy, never mind begin movement to one based on workplace democracy and popular coordination. Indeed, it was the conditions of IMF loans imposed on Yugoslavia that led in the early 1990s to the dismantling of the Titoist economy, stuck partway between a Leninist command economy and genuine economic democracy.

The division of Bosnia-Herzegovina along ethnic lines in many ways legitimizes the ethnic chauvinism that was one of the root causes of the conflict. By separating Bosniaks and Serbs into their own political "entities," the Dayton Accords reinforced the notion that the two groups can't live together peacefully. The UN and NATO's approach to dealing with ethnic tensions and the aftermath of the civil war have been overwhelmingly bureaucratic, including international supervision of the police, a Human Rights Ombudsperson, repatriation efforts, and textbook corrections. While these may do some good, given the racism entrenched in Bosnian institutions, they don't deal with the more complex psychological and cultural legacies of war. The trauma of war has left the people of Bosnia-Herzegovina psychologically devastated, their formerly multi-ethnic communities torn asunder, many fearful of returning to their hometowns because of the unresolved ethnic tensions. This potent mix of personal and communal trauma could all too easily break out into open conflict again, further ravaging the Balkans. These are issues that bureaucracies, however well-meaning their members, simply cannot address—they need to be dealt with in face-to-face, community-based forums.

Similar neo-colonial structures are now being put into place in Kosovo and East Timor in the guise of peacekeeping. The East Timorese have been treated with sickening contempt by their supposed UN liberators. Many UN bureaucrats and their partners in giant NGOs, such as World Vision, have treated the East Timorese with blatant racism—East Timorese workers have been denied their wages and even been beaten up by representatives of international "aid" groups. There remains a huge gap in living standards as UN staff took over the best buildings and drive around in shiny new SUVs, while the vast majority of East Timorese (including many resistance leaders) remained destitute and often homeless.

UNTAET (the United Nations Transitional Administration in East Timor) showed no signs of preparing the way to true independence for East Timor. Initially, no East Timorese were in decision-making roles in "their" UN "provisional" government. The National Council of Timorese Resistance (CNRT, the umbrella East Timorese resistance group), although hobbled by lack of resources, began setting up a parallel government from the village level up, with local commissions on health, education, agriculture, etc. Probably in response to this, the UN allowed various East Timorese factions (including pro-Indonesian ones) to appoint representatives to a National Consultative Council, although UNTAET retains all actual authority. A couple of UN bureaucrats stricken with consciences have resigned in protest. The

> *Similar neo-colonial structures are now being put into place in Kosovo and East Timor in the guise of peacekeeping. The East Timorese have been treated with sickening contempt by their supposed UN liberators.*

most outspoken, Jaret Chopra, a British director of district administration in East Timor, has described UNTAET as "colonial" and even "Stalinist" (Mark Dodd, "UN Staff Battle Over Independence Policy," *Sydney Morning Herald*, March 14, 2000).

Meanwhile, Francisco Gutteres, a spokesperson for the CNRT, has threatened massive civil disobedience against the UN if they do not begin including the CNRT more actively in making plans. A similar system of incorporating the people of Kosovo into the United Nations Mission in Kosovo while leaving the UN firmly in charge, has been set up in Kosovo—although the Kosovars were included right from the beginning (perhaps because, unlike the East Timorese, they are white). The people of Kosovo have shown themselves quite capable of self-governance. The nonviolent separatist movement, led by the Kosovo Democratic League (KDL), had arranged popular elections and created an entire shadow government, while committing itself to the protection of ethnic minority rights. No effort, however, was made to incorporate any of this incredible work into new "provisional" government. It was ignored and the KDL was initially given equal formal status with the Kosovo Liberation Army (KLA), an ugly ultra-nationalist mixture of Leninists and fascists, unconcerned with either democracy or pluralism.

Now the KDL is being edged out of the "provisional" government in favor of the KLA, which has been allowed to preserve its guerrilla army, albeit supposedly transformed into an emergency disaster relief force—the Kosovo Protection Corps (KPC). The KLA/KPC is still acting like a guerrilla army and the UN's attempts to make the government multi-ethnic have foundered as the Serbs appointed (not elected) to positions within it flee in fear of their lives from unreformed KLA terrorists.

Immediately following the arrival of UN troops, the IMF and World Bank began setting up shop in East Timor. Most "aid" agencies had ignored local initiatives and aid took the form of hand-outs, creating the beginnings of a culture of dependency on foreign bureaucracies. The major exception, bizarrely enough, may prove to be the World Bank; although it remains overall an unsound institution, the pressure of the 50 Years is Enough campaign has forced it to create a few decent programs. This—probably in combination with pressure from the CNRT, which made it clear that the resistance's vision for East Timor is a just, egalitarian, ecologically sustainable one—has lead the World Bank to create a program of grants to rebuild East Timorese institutions, the use of which is to be decided on by democratically-elected local councils. We may never get a chance to see if this is the no strings attached program the World Bank claims it is, because UNTAET is dead set on eliminating all the democratic aspects of the program. The IMF, meanwhile, remains the UNTAET's primary economic advisor and has dictated taxes that are both wildly unpopular and have been described as "lunacy" by at least one independent economist (Wilson da Silva, "Timor Ire at Coffee Tax," *Australian Financial Review*, February 29, 2000).

The European Union has been placed in charge of economic reconstruction in Kosovo and has been working with the usual suspects, dismantling the Titoist economy and creating a "modern" market economy as they did in Bosnia. Members of the KLA are taking over many of the formerly state-owned enterprises and banks as they are privatized, giving Western corporations the compliant, authoritarian partners they need. Meanwhile the entire banking system has been handed over lock, stock, and barrel, to a German firm, Commerzbank A.G. (Michel Chossudovsky, "State Terror and the 'Free Market'.") The European Union and World Bank see their work in Kosovo as the starting point of a mandate (from the Western powers) to begin dogmatically restructuring the economy of the entire Balkan region along neoliberal lines ("The World Bank's Role in Reconstruction and Recovery in Kosovo"), despite extensive experience showing that this will plunge the bulk of a country's population into miserable poverty.

UN attempts to try to promote inter-ethnic reconciliation in Kosovo are going nowhere fast. The UN has delegated oversight of human rights to the OSCE (Organization for Security and Cooperation in Europe), which is relying on the same bureaucratic measures that have not created any substantial social healing in Bosnia-Herzegovina. The situation in Kosovo remains far worse than in Bosnia—the KLA is forcing Serbs to flee Kosovo in fear of their lives right under the nose of NATO "peacekeepers." Programs to encourage dialogue, create a grassroots leadership that can undercut both Albanian and Serbian nationalists, and heal both community and individual war trauma are needed all the more desperately.

The need for reconciliation is perhaps less obvious in East Timor, but it is still there. Many of the East Timorese members of the pro-Indonesian paramilitary groups were forcibly recruited on pain of death. Understandably, there have been outbreaks of violence against suspected paramilitary member. There is an urgent need to find some way to help these lost souls to become members of the East Timorese community again. The East Timorese have also been through 25 years of hell and many of them are suffering from war trauma. The effects of the long-term violence are showing, as it is reported that some CNRT officers are bullying people, accusing them of being paramilitary members, in order to control the local political scene.

The UN has no programs of any sort in place to address these problems and has often shown gross insensitivity to what the East Timorese have been through at the hands of the Indonesian army and government. On the other hand, the leaders of the main resistance group FRETILIN and its guerrilla wing FALANTIL have taken the initiative and both arranged a meeting with paramilitary leaders in Singapore to discuss reconciliation efforts (Anastasia Vranchos, "Why Falintil Guerrillas are Now Rebels Without a Cause"), while acknowledging and apologizing for war crimes committed by their own troops.

In East Timor, the UN has proven to be even more reactionary than the World Bank. More generally, the UN works hand-in-hand with the IMF, World Bank, and other neoliberal institutions to advance the domination of Western-based multinational corporations and "free" market economics. Despite a lot of rhetoric about partnership, there are few attempts to engage local communities and create an alternative, grassroots, ecologically sustainable economy in war-ravaged lands. Even if the UN should actually pull out of Kosovo, Bosnia, or East Timor, the tyranny of the "free" market will already have been imposed, without consultation, on these countries.

This is not to say that everyone in the UN is happy with being a Western tool. Secretary General Kofi Annan and the UN leadership do seem to be resisting great power manipulation, at least partly in the hopes of making the UN an independent force for humanitarianism. They are still, however, members of the global elite—of a different faction than that represented by the Clinton administration, but elites nonetheless—and, like elites every-

where, they have an undemocratic mentality and worldview. Although some UN agencies do positive, even essential humanitarian work, they are still top-down bureaucracies that make no place for democratic participation by the people they are helping. The elitist orientation of the UN should not really be a surprise. The UN is not a global democratic coordinating body, but an assembly of the rulers of

> *The UN is not a global democratic coordinating body, but an assembly of the rulers of the world's nation-states who aren't exactly going to pick radical democrats to administer the world body*

the world's nation-states who aren't exactly going to pick radical democrats to administer the world body. At this stage in the game though, we are not going to get along without the UN. Too many UN agencies such as UNICEF and the World Health Organization, despite their bureaucratic organization, perform essential social functions. Surely we can do better than current UN "peacekeeping" though—both in terms of what we call on the UN and other such institutions to do and in terms of building radical alternatives. Calling for an end to intervention is too simplistic. Given problems like the entrenched racism of the governments of Bosnia's two entities, the continued violence in Kosovo and the need to control the pro-Indonesian paramilitaries in East Timor, we need to experiment with new forms of intervention—ones that are non-imperialist and leave open room for the growth of grass-roots political and economic democracy and a lasting, multicultural peace.

The conflict in Kosovo actually demonstrates one possibility—one that was sabotaged by the U.S. Before NATO went on its bombing rampage there were unarmed human rights monitors from the Organization for Security and Cooperation in Europe (OSCE) present. The OSCE—an official body, composed of 54 nation-states, unlike

NATO, which is simply a military alliance—officially committed to promoting human rights in a manner similar to the United Nations. At the time NATO ordered them out, there were 1,400 human rights monitors present; the total was supposed to eventually reach 2,000.

Despite being primarily from military backgrounds and having only four days training, they still could have been effective. The simple presence of international observers kept the Serbian paramilitaries and police in check initially. Unfortunately, the monitoring operation was headed by an American, William Walker, who was an old hand from U.S. proxy wars in Central America. He worked to undermine the whole operation by building ties with the KLA, ignoring their attacks on Serbian police

There are several reasons for using a combination of these nonviolent approaches instead of using conventional ground troops. Sending in trained killers to end mass killing is, as Barbara Ehrenreich notes, "a little like recruiting your local arsonists into the volunteer fire department."

and paramilitaries, prompting the latter to respond in kind, which was then seized on as the excuse NATO wanted for bombing (Diana Johnstone, "Humanitarian War: Making the Crime Fit the Punishment"). But, with all its faults, when the monitoring mission pulled out, there was a dramatic increase in violence on both sides, as the check of outside scrutiny, however biased, disappeared.

Unofficial activist groups—unhampered by members with an alternative agenda—have had real successes with using unarmed human rights observers. For instance, the officially non-partisan Peace Brigades International sends volunteers from powerful Western nations to conflict-torn regions to accompany progressive activists who fear brutal government repression. "Armed" only with cameras, they rely on a large worldwide network of human rights and media organizations to get out

the word of any human rights abuses they witness—the threat of which is often enough to keep repressive governments in check. Shanti Sena (Army of Peace) was a Gandhian organization in India that intervened to end violent conflicts such as Hindu-Muslim riots, by working with both sides to dispel rumors and stereotypes. They would also patrol the streets of troubled areas and, when necessary, risk their lives and physically stand in the way of rioters, calling on them to act peacefully.

In addition to the immediate peacekeeping work of unarmed intervention, there is a need to get at the root causes of the inter-ethnic conflict in the Balkans and elsewhere. Often dialogue needs to be created between groups in conflict so they can see what points they have in common and work out their differences in an atmosphere of understanding and mutual respect. Shanti Sena combined this long-term work with their immediate peacekeeping.

A number of other groups make peace-building their main focus. For instance, the Karuna Center, based in Massachusetts, has done this sort of work with Bosniaks and Serbs in Bosnia-Herzegovina, Arabs and Jews in Israel/Palestine, and elsewhere. It also teaches skills in nonviolent social change (as does PBI sometimes) giving these people the tools to pressure elites and to reshape society in a constructive manner, instead of relying on nationalist scapegoating to solve problems.

The Karuna Center also attempts to help people heal their communal and individual war trauma. There are several reasons for using a combination of these nonviolent approaches instead of using conventional ground troops. Sending in trained killers to end mass killing is, as Barbara Ehrenreich notes, "a little like recruiting your local arsonists into the volunteer fire department" ("Don't Send the Air Force to Do an Angel's Job," The *Progressive*, June 1999). Soldiers are trained in war-making, not peacemaking and—even when they have good intentions—they generally do not have any idea how to go about constructively resolving conflicts. The presence of armed troops with the backing of the "international community" legitimates the idea of solving social conflicts through violence, an idea that is often part of the problem in the first place.

It is also extremely difficult to engage in imperialism without guns. It can still be done by such measures as forcing IMF loans on countries, but even then a greater amount of local self-governance remains. The dialogue and reconciliation work done by groups like the Karuna Center is also critical in defusing the grounds for future conflicts, something that the standard UN military-bureaucratic approach seems totally unfit for, as witness the on-going KLA violence against Serbs and other ethnic minorities in Kosovo. Groups like PBI and the Karuna Center wait to go into an area until they have been invited by a local activist group instead of imposing their own agenda from without. The Karuna Center also draws on local customs to help people build their own modes of reconciliation and nonviolent action. We need to work at building more such alternatives so that where there is the need, radicals can intervene in ways consistent with their values and visions for the future. Such nonviolent peacekeeping needs to be tied to grassroots sustainable economic development to provide an alternative to the "reconstruction" and "development" plans of the IMF and World Bank. At the same time, we need to recognize that there will be situations that are beyond the capabilities of activist groups to handle. Therefore, we also need to pressure the UN to alter its peacekeeping program so it is centered around unarmed human rights monitors, genuine partnership with local communities, and reconciliation-build-

ing, not around sending in bureaucrats backed by heavily armed soldiers. Being composed of the representatives of the governing elites of nation-states the UN will never be a perfect tool for peacekeeping, but there is a lot of room for improvement.

There may be situations where the UN is unwilling to engage in entirely unarmed peacekeeping efforts. There will also probably be situations to which we aren't wise enough to offer any nonviolent solutions yet, but that require urgent attention. East Timor may well have been one of those situations where some sort of armed force was the lesser of two evils—even some pacifists were reluctantly calling for armed peacekeepers in response to the atrocities by the Indonesian military and para-militaries. There are still alternatives to sending in regular ground troops. Ehrenreich has suggested a corps of peacekeepers who are lightly armed and capable of defending themselves, but are primarily trained in mediation and similar peace-making skills ("Peacekeeping"). This would be a massive step up from the current system, mired in militaristic thinking, and might hamper some of the imperialist excesses of the UN by making intervention less of a military occupation.

Working for this new orientation in peacekeeping requires a reorientation in anti-imperialist activist thinking. Imperialism is growing more insidious in the New World Order, working not just through U.S. armies and IMF loans, but through organizations like the UN that many progressives support. As radical peace activists, we have to develop new networks and new strategies to work for international grassroots democracy and peace.

From Z Magazine, *September 2000*
Volume 13, Number 9

11

NATO: The Imperial Pitbull

By Edward S. Herman

ONE OF THE DECEPTIVE clichés of Western accounts of post-World War II history is that NATO was constructed as a defensive arrangement to block the threat of a Soviet attack on Western Europe. This is false. It is true that Western propaganda played up the Soviet menace, but

> *One of the deceptive clichés of Western accounts of post-World War II history is that NATO was constructed as a defensive arrangement to block the threat of a Soviet attack on Western Europe. This is false.*

many key U.S. and Western European statespeople recognized that a Soviet invasion was not a real threat. The Soviet Union had been devastated and, while in possession of a large army, it was exhausted and needed time for recuperation. The United States was riding high, the war had revitalized its economy, it suffered no war damage, and it had the atomic bomb in its arsenal, which it had displayed to the Soviet Union by killing a quarter of a million Japanese civilians at Hiroshima and Nagasaki. Hitting the Soviet Union before it recovered or had atomic weapons was discussed in Washington, even if rejected in favor of "containment," economic warfare, and other forms of destabilization. NSC 68, dated April 1950, while decrying the great Soviet menace, explicitly called for a program of destabilization aimed at regime change in that country, finally achieved in 1991.

Thus, even hardliner John Foster Dulles stated back in 1949 that, "I do not know of any responsible high official, military or civilian...in this government or any other government, who believes that the Soviet now plans conquest by open military aggression." But note Dulles's language—"open military aggression." The "threat" was more a matter of possible Soviet support to left political groups and parties in Western Europe. Senator Arthur Vandenberg, a prime mover of NATO, openly stated that the function of a NATO military buildup would be "chiefly for the practical purpose of assuring adequate defense against internal subversion." The much greater support of right-wing forces by the United States was, of course, not a help to internal subversion and a threat to democracy—only possible Soviet help to the left fit that category. (Recall Adlai Stevenson's claim in the late 1960s that the resistance within South Vietnam by indigenous forces hostile to the U.S.-imposed minority regime was "internal aggression.")

The non-German Western European elites were more worried about German revival and a German threat. Like U.S. officials, they were more concerned about keeping down the power of the left in Europe than any Soviet military threat—and the United States was pressing the Europeans to build up their armed forces and buy arms from U.S. suppliers. Although knowingly inflated or even concocted, the Soviet military threat was still very

> *The United States, the dominant NATO power, supported right-wing politicians and former Nazis and fascists elsewhere, while, of course, claiming to be pro-democratic and fighting against totalitarianism*

useful in discrediting the left by tying it to Stalin and Bolshevism and an alleged Soviet invasion and mythical world conquest program.

In fact, the Warsaw Pact was far more a "defensive" arrangement than NATO. Its organization followed that of NATO and was clearly a response. It was a structure of the weaker party with less reliable members and, in the end, it collapsed, whereas NATO was important in the long-term process of destabil-

izing and dismantling the Soviet regime. For one thing, NATO's armament and strength were part of the U.S. strategy of forcing the Soviets to spend resources on arms rather than provide for the welfare, happiness, and loyalty of their population. It also encouraged repression by creating a genuine security threat, which, again, would damage popular loyalty and the reputation of the state abroad. Throughout this early period the Soviet leaders tried hard to negotiate some kind of peace settlement with the West, including giving up East Germany, but the United States and hence its European allies/clients would have none of it.

As noted, in the U.S., official—therefore mainstream media—view, only Soviet intervention in Western Europe after World War II was bad and threatened "internal subversion." But in a non-Orwellian world it would be recognized that the United States far outdid the Soviet Union in supporting not only "internal subversion," but also real terrorism in the years after 1945. The left had gained strength during World War II by actually fighting against Nazi Germany and Fascist Italy. The United States fought against the left's subsequent bids for political participation and power by any means, including direct warfare in Greece and by massive funding of anti-left parties and politicians throughout Europe.

In Greece, it supported the far right, including many former collaborators with fascism and succeeded in putting in place a nasty right-wing authoritarian regime. It continued to support fascist Spain and accepted fascist Portugal as a founding member of NATO, with NATO arms helping Portugal pursue its colonial wars.

The United States, the dominant NATO power, supported right-wing politicians and former Nazis and fascists elsewhere, while, of course, claiming to be pro-democratic and fighting against totalitarianism.

Perhaps most interesting was the U.S. and NATO support of paramilitary groups and terrorism. In Italy, they were aligned with state and right-wing political factions, secret societies (Propaganda Due or P-2), and paramilitary groups that, with police co-operation, pursued what was called a "Strategy of Tension," in which a series of terrorist actions were carried out that were blamed on the left. The most famous was the August 1980 bombing of the Bologna train station, killing 86.

The training and integration into police-CIA-NATO operations of former fascists and fascist collaborators was extraordinary in Italy, but common elsewhere in Europe (for the Italian story, see Herman and Brodhead, "The Italian Context: The Fascist Tradition and the Postwar Rehabilitation of the Right," in *Rise and Fall of the Bulgarian Connection*. For Germany, see William Blum, on "Germany 1950s," in *Killing Hope*).

NATO was also linked to Operation Gladio, a program organized by the CIA, with collaboration from NATO governments and security establishments that in a number of European states set up secret cadres and stashed weapons, supposedly preparing for the threatened Soviet invasion, but actually ready for "internal subversion" and available to support right-wing coups. They were used on a number of occasions by right-wing paramilitary groups to carry out terrorist operations (including the Bologna bombing and many terrorist incidents carried out in Belgium and Germany).

Gladio and NATO plans were also used to combat an "internal threat" in Greece in 1967: namely, the democratic election of a liberal government. In response, the Greek military put into effect a NATO Plan Prometheus, replacing a democratic order with a torture-prone military dictatorship. Neither NATO nor the Johnson administration objected.

Other Gladio forces, from Italy and elsewhere, came to train in Greece, during its fascist interlude to learn how to deal with "internal subversion."

> *They were used on a number of occasions by right-wing paramilitary groups to carry out terrorist operations (including the Bologna bombing and many terrorist incidents carried out in Belgium and Germany)*

In short, from its inception, NATO showed itself to be offensively, not defensively, oriented, antagonistic to diplomacy and peace, and intertwined with widespread terrorist operations and other forms of political intervention that were threats to democracy (if traceable to the Soviets would have been denounced as brazen subversion).

The Post-Soviet NATO

With the end of the Soviet Union and the menacing Warsaw Pact, NATO's theoretical rationale disappeared. That rationale was a fraud, for public consumption NATO still needed to redefine its reason for existence and it took on a larger and more aggressive role. With no need to support Yugoslavia after the Soviet demise, NATO soon collaborated with its U.S. and German members to wage war on and dismantle that former Western ally, in the process violating the UN Charter's prohibition of cross-border warfare (i.e., aggression).

Amusingly, during the NATO bombing war against Yugoslavia in April 1999, NATO held its 50th anniversary in Washington, DC, celebrating its successes and, with characteristic Orwellian rhetoric, stating its devotion to international law in the midst of its ongoing blatant violation of the UN Charter. In fact, the original 1949 NATO founding document had begun by reaffirming its members' "faith in the UN Charter" and in Article 1, undertaking, "as set forth in the UN Charter, to settle any international disputes by peaceful means."

The April 1999 session produced a Strategic Concept document that laid out a supposedly new program for NATO, now that its "mutual defensive" role in preventing a Soviet invasion had ceased to be plausible ("The Alliance's Strategic Concept," NATO Press Release, Washington, DC, April 23, 1999). The Alliance still stressed "security," though it "committed itself to essential new activities in the interest of a wider stability." It welcomed new members and new "partnership" arrangements, though why these were necessary in a post-Cold War world with the United States and its closest allies so powerful is never made clear. It admits that "large-scale conventional aggression against the Alliance is highly unlikely," but it never mentioned the possibility of "large-scale conventional aggression" by members of the Alliance and it brags about the NATO role in the Balkans as illustrative of its "commitment of a wider stability." Not only was this Alliance effort a case of legal aggression—"illegal but legitimate"—but NATO played a major destabilization role in the Balkans, helping start the ethnic warfare and refusing to pursue a diplomatic option in Kosovo in order to justify its attack on Yugoslavia in a bombing war that was in process while this document was being handed out.

Strategic Concept also claims to favor arms control, but, in fact, from its very beginning NATO promoted more armaments and all new members, like Poland and Bulgaria, were obligated to build up their "inter-operable" arms, meaning get more arms and buy them from U.S. and other Western suppliers. Since the document was produced in 1999, NATO's leading member, the United States, has more than doubled its military budget and greatly increased arms sales abroad. It has also pushed further into space-based military operations. It has withdrawn from the 1972 ABM treaty, refused to ratify the Comprehensive (Nuclear) Test Ban Treaty and rejected both the Land Mine treaty and UN Agreement to Curb the International Flow of Illicit Small Arms. With NATO's aid it has produced a new arms race, which many U.S. allies and clients, as well as rivals and targets, have joined.

The 1999 document also claims NATO's support for the Nuclear Non-Proliferation Treaty (NNPT), but it stresses how important nuclear arms are for NATO's power—it therefore rejects a central feature of the NNPT, which involved a promise by the nuclear powers to work to eliminate nuclear weapons. What this means is that NATO is keen only on non-proliferation by its targets, like Iran. Nuclear weapons "make a unique contribution in rendering the risks of aggression against the Alliance incalculable and unacceptable." But if Iran had such weapons, it could make Alliance "risks of aggression"—which Alliance member the U.S. and its partner Israel have threatened—unacceptable. Obviously, that would not do.

In its Security segment, Strategic Concept says that it struggles for a security environment "based on the growth of democratic institutions and commitment to the peaceful resolution of disputes, in which no country would be able to intimidate or coerce any other through the threat or use of force." The hypocrisy here is mind-boggling. The very essence of NATO policy and practice is to threaten the use of force and U.S. national security policy is now explicit that it plans to maintain a military superiority and prevent any rival power from challenging that superiority in order to hold sway globally—that is, it plans to rule by intimidation.

NATO now claims to threaten nobody and even talks in Strategic Concept about possible joint "operations" with Russia. Again, the hypocrisy level is great. As we know, there was a U.S. promise made to Gorbachev when he agreed to allow East Germany to join with the West, that NATO would not move "one inch" further East. Clinton and NATO quickly violated this promise, absorbing into NATO all the former Eastern European Soviet satellites as well as the Baltic states. Only self-deceiving fools and/or propagandists would not recognize this as a security threat to Russia, the only power in the area that could even theoretically threaten NATO members. But Strategic Concept plays dumb and only threats to its members are recognized.

Although "oppression, ethnic conflict" and the "proliferation of weapons of mass destruction" are alleged of great concern to the new NATO, its relations with Israel are close and no impediment whatsoever has been placed on Israeli oppression, ethnic cleansing, or its semi-acknowledged substantial nuclear arsenal. Neither its war on Lebanon in 2006 nor its current murderous attacks on Gaza impeded warm relations, any more than the U.S.-UK unprovoked attack on Iraq reduced NATO-member solidarity. If Israel is a highly favored U.S. client, it is then by definition free to violate all the principles mentioned by Strategic Concept. In 2008, NATO and Israel signed a military pact, so perhaps NATO will soon be helping Israel's "security" operations in Gaza. (In fact, Obama's choice as National Security Adviser, James Jones, has over the past year or so been clamoring for NATO troops to occupy the Gaza Strip and even the West Bank).

The new NATO is a U.S. and imperial pitbull. It is currently helping rearm the world; encouraging the military buildup of the former Baltic and Eastern European Soviet satellites (now U.S. and NATO satellites); working closely with Israel as that NATO partner ethnically cleanses and dispossesses its untermenschen; helping its master establish client states on the Russian southern borders, officially endorsing the U.S. placement of anti-ballistic missiles in Poland, the Czech Republic, Israel, and threateningly elsewhere, at a great distance from the United States and urging the integration of the U.S. plans with a broader NATO "shield." This virtually forces Russia into more aggressive moves and accelerated rearmament (as NATO did in earlier years).

Of course, NATO supports the U.S. occupation of Iraq. NATO Secretary-General Scheffer regularly boasts that all 26 NATO states are involved in Operation Iraqi Freedom, inside Iraq or Kuwait. Every single Balkan nation, except for Serbia, has had troops in Iraq and now has them in Afghanistan. Half of the former Soviet Commonwealth of Inde-

The new NATO is a U.S. and imperial pitbull. It is currently helping rearm the world; encouraging the military buildup of the former Baltic and Eastern European Soviet satellites (now U.S. and NATO satellites); working closely with Israel as that NATO partner ethnically cleanses and dispossesses its untermenschen

pendent States has also provided troops for Iraq with some of them also in Afghanistan. These are training grounds for breaking in and "inter-operationalizing" the new "partners" and developing a new mercenary base for the growing "out of area" operations of NATO, as NATO participates more actively in the U.S. wars in Afghanistan and Pakistan.

As noted, NATO brags about its role in the Balkans wars and both this war and the wars in Iraq, Afghanistan, and Pakistan are violating the UN Charter. Lawlessness is built-in to the new Strategic Concept. Superceding the earlier (fraudulent) "collective self defense," the ever-expanding NATO powers give themselves the authority to conduct military campaigns "out-of-area" or the so-called "non-Article V" missions beyond NATO territory. As the legal scholar Bruno Simma noted in 1999, "The message which these voices carry in our context is clear. If it turns out that a Security Council mandate or authorization for future NATO 'non-Article 5' missions involving armed force cannot be obtained, NATO must still be able to go ahead with such enforcement. That the Alliance is capable of doing so was demonstrated in the

Kosovo crisis" ("NATO, the UN, and the Use of Force: Legal Aspects," *European Journal of International Law*, Vol. 10, No. 1, 1999).

The new NATO is pleased to be helping its master project power across the globe. In addition to helping encircle and threaten Russia, it pursues "partnership arrangements" and carries out joint military maneuvers with the so-called Mediterranean Dialogue countries (Israel, Egypt, Jordan, Morocco, Tunisia, Mauritania, and Algeria). NATO has also established new partnerships with Gulf Cooperation Council states (Bahrain, Kuwait, Saudi Arabia, Oman, Qatar, and the United Arab Emirates), thereby expanding NATO's military ambitions from the Atlantic coast of Africa to and throughout the Persian Gulf. In the same time frame, there have been an unbroken series of NATO visits to and naval exercises with most of these new partners, as well as the first formal NATO-Israeli bilateral military treaty.

The pitbull is well positioned to help Israel continue its massive law violations, to help the United States and Israel threaten and perhaps attack Iran and to enlarge its own cooperative program of pacification of distant peoples in Afghanistan and Pakistan—no doubt elsewhere—all in the alleged interest of peace and that "wider stability" mentioned in Strategic Concept. NATO, like the UN, provides a cover of seeming multilateralism for what is a lawless and virtually uncontrolled imperial expansionism. In reality, NATO, as an aggressive global arm of the U.S. and other local affiliated imperialisms, poses a serious threat to global peace and security. While it should have been liquidated in 1991, it has instead expanded, taking on a new and threatening role spelled out in its 1999 Strategic Concept while enjoying a frighteningly malignant growth.

From Z Magazine, *February 2009*
Volume 22, Number 2

12.

Eco-Imperialism: War on the Earth

An interview with Vandana Shiva

By David Barsamian

VANDANA SHIVA PROVIDES an international voice for sustainable development and social justice. She's a physicist, scholar, social activist, and feminist. She is director of the Research Foundation for Science, Technology and Natural Resource Policy in New

> *This war has its roots in an economy which fails to respect ecological and ethical limits*

Delhi and a recipient of the Right Livelihood Award, the alternative Nobel Prize. She is the author of many books, including *Water Wars, Earth Democracy,* and *Soil Not Oil*.

BARSAMIAN: On receiving the Sydney Peace Prize in November 2010, you said, "When we think of wars in our times, our minds turn to Iraq and Afghanistan, but the bigger war is the ongoing war against the Earth. This war has its roots in an economy which fails to respect ecological and ethical limits." Tell me more about this war.

SHIVA: This war is being fought, for example, in India across the country, wherever there are minerals, which happens to be where there are forests, which happens to be where tribals live. And it's fueled by the very investor-speculators who brought down the world economy. Huge money is to be made out of iron ore and bauxite mining. And then to push consumption, to use more and more of these nonrenewable resources.

India until 20 years ago never had landfills. But our laws are saying they want us to move from one kilogram of aluminum use to 15 kilograms per capita of use. Fifteen kilograms multiplied by a billion Indians means that every mountain will have to be mined, every forest destroyed. This generates a war against nature because it devastates ecosystems. But it's also a war against people, because every human right must be violated and a war economy, in a real sense, has to be created.

You say that the war against the Earth begins in the mind. How does that happen?

The moment you take an Earth in which systems are mutually supporting, in which forest systems create the weather systems and create the water systems, where the soil gives us the food—a reductionist, mechanistic world-view chops up that interconnected nature. That chopping up, reductionism, is the beginning of the war in the mind.

And this "eco-imperialism" has its roots—are we talking a couple of hundred years now?

All of this was a synergy between colonialism, a conquest of the South, and defining the people of the South as if we weren't fully human. A conquest of nature through redefining nature as dead, inert, manipulable matter. And it

> *All of this was a synergy between colonialism, a conquest of the South, and defining the people of the South as if we weren't fully human*

was a conquest over the feminine aspect of every society. The witch hunts were part of it in America and in Europe because what was being hunted was not women who were witches,

but holistic knowledge and expertise by women. This triple colonization is really only a few hundred years old, and it has reached its limits. But those who gain from it, whether its power or its money would like to push that limit a little longer by commodifying every aspect of nature.

There are multiple crises facing the planet. They're fairly obvious and are interlinked.

The interconnections have actually just intensified in the last two years. We see the financial crisis that created the unraveling of the economy. Ordinary, hard-working people are paying the price, sometimes with their lives.

The financial crisis, then, is linked to the energy crisis, because a fossil fuel-driven economy can only carry on its path of growth by converting the living earth into oil rather than finding an alternative economy based on non-renewables, and they would like to take renewables and turn them into nonrenewables. The biofuel grab is part of it. And that biofuel grab is leading to the land grab in Africa. All of this is also creating the climate-induced catastrophes, which are then feeding back into food insecurity. So 2010 saw forest fires in Russia, floods in Pakistan, flooding and then cyclones in Australia—after about six years of an intensive drought.

Meantime, that same financial gambling game is speculating on food as a commodity, driving up food prices, which is a big issue in Indian politics. Recently, nine opposition parties came together to fight the price rise. We are tied up in these interconnections of a vicious cycle, where each crisis feeds the other crisis. And bio-imperialists, who want to use the planet's resources for their own gain and extension of their power, now use the crisis they have created to say, "Okay, let's grab Africa. Let's grab the farmlands of India. Let's grab the last mineral. Let's commodify every bit of food and grain on this planet," never answering the question, "What happens to 80 percent of humanity?"

The UN's Food and Agricultural Organization said prices in 2010 were the highest in history.

In 2008 there was a spike in food prices and 2010 has gone beyond that because 2010 has been a combination of real scarcity due to climate catastrophes, along with the artificial scarcity created by speculation. And when you have two forces driving prices upwards, and they are structural, that is why any government who says, "Oh, next month the weather will be fine" or "the harvest will come," is not realizing two things. One, industrial globalized agriculture as well as other fossil-fuel-driven systems have given us climate chaos. It's not a future issue, it's not a future debate of what will happen in 100 years. People are dying today. The second thing they don't realize is politicians still try and respond to these crises as if they're living in isolated nation states, when they themselves have signed a WTO agreement interlinking the global food system, which means a problem in one part of the world gets transmitted to the rest of the world—whether it be a speculation or climate damage.

You mentioned Australia—drought, floods, cyclones. Is extreme weather an anomaly or is it part of a pattern we're going to see more of?

Climate chaos, as I call it, is a pattern. That's why I am reluctant to use the words "global warming," in which case you get one snowstorm and the climate skeptics say, "Oh, this is global cooling? Didn't we tell you?" As if all the time the temperature will be rising everywhere rather than what the climate scientists say, average temperatures across the planet are rising. The second is, when you talk "cli-

mate change," you get other climate skeptics saying, "Oh, we just adapt to it. And Swedish beaches will become like the tropics, so isn't that wonderful?" Or "England will get warmer and will now grow grapes and will become wine country." That kind of stupidity does not take into account that the same England gets a snowstorm and gets stalled for two weeks because they are not a heavy snow country and have none of the equipment to clean up Heathrow airport.

> *It's not a future issue, it's not a future debate of what will happen in 100 years. People are dying today. The second thing they don't realize is politicians still try and respond to these crises as if they're living in isolated nation states.*

A large number of Americans doubt there is such a thing as global warming. You've studied the issue, you're a scientist. Is the science solid?

There are reasons why we have to take climate science seriously. It's not just one or two scientists or single discipline. The Intergovernmental Panel on Climate Change, the IPCC, is a multidisciplinary group of 2,500 scientists.

Never in the history of humanity have 2,500 scientists, trained in different aspects of the environment, resources, the planet, the climate, the atmosphere, put together their collective expertise from 1988 onwards.

Every ecosystem with an additional burden will have a different behavior. A river with too much pollution becomes a dead river. An atmosphere with too much pollution will start having different patterns, too much snow where there should be no snow, and no rain where there should be rain. All of this unpredictability needs to be seen as a phenomenon that people are living through.

Mining issues are key in India. There is the Niyamgiri Mountain issue in Orissa in eastern

India. You've been there. Talk about that and why it is significant and the push-back and resistance from the people.

They talk of something called the India story. And the India story is a high-growth story built on the outsourcing of software, creating Silicon Valleys in Bangalore. But the untold part of the India story is the outsourcing of pollution and resource extraction. So while most aluminum and steel manufacturing has shut down in Europe, the U.S., and Japan, the consumption of all of these items is being pushed

> *De facto privatization is happening everywhere. When you look at Vedanta, their aluminum factory has totally rerouted the Indravati River that flows southward, moved it northward, had it dropped into a river called Hati Tel River to then service this huge aluminum smelter*

even further with everything that makes this global economy run. Aluminum is vital to it. Bauxite is the raw material for aluminum.

Vedanta, a UK-based company owned by an Indian, wanted to mine a mountain called Niyamgiri, which means the mountain that upholds the sacred law. Niyam means the law of the universe and giri means mountain. The most ancient tribes of the Dongria Kondh have been living on this mountain since the beginning of their own memory. They've resisted the bauxite mining. In spite of it, Vedanta managed to set up a refining plant and a smelter in the valley and further downstream. Because of the protests, they were never able to get to the bauxite, even though the courts and the Ministry of Environment were manipulated.

The interesting thing is there is another plant in Orissa which is called Posco. It is a Korean steel plant, but our research shows it's actually owned by Wall Street. The majority of shares are owned by Citigroup and JPMorgan Chase. The World Bank forced the privatization of this plant in the Southeast Asia financial crisis. They want 4,000 acres of the coast

with a captive port and parkland. Then, of course, they want mines. Most of the iron ore they mine will go straight out to Korea and China. Some will be processed in an export zone, also for export.

Tell me how rivers can be sold.

Both aluminum and steel making are highly energy-intensive and resource-intensive processes. They are extremely water-intensive processes. Entire rivers are being rerouted for steel and aluminum making. The River Shivnath in Chhattisgarh is flowing through tribal areas. We use our rivers to go down and wash our clothes, to bathe. Our buffalos and our cows go to the river. The river recharges all of the groundwater around it. The River Shivnath, 22 kilometers of it was privatized, to bring water to Jindal's steel plant. In order to privatize it, people could not access the river water, they could not access the groundwater in their own fields and wells.

It's very much like the privatization of water in Bolivia where, when Bechtel faced resistance, they said, "You can't have this water on your roof, you can't take water in your well." And the Bolivian people said, "So you now own the rain and you own the groundwater?" That's what the people of Chhattisgarh said. That project had to be cancelled. This was a direct legal transfer of a river to a private company.

De facto privatization is happening everywhere. When you look at Vedanta, their aluminum factory has totally rerouted the Indravati River that flows southward, moved it northward, had it dropped into a river called Hati Tel River to then service this huge aluminum smelter. The Tatas, when they expanded their Jamshedpur factory, put dams on two tributaries of Suvernarekha River, and that was 100 percent water for Jamshedpur. We fought the privatization of Delhi water, which was going to bring water up into the Himalaya from the Tehri Dam, and Suez was going to then sell it at 10 times the normal price that we pay for water. So whether it's for a city or a steel plant, an aluminum plant, they're such thirsty projects that they have to steal water from people and from nature.

But this other story of the emerging economy, the giant with 9 percent growth, is a joint construction of the Indian elite and the global elite. The global elite, of course, spun the globalization story. The global elite need the success of the model of globalization, of free trade, of corporate- driven economies. They have to sell that.

They first tried to sell it through the Southeast Asian countries. You remember there was a period when the East Asian tigers and the dragons were the poster children of globalization. In 1997 that collapsed. The West was its own poster child. After 2008 that collapsed. So if that fake story of globalization and corporate control has to continue, they've got to have some poster child. They're hanging on desperately to the India of today, with its billionaires, but constantly more and more impoverished people. We have some of the richest people in the world today—the Ambani brothers, the Mittals, and Anil Agarwal sitting in England. They are using India as a subcomponent of the globalization story.

But nobody tells the story that this has pushed half of Indian children to severe malnutrition, that every fourth Indian is today hungry. That the land wars are being fought between the poor, who want to defend their quarter-acre land, against the richest of these people, who are engaged in a big land grab.

You also talk about agriculture and militarized language.

The Copenhagen Treaty agreement on climate change should have brought us to the next level of legally binding agreements to bring down emissions because the Kyoto Protocol period was running out, climate catastrophes were getting worse, and something needed to be done. Instead, President Obama came, bullied four other countries—the so-called rising powers of China, India, South Africa, Brazil—and signed this Copenhagen Accord, which is a non-accord in terms of legally binding commitments.

The world is waiting for another paradigm, another worldview, another way of centering our lives. The West needs it because their economies are collapsing. The South needs it to prevent their economies from being totally wiped out, because I believe it's cultures that define their rights through the Earth that have the strongest struggle even for their own rights. I've seen it with every land movement.

Is there a connection between capitalism and environmental degradation?

There is a very intimate connection with the rise of capitalism and the plunder of nature, because capitalism located wealth in capital, which is just a construct. It's in human imagination. It gave power to those who owned capital to start owning the resources of the Earth. The privatization of rivers, the privatization and patenting of seeds (the basis of my work in Navdanya) the privatization of the atmosphere for emissions trading, all of these privatizations are defending the rights of capital and allow capital to expand its control, because capital is an abstract.

Given the urgency, it seems that collective action is required.

Individuals acting consciously as members of society and collectives is what we need. The two things we need that everyone can do are, first, a shift in the mind. If these wars are wars in the mind, then the place to make peace is in the mind, peace with nature and peace with each other. Creating living economies, a movement we've tried to build through Navdanya here, local living economies, but a movement that's very strong in the U.S., is something people can start engaging in today. If they don't, they will have nowhere to turn to. Our calculations show that even though global corporations have the power to reach the last resource, they only have the power to generate employment for 3 percent of humanity. You can't have a system where 100 percent of resources are owned by probably 15 to 20 corporations, and 3 percent are hired for them to do the stealing of the planetary wealth. So you need to have other ways for people to look after themselves.

You cannot do that individually. You can begin the shift in your mind, but framing other economies and framing other ways of structuring society has to be a collective enterprise, because what was killed by the privatization of the economy was a very collective identity, the identity that we are interconnected. And Margaret Thatcher saying, "There is no society, there is only individuals," is part of that market individualism of atomizing us, making us lonely, isolating, and telling us we have nowhere to turn.

Just like Evo Morales removed the censorship on the rights of Mother Earth, India is a civilization based on the recognition of the Earth as a living system, as our living support, and peace with the Earth as our duty.

This ancient prayer has always been my inspiration. It is from the Bhoomi Sutra of the Athara Veda. And it says:

> May there be peace with space
> and the skies,
> Peace with the atmosphere,
> Peace with the waters.
> May there be peace with the earth.
> May there be peace with the herbs,
> the plants, the trees.
> May all the divine beings pervade peace.
> May the peace that pervades all creation
> Be with you.

From Z Magazine, *June 2011*
Volume 24, Number 6

13.

Key Words In The
New World Order

By Edward S. Herman

A S THE 21ST CENTURY begins, with the U.S. transnational capitalism roaming the earth like the dinosaurs of the distant past, we should take stock of the key words that help rationalize their rampages. Many are

> *But the word usage is effective because the rulers dominate the communications system and are free to reengineer meaning and rewrite history.*

heart-warming "purr" words like "democracy," "empowerment," "freedom," "reform," and "responsibility," which are applied to arrangements and policies that are antidemocratic, disempower, diminish freedom, and abandon responsibility on the part of the rulers of the New World Order (NWO). But the word usage is effective because the rulers dominate the communications system and are free to reengineer meaning and rewrite history.

These words are linked together and they serve as important components of an ideological and propaganda apparatus. The language of economics—market, commodities, commodification, free trade, growth—flows smoothly into political lingo—freedom, democracy, elections, reform, deregulation—and into the key words relating to personal behavior and social issues—consumption, compassion, morality, family values, law and order, crime, prisons—and also into the language of global expansion and the maintenance of global law and order ("stability")—free trade, globalization, security, ethnic cleansing, human rights, and humanitarian intervention. "Free trade" sits astride both the language of economics and that of global issues of expansion, and so do other words in this evolving system.

Free Trade and Protectionism

Many of the key words that purr have their counterparts that hiss and snarl—free trade has its snarl partner in "protectionism," and "market" has a set of negative partners—"government," "government control," and "regulation." Typically, the ideological/propaganda system arranges the "facts" and history to idealize the purr word and cast the snarl word into outer darkness. In the case of free trade, for example, the establishment wants us to perceive the freedom to trade as generally beneficial, protectionism helping only the "special interests" to evade competition. The *Wall Street Journal's* Bernard Wysocki Jr. states that, "The first rule of trade agreements is that the benefits are widely dispersed, the costs are very concentrated and the losers are very vocal" (December 6, 1999). *Philadelphia Inquirer* business columnist Andrew Cassel asserts that trade openness "leads to higher living standards for everyone" (December 6, 1999). But support for the trade agreements is very concentrated and opposition very widespread, despite the alleged wide benefits. The majority who oppose are presumably irrational; the big boys who fight so furiously for the agreements are showing once again their community spirit.

The freedom to trade as sponsored by the great powers is not really free at all. Among other unfree features, it restricts the right to trade the patented goods of the big boys, allowing them to capture their monopoly profits. It directly benefits several hundred transnational corporations, but in the NWO this is deemed to be serving the "national interest." Protectionism, which serves the "special interests," is opposed by the media and economists, except in countries and at times when those who define the national interest feel that they need it. The economics profession "follows the flag," like the mainstream media. When industry needs protection from powerful foreign firms that benefit from economies of scale and

that work far down the learning curve, as in the United States and Germany in much of the 19th century, protectionist thought and the "infant industry argument" flourishes. When a country's industries are in the advanced and advantaged state of the United States and Germany today, free trade theory rules uncontested. This pattern is reversed in Third World and ex-Soviet bloc countries today, where the loss of autonomy and the influence of transnational corporate money and ideology causes the indigenous politicians, economists, and media to serve foreign and affiliated local comprador interests.

Free trade can increase income and wealth and provide some trickle-down benefits, but so can controlled trade and protectionism. In one of the great collective acts of historical revisionism, the western establishment claims that the takeoffs into sustained growth of Japan, the United States and other great Western powers, and the Asian "tigers" occurred under regimes of free trade. They didn't; all benefitted from the dread protectionism. The point today is to deny less developed countries the right to choose their paths to development and to force them into the global market system and domination by the great powers, their transnationals, and their international agencies—IMF, World Bank, WTO.

Economics

Basic words in the NWO lexicon are "commodity," "commodification," and "markets." A commodity is something bought and sold. The market is where the buying and selling takes place and commodification is the process of making into a commodity something that was formerly outside the market, as in privatizing public services like schools, hospitals, prisons, railroads, and parks.

Commodification and privatization are allegedly good because they enhance "efficiency," another key word in the NWO lexicon. Government and public ownership and control are bad because they are detrimental to efficiency.

As with free trade, these purr words purr and the snarl words snarl by the use of selective history, biased economic analysis, and an ignoring of socially important considerations that are of no interest to the NWO rulers. Commodification of everything weakens government, which can be an instrument of a democratic society, in favor of an increasingly concentrated corporate community that can more easily dominate politics and public policy. It strengthens individualism and the spirit of acquisition at the expense of any sense of the collective.

The efficiency advantages of global commodification are also highly debatable. Competition can involve enormous waste in duplication and marketing efforts and the privatized economy entails systematic market failure in its neglect of externalities, which are increasingly important in an integrated chemicalized world that is threatening the biosphere. These enormous costs and threats are simply ignored or played in very low key in the media and by the intellectuals that serve the NWO interests. The focus is on private, not social, efficiency, but social efficiency is the real efficiency for the community and world.

The same kind of bias applies to the treatment of "growth," another purr word favorite in the NWO. One merit of the word is that growth can clearly be stimulated by making things good for business, which will then invest and bring advanced technology to the community, with trickle-down jobs and other benefits. A focus on growth and technology is commonly accompanied by a failure to note their distributional or externalities effects.

A sufficiently bad distributional effect of growth could result in a decline in human welfare; and sufficiently large negative externalities (social inefficiencies) could cause properly measured growth to show negative values. But combined with a worry about inflation and employment levels above the "natural rate,"

the focus on growth per se provides a word structure perfectly attuned to a policy of serving business first, with others benefitting, if at all, as a spinoff. Income distribution, inequality, equity, externalities, market failure, and ecocide are, if not snarl words, words to be avoided.

"Globalization" also has a warm glow, implying an international division of labor voluntarily undertaken, international peace and goodwill, and the ending of nationalism, cross-border enmity and war. But war, ethnic conflict, and nationalism have flourished in the NWO, as TNCs, with the aid of their governments and IMF, have destabilized many weak countries and created a new order of "chaotic ungovernable entities" (Oswaldo De Rivero, "Les entites chaotique ingouvernables," *Le Monde Diplomatique*, April 1999).

Globalization activities have been carried out by TNCs for their own advantage, without regard to secondary effects on employment and the social or ecological environment. Their power to influence politics has grown with their wealth and mobility and their success in pushing globalization has been based on power and coercive threat, not truly voluntary or democratic approval. The counterpart word describing globalization's coercive base and negative effects is "imperialism," but as that word snarls at something clearly beneficent it has dropped out of the establishment lexicon.

Politics

NWO politics is the politics of "golden rule." Gold rules by its power over ideology—through advertising, a controlled media, and friendly and funded intellectuals—by the impact of mainly business money in elections and because of capital's increasingly effective threat to go on strike (by money flight abroad as well as by a reallocation of production and investment to more hospitable environments). Politicians operate within very narrow constraints and in less developed countries cannot afford to offend foreign bankers, the IMF, the United States, and its allies, and the internal gendarme armies overseeing things for their masters, in a now longstanding tradition.

The function of these political lackeys is to carry out "reform," which means deregulation, privatization, opening up of market opportunities to the global sharks, and cutting back on unnecessary expenditures on food, education, housing, and health care for the people without gold. (With amazing cynicism, the World Bank periodically announces a new focus on helping the goldless people that its primary

> *"Freedom" is a key word linking economics and politics. Freedom has come to mean the freedom of individuals to do business and of corporations to operate without restraint.*

policies systematically damage.) Politicians who actually tried to do something for the goldless, like former German finance minister Oskar LaFontaine, are quickly vilified and ousted, but in the NWO such politicians rarely attain even brief power, whatever the desires and interests of the masses.

This means, of course, that "elections" have been drained of substance and can no longer effect any useful changes, except for the dominant class and their foreign supporters, as in Russia with its devastating "reform" process. The function of elections in Russia was to convince the victimized populace that they had a democratic choice, when they didn't have one, and to diffuse any threat of a rational and more forceful response to the destruction and looting of their society. A Latvian-Canadian businessperson explained to historian Jeff Sommers that he favored lifting the prohibition of the Communist Party in Latvia for its benefits displayed in Russia where people could vote for CP candidate Zhuganov, without the slightest chance of his winning, but providing an outlet to diffuse a potentially volatile situation.

"Freedom" is a key word linking economics and politics. Freedom has come to mean the freedom of individuals to do business and of corporations to operate without restraint. The political component has been relegated to the background and Chicago School and other apologists for regimes of murder like Pinochet's have long argued that his creation of market institutions would assure political freedom in the long run. But their complaisance at the murders and terror, and their undetectable efforts on behalf of political freedom, point to the clearly towering dominance of market freedom in their value systems. More generally, the establishment's regular support of political gangsters like Suharto, who brutalize and kill, but provide a favorable climate of investment, allow us to understand the subtle transformation of the meaning of "freedom" to "economic freedom."

As noted, globalization purrs because its meaning is confined to the spread of business overseas with accompanying productivity advances, greater cultural intercourse, and the other good things—the bads, the weakening of governments' ability to serve their local populations, the disrupting effects, the one-sidedness of the cultural intercourse, the coercive elements, are associated with "imperialism," a word now mentioned only within quote marks. In NWO ideology "imperialism" refers to the colonialism of a bygone age, not to the indirect form of domination being carried out on a global scale today.

Personal Behavior and Morality

Privatizing values and morality have been important for the rulers of the NWO for three reasons. One is that it gears personal objectives to the aim of business to sell goods; a second is that it helps rationalize privatization of everything else; and a third is that by stressing the individual and downgrading the group, the community, and government, it makes it easier for the corporate community to dominate, faced only with an atomized populace.

The success of the business system in extirpating the threat of the ideas that materialism is bad, that, "The love of money is the root of all evil" and that rich people might have a tough time getting into heaven, goes back a long way. But it continues to amaze how successfully the system escapes condemnation for putting personal material gratification front and center and how, with the help of the "bell curve intellectuals" and media, the system's victims are made into autonomous causes of social problems.

In our time, this process has involved demonizing welfare mothers, who represent a congerie of bads, easily linked to crime in the streets by the black "underclass." This demonization helps reinforce the "family values" ideology of patriarchy, work, shopping, saving, and avoidance of government handouts. In this structure of privatized morality, people can take pride in their difference from the demonized and genetically deprived criminals who society is properly disposing of through welfare "reform" in "personal responsibility" legislation and via incarceration in "corrections" facilities. These folks will be only dimly aware that the corporate world is running things, is getting huge welfare largess of its own and that foreign policy is devoted to carving out opportunities for transnationals.

The family values people will also not see that their morality represents an abandonment of all that is generous, social, community oriented, and reflective of the strand of the Western tradition that speaks of all people as brothers and sisters. The ease with which they swallow "tough love" and "compassionate conservatism"—or plain vanilla uncompassionate liberalism ("liberals with guts," in the *New Republic*) and conservatism—all of which amounts to a ruthless abandonment of com-

passion and genuine "responsibility," is striking. So also is the ease with which they accept the mass killing and starvation of demonized foreigners—expressed in the Vietnam War era as "the mere gook rule"—in contrast with the unacceptability of deaths of their own military personnel.

Humanitarian Intervention

In NWO ideology globalization is portrayed as technologically driven, inevitable, and beneficial to all but a few "special interests." But globalization runs into difficulties with "rogues" and others who fail to appreciate its wonders. The ongoing global polarization of incomes, the widespread ethnic conflict, and the growth of "chaotic ungovernable entities" are not seen as a product of globalization (which they are in considerable measure), but as fortuitous happenings that interfere with the wondrous process. As in the case of Rus-

> *So also is the ease with which they accept the mass killing and starvation of demonized foreigners—expressed in the Vietnam War era as "the mere gook rule"*

sian "reform," the answer to seriously negative consequences is an intensification of their causes. As with crime in the streets at home, the cure is not in altering the workings of the economy serving the elite so well, it is in prisons at home and putting the rogues in their place abroad.

This fits well with domestic policy, where "military Keynesianism" has long been the acceptable base of macro-stabilization and Pentagon subsidization of high tech industry in the acceptable form of welfare. It is also useful to have a large military establishment available to keep the lid on any future internal security threats. Furthermore, as Thorstein Veblen pointed out in 1904, a militarized society not only conduces to "the orderly pursuit of business," it "directs the popular interest to other, nobler, institutionally less hazardous matters than the unequal distribution of wealth or of creature comforts," and affords "a corrective for 'social unrest' and similar disorders of civilized life."

Nice little wars against rogues bring us together (around our TV sets, as in watching the Super Bowl), demonstrate our high moral virtue in willingness to prevent "ethnic cleansing" with "humanitarian bombing" and demonstrate to the rest of the world that we are the police of the globalization process from which almost everybody benefits. Of course, when it gets to the condition of the Kurds in Turkey and the East Timorese under Indonesian assault, we must recognize that we "can't do everything," and that there are cases where "constructive engagement" is more helpful than threats and the use of force. But otherwise, this is clearly the best of all possible worlds.

From **Z** *Magazine, April 2000*
Volume 13, Number 4

14.

The Global Media

An interview with Edward S. Herman & Robert W. McChesney

By David Peterson

EDWARD S. HERMAN and Robert W. McChesney are two of the most important critics of the global media scene. A Professor Emeritus of Finance at the Wharton School of the University of Pennsylvania, and a contributor to *Z Magazine* since its founding in 1988, Edward Herman is the author of numerous books, including a number of corporate and media studies. These include *Corporate Control, Corporate Power* (1981), the two volume *Political Economy of Human Rights* (1979) and *Manufacturing Consent: The Political Economy of the Mass Media* (1988), both of which he co-authored with Noam Chomsky, as well as *The "Terrorism" Industry: The Experts and Institutions That Shape Our View of Terror* (1989), which he co-authored with Gerry O'Sullivan. Robert McChesney is an Associate Professor of Journalism and Mass Communication at the University of Wisconsin, Madison. McChesney is the author of T*elecommunications, Mass Media and Democracy: The Battle for the Control of U.S. Broadcasting, 1928-1935* (1993), *Corporate Media and the Threat to Democracy* (1997). Last summer, Cassell published their recent collaboration, a study called *The Global Media: The New Missionaries of Corporate Capitalism*.

> *You argue in* The Global Media *that before we'll ever be able to understand what's new about the "global media," we'll need to understand the "institutions of global capitalism"*

PETERSON: *You argue in* The Global Media *that before we'll ever be able to understand what's new about the "global media," we'll need to understand the "institutions of global capitalism." Well, what are the major institutions?*

HERMAN: The major institutions of global capitalism are the transnational corporations (TNCs), the international organizations formed to serve global capital or adapted to that service over time, and the national governments that also work in the interest of global capital. The most important of the international organizations are the International Monetary Fund (IMF), World Bank, and World Trade Organization (WTO), although there are many others. As global capital has strengthened, more and more institutions are bent to serve its interests, and an organization like the WTO, formed under the GATT agreement in the late stages of this evolution, is explicitly designed to serve the needs of global capital.

Global capital wants international trade and investment rights to prevail over the desires of local populations. It also wants to minimize welfare state expenditures, business tax burdens, threats of inflation, union organization, and environmental constraints; and the IMF, World Bank, and WTO strive to carry out these aims. These organizations have a common set of goals, reflecting the power of TNCs, transmitted to them by the national governments serving the same interests.

Both in terms of the depth of the changes that have taken place, and their rapidity, the past two decades have seen major transformations in the nature of corporate capitalism. But which changes have been the most important?

EH: The most important changes over the past several decades have been corporate capitalism's increasingly global perspective and reach, its increasing intolerance of welfare state commitments and labor organization and the social contract, and its willingness to attack these in various modes of intensified class warfare. But the list continues. An increase in the centralization of economic power, both within states and globally, at the same time has been matched by an increasing competition be-

tween the media giants, and by their willingness to attack rivals by crossing product lines, vertically integrating, and invading one another's territories.

And whether national or transnational, corporate capital has a certain ideology, a veil that surrounds it that helps it to justify its consequences to its victims.

EH: That's right. The main element in corporate ideology is the belief in the sublimity of the market and its unique capacity to serve as the efficient allocator of resources. So important is the market in this ideology that "freedom" has come to mean the absence of constraints on market participants, with political and social democracy pushed into the background as supposed derivatives of market freedom. This may help explain the tolerance by market-freedom lovers of market-friendly totalitarians—Pinochet or Marcos.

A second and closely related constituent of corporate ideology is the danger of government intervention and regulation, which allegedly tends to proliferate, imposes unreasonable burdens on business, and therefore hampers growth. A third element in the ideology is that growth is the proper national objective, as opposed to equity, participation, social justice, or cultural advance and integrity. Growth should be sustainable, which means that the inflation threat should be a high priority and unemployment kept at the level to assure the inflation threat is kept at bay. The resultant increasingly unequal income distribution is also an acceptable price to pay.

Privatization is also viewed as highly desirable in corporate ideology, following naturally from the first two elements—market sublimity and the threat of government. It also tends to weaken government by depriving it of its direct control over assets, and therefore has the further merit of reducing the ability of government to serve the general population through democratic processes. It is of course a coincidence that privatization yields enormous pay-offs to the bankers and purchasers participating in the sale of public assets.

The Global Media characterizes the United States as "the country in which market domination of the media has been most extensive and complete." Tell me what, exactly, it means for the "market" to "dominate" the media?

McCHESNEY: It means that capitalists control the media and they do so to maximize profits, often through selling advertising to other large corporations. In most other nations there has been a long tradition of having a large segment of the media—especially broadcasting—removed from commercial control and operated by some sort of non-profit, noncommercial agency. But it was not exclusively broadcasting. In Scandinavia there has been the practice of subsidizing newspapers and magazines to keep alive diverse points of view. Left to the market, the media system tends to produce a narrow range of viewpoints that comports to those of the upper class, and commercial pressures also downplay public affairs and journalism.

In the current era of neoliberalism all of these subsidies for diverse print media and for nonprofit broadcasting are under attack. Around the world the trend is toward predominately commercial systems. In Germany and Sweden, for example, the public broadcasters have seen their audience shares cut in half in the 1990s, as they face new competition from the proliferation of commercial channels on cable and satellite systems. The British Broadcasting Corporation, arguably the most successful public broadcaster in the world, has effectively become a full blown commercial enterprise in its global operations. It is a partner with the U.S. cable company TCI and some of TCI's subsidiaries. The BBC recognizes that it will eventually see its public sub-sidy cut so it hopes that by becoming profitable outside of Britain it can continue to be a noncommercial venture in the UK. The jury is out on that strategy, but on the surface it seems like the logic of commercialism should permeate every aspect of the BBC's being.

Your book characterizes the U.S. media model as an "outlier"—one that goes beyond any other country's in institutionalizing private ownership of the means of communications in profit-seeking corporations whose major source of revenue, and survival, derives from the advertising dollars of other corporations. How did the U.S. model come about?

RM: Well, the one thing we know for sure is that the current U.S. system is a 20th century development. But it is nothing like the media system we had during the first few generations

> *It means that capitalists control the media and they do so to maximize profits, often through selling advertising to other large corporations*

of the republic. The press system of the early republic was highly partisan and not especially profitable. Many of the major newspapers were subsidized by political parties or by the government through printing contracts. The current system evolved gradually as a commercial entity. By the early part of this century it had become dominated by large firms operating in oligopolistic markets, and advertising had emerged as an important source of revenues. This all followed the logic of capitalism: firms get bigger and eliminate competition to enhance their profitability and reduce risk.

In the past generation the two crucial developments for U.S. media firms is that they have conglomerated and globalized. By conglomeration I mean that the largest media firms all have major holdings in several different media sectors, like film and TV show production, cable TV channels, music production, book publishing, magazine publishing, retail stores, etc. Firms found they had to be conglomerates or they could not compete with their rivals. Globalization refers to the fact that the media industry may be at the forefront of the process of globalization. Firms like Disney and Time Warner did just over 10 percent of their business abroad in 1990 and will do around one-third of their business abroad in 1997. Sometime in the next decade they expect to do a majority of their business outside of the United States.

It is worth noting that the American people did not accept the development of the corporate media system without opposition. There were significant protests. Partially as a result of this came the professionalization of journalism, that is, the notion that the news would be provided by trained objective professionals who could not be influenced by media owners or advertisers. In addition, in the 1930s there was a fairly widespread movement to establish a nonprofit and noncommercial radio broadcasting system. It collapsed following the passage of the 1934 Communications Act, which was pushed through with minimal publicity by the powerful radio lobby.

Hand-in-hand with the U.S. media model goes an ideology that states that thanks to First Amendment guarantees of "freedom of speech or of the press," neither the government nor the public have any more than a very weak, if any, right to interfere with the free speech of the corporations that own the media. Has this belief always been as widely held as it seems to be today?

RM: No. Not at all. This is a recent development, one that has much more to do with the power of corporations than it does with the First Amendment or democratic theory. In the early 1940s, when the U.S. Supreme Court first considered whether advertising should be exempt from any government regulation on the grounds that advertising was protected by the First Amendment, the Court voted 9-0

that advertising was not covered by the First Amendment. This was a court that had several right-wingers who detested the New Deal and government regulation. It was seen as absurd that selling something for a profit should be equated with political speech and democracy. Over the past 50 years the matter has shifted and now the Supreme Court has extended the First Amendment to cover advertising in significant ways. This reflects the power of corporations in our society.

The irony of course is that advocates of this "extension" of the First Amendment argue that the more that is protected from the government, the more freedom there will be and the more likely democracy will prosper. But these proponents have an idiotic, untenable, and myopic view of where power lies in our society. Extending the First Amendment to advertising removes it, as well as corporate power, as legitimate political topics and shrinks the range of political debate to an ever-narrower scope.

The ACLU is the most egregious in this regard. It might as well set up its headquarters on Wall Street because its silly view that there is no reason for public concern about private control over media plays directly into the hands of the largest media firms. In the 1930s Morris Ernst, Roger Baldwin, and Norman Thomas pushed the ACLU in a far more enlightened direction. They argued that corporate commercial control over broadcasting significantly prevented the coverage of public affairs and discriminated against pro-labor and anti-business perspectives. They argued that establishing a viable democratic nonprofit, noncommercial broadcasting system was a First Amendment issue for the ACLU. The ACLU even had a radio committee that lobbied Congress to take control of broadcasting away from capitalists and advertisers. But when the movement failed, the ACLU gradually moved toward its present position of accepting the corporate system as the appropriate model for democracy. But the ACLU did not adopt this modern position because of principled debate; rather, it was adopted due to the admitted inability to defeat the corporate media giants on Capitol Hill. But I doubt anyone at the ACLU today knows this history. To them it seems that protecting corporate power to make money and dominate society is the purpose of the First Amendment and the cornerstone of a democratic society.

Your book calls the U.S. Telecommunication Act of 1996 the "single most important law" affecting not only U.S. telecommunications, but global telecommunications as well. How so?

RM: The 1996 U.S. Telecommunications Act specifically is a global law because, by providing for the deregulation of U.S. markets, it permits the dominant firms to get considerably larger through mergers and acquisitions. And the dominant U.S. firms provide a majority of the dominant global firms. So other countries are now facing a larger and more powerful set of firms, like the merged Nynex-Bell Atlantic, and the proposed merger of AT&T and SBC Communications. All of the media firms have gotten bigger in the past year too.

It is worth noting that the 1996 Telecom Act was rushed through Congress with almost no debate. There was virtually no press coverage outside of the business press and almost no public participation. The only debate concerned which sector—long distance telephone, local telephone, computer firms, broadcasters, or cable companies—would get the best deals in the legislation. That a handful of corporations were being granted the right to rule the entire range of our communication system to maximize profit with almost no strings attached was simply not subject to debate. That's because all the interested parties agreed on that as a given and the public was not invited to the debate.

This was an incredibly corrupt law. The Internet was never discussed at all, but this is the law that provides for the commercial development of cyberspace. The broadcasters, for example, snuck a clause into the law requiring the FCC to give them free spectrum for digital broadcasting. This was outrageous. Even the other communication firms have to pay for the use of their spectrum for the most part. It is incumbent on us to get another telecom bill passed, one that reflects the public interest.

Another major theme of your book is that, much as the rest of the world is moving towards or being pushed towards a socio-economic model similar to that in the United States, so, too, the rest of the world's media are being pushed towards a model similar to that found in the United States.

EH: Yes, and the two processes are closely linked. The socio-economic model is one of market hegemony, minimal state provision, the supplanting of the citizen by the consumer, and a commercial media providing the entertainment-cum-advertising culture appropriate to the socio-economic model. In much of the rest of the world public broadcasting has been important, so that one of the crucial global struggles has been over the status of public broadcasting.

Public broadcasting has been under steady attack by the dominant forces of global capitalism and is being weakened and displaced by commercial, advertising-based media.

The spread of the U.S. media model to the rest of the world is weakening their public broadcasting systems in countries where these are important, and strengthening the commercial media and the domination of advertisers in shaping media performance and standards. What it means for the rest of the world is more light entertainment, sex and violence on TV, and a lightening up of other media forms, with a parallel weakening of the public sphere —hard news, investigative reporting and documentaries, debates on public and community issues, enlightening children's programs, and the like. The rest of the world can look forward to a growing culture of entertainment and perhaps, in Neil Postman's phrase, "amusing themselves to death."

The U.S. Trade Representative Charlene Barshefsky cheered February's signing of the telecommunications agreement as "one of the most important trade agreements of the 21st Century." Then she added: "U.S. companies are the most competitive telecommunications providers in the world. They are in the best position to compete and win under this agreement." Might Barshefsky's elation tell us something else about the nature of the agreement?

EH: Yes. The telecommunications agreement of last February is a coup for powerful global providers of telecom services. It is essentially a market opening agreement, with clear benefits to the big boys who can participate, less clear benefits to the consumers and societies in the

> *Ad-based and concentrated, this system is a servant of the Brazilian elite and is destined to inculcate the individualist, consumerist ideology of the neoliberal order*

countries opening their doors. There may be efficiency gains, but there may be reduced universality of service, greater unregulated monopoly power, and a loss of national autonomy.

In Latin America a similar process was crucial in bringing about the domination of commercial broadcasting and assuring that the European model of strong public broadcasting did not prevail. From the earliest years U.S. equipment manufacturers, advertisers, broadcasters, and publishers pushed the governments of the region toward commercial systems, so that public broadcasting was marginalized or never came into existence at all, preempted by a commercial system, as in Brazil.

The experience of Brazil was a telling one. In our book we characterize it as a case of "media neo- and sub-imperialism." As just noted, a commercial system was installed from the beginning, with U.S. help and under U.S. pressure. By the early 1960s, U.S. transnationals already had a major presence in the Brazilian economy, Brazil's media included. In the years prior to the 1964 coup, Brazil's media had been heavily penetrated by U.S. economic and political agents. The *O Globo* newspaper, Brazil's largest, was receiving infusions of cash from Time-Life, and may have been CIA-controlled. Time-Life justified its invasion of the Brazilian media by the need to combat what it referred to as "Castroism."

Following the 1964 coup, the Globo media empire grew to virtual monopoly status. The junta supported Globo financially and in regulatory practice, and the media giant served the military and Brazilian elite well. During the dozen years following the coup, Brazil's commercial media system was consolidated and integrated into the global system. Ad-based and concentrated, this system is a servant of the Brazilian elite and is destined to inculcate the individualist, consumerist ideology of the neoliberal order.

India provides an important contrasting example. There, the British model was imported and a public broadcasting system was imposed and became a heritage of the colonial system after the British exit. Admittedly, its performance has not been inspiring, but it is regrettable to see it being commercialized rapidly without having realized the potential of a more autonomous public broadcasting system such as developed in the imperial country.

A little earlier, Ed Herman mentioned the "public sphere," a concept that you use widely in your book, and that you draw from the German philosopher Jurgen Habermas. You write that by the "public sphere," you mean "all the places and forums where issues of importance to a political community are discussed and debated, and where information is presented that is essential to citizen participation in community life." But your analysis is anything but sanguine about the fate of the public sphere in the U.S.

EH: We are definitely not optimistic at this juncture. The U.S. model entails a displacement of the public sphere with entertainment. Advertisers don't like public sphere programs, which do not provide a good selling environment and do not draw as heavily as mayhem and sex. We have a 70-year record in this country of the gradual abandonment of "public service" programming under the pressure of market interest.

Contrary to the claims of the market beneficiaries of this transformation, it has not been catering to "what consumers want," because a substantial minority want public service programs, and many others believe that such programs ought to be available. It's what proprietors and advertisers want. The corporate system prefers a culture of entertainment and light news mixed with serviceable propaganda to a public sphere that would address serious issues.

So, in your eyes, corporate control and manipulation pose a serious anti-democratic threat?

EH: Yes. But the real problem isn't "manipulation." The real problem lies in the normal operations and effects that corporate media have on the public sphere, and with the structural changes now going on, which are putting in place profoundly undemocratic arrangements. The Enlightenment project is one of people moving into control of their lives, winning their emancipation through knowledge and action, whereas transnational media corporations want the conditions that have prevailed in the United States for decades to ex-

tend everywhere, with people treated strictly as audiences to be sold to advertisers. The contradiction between the project of the Enlightenment and the project of transnational media corporations is immense. The global media are carrying out what we might call an "entertainment revolution" which is implemented from above. They are not agents of a democratic "information revolution."

> *The global media are carrying out what we might call an "entertainment revolution" which is implemented strictly from above. They are surely not agents of a democratic "information revolution."*

And, therefore, contrary to Nicholas Negroponte, Alvin Toffler, Newt Gingrich, and a host of other luminaries who praise the democratic miracles awaiting us on the Information Superhighway. The two of you would argue that, given the current political climate in the United States (not to mention the rest of the world), the "egalitarian potential" of the "media revolution" isn't likely to be realized.

RM: That's correct. Although some technologies—like digital communication, say—have immense influence over societies, they do not have magical powers. Unless there is explicit social policy to develop cyberspace as a noncommercial, nonprofit entity, it is going to be taken over by the most powerful elements in our society. That is exactly what is happening. The largest computer, telecom, and media firms are doing everything in their considerable powers to see the Internet brought within their empires.

A telling sign was Microsoft's purchase of WebTV and its billion dollar investment in Comcast, the cable TV company. Right now the smart money seems to be betting that the Internet can be used as a commercial entertainment medium like television, in addition to being a business tool and a place for commerce.

All that stuff from a few years ago about how the Internet was going to create some democratic Valhalla and eliminate the corporate communication giants might as well as have been written in the 15th century. That is just nonsense. The Internet is becoming a hierarchical commercial entity. Some people will have full service, others lower-grade service, and still others none at all. Yet, at the same time, the Internet is a remarkable and revolutionary tool for activists. It will continue to be just that. But we cannot extrapolate from the activist experience to society as a whole. Not unless we get policies to enforce that as a goal.

"The ultimate goal [of media activists]," The Global Media concludes, "must be the establishment of a global, nonprofit public sphere to replace, or at least complement, the global commercial media market." But that sounds far more utopian than practical. Doesn't it?

RM: To the contrary, I think that the most utopian notion is that the market system can ever provide the basis for a democratic society. Everywhere across the world democratic left parties and movements are battling neoliberal "free market" policies. In almost all cases these democratic forces have highlighted taking control of the media from corporations and advertisers as central to the project of building a democratic society. In Sweden, New Zealand, Australia, India, Brazil—the list goes on and on—there are viable left parties and movements that are talking about ways to build and develop nonprofit, noncommercial, and democratically accountable media systems. They are finding considerable popular support for these positions. In view of the global trend toward a commercial media system there is every reason to believe this will be an area of democratic political activity. Can they succeed? Who knows, but what other choice is there? When you see the scope of these activities, you become optimistic.

The United States is the laggard in media activism. So, based here in the most depoliticized society on earth—with the possible exception of Russia—it is easy to think social change is impossible. But even here there has been tremendous growth in media activism and political activism in the 1990s. Perhaps the period we are in now is like the civil rights movement in the early 1950s, when it appeared to be quiescent but we now know it was laying the foundation for the great victories to follow. At any rate, I think the best has yet to come.

From Z Magazine, March 1995
Volume 8, Volume 3

15.

The Great Game

By Nicolas J.S. Davies

AFGHANISTAN IS KNOWN as the "graveyard of empires." But just why do empires keep sending thousands of their young people to die in Afghanistan? American bloodletting there is generally explained in terms of the Taliban and al-Qaeda, but it was U.S. involvement in Afghanistan that led to the emergence of these

> *A Dutch friend of mine tried to have a rational conversation with an American co-worker about September 11 and the so-called war on terror and was told, "You can't possibly understand. Your country has never been attacked like this." The puzzled Dutch woman had to ask, "Did you never hear anything about the Second World War?"*

movements in the first place, not the other way around. Nevertheless, the United States government has used the terrorist attacks of September 11, 2001 to justify foreign invasions and occupations, flagrant war crimes, and its largest military budget since 1945. It has persuaded an influential minority of Americans that their country faces a unique and unprecedented threat that justifies all these measures, not least its savage war in Afghanistan.

A Dutch friend of mine tried to have a rational conversation with an American co-worker about September 11 and the so-called war on terror and was told, "You can't possibly understand. Your country has never been attacked like this." The puzzled Dutch woman had to ask, "Did you never hear anything about the Second World War?" Of course, it is precisely the relative safety of America that makes us so vulnerable to panic and propaganda when faced with such a limited threat.

While Americans think of the war in terms of September 11 and terrorism, Afghans are not afflicted with such a myopic view. They see the war in the context of a much longer history that is shaped by their country's mountainous geography and strategic location between Iran to the West, Russia to the North, and India and Pakistan to the South and East—and of their own ability to defend their country against the world's greatest empires. Or, as noted in the resignation letter of Matthew Hoh, an American diplomat who resigned from his post in protest in 2009: "I have observed that the bulk of the insurgency fights not for the white banner of the Taliban, but rather against the presence of foreign soldiers and taxes imposed by an unrepresentative government in Kabul. The United States military presence in Afghanistan greatly contributes to the legitimacy and strategic message of the Pashtun insurgency."

Fall of the Safavid Empire of Persia

The first modern empire brought down by the Afghans was the 200-year old Safavid Empire of Persia. Local Pashtun tribespeople rebelled under Mirwais Khan Hotak in 1706 and expelled Persia from Western Afghanistan. Mirwais's son, Mir Mahmud Hotaki, continued the war and sacked the Persian capital of Isfahan in 1722. The Safavid dynasty was already economically weak, as Dutch merchant ships were sailing away with the bulk of regional trade from its formerly lucrative trade routes. But the Afghans delivered the coup de grace.

As the Russian Empire expanded in the Caucasus and Central Asia in the early 19th century, a weakened Persia gradually lost territory. The British came to see Persia as a Russian puppet and adopted a "forward policy" to keep Afghanistan as a buffer between British

India and the expanding Russian Empire. This effectively made Herat in Western Afghanistan the new outer frontier of the British Empire that Britain was committed to keeping out of the hands of Russia and Persia.

A Persian army besieged Herat for 280 days in 1837-38. The failure of the siege exposed the weakness of Persia, which continued to disintegrate. But it also highlighted the vulnerability of Afghanistan, which was ruled at the time by different tribal leaders in Herat, Kandahar, and Kabul, following the collapse of the Durrani dynasty. So the British and their Sikh allies from the Punjab marched into Afghanistan to restore the former Amir, Shah Shuja, who had been deposed and exiled in 1809.

This is called the first Afghan war. In a parallel with the present crisis, the British plan was to stay only as long as necessary to leave Shah Shuja in firm control of the country, but this proved to be impossible. He effectively ruled only Kabul where he owed his position to the presence of British and Indian troops and officials. The longer the British stayed, the more they alienated the Afghans. British officials brought their families to Kabul and established a small colony, complete with soirees and cricket matches. Their expenditures caused runaway inflation, which alienated the merchant class of Kabul and a riot there in November 1841 soon grew into a full-blown rebellion against the British occupation. Mohammed Akbar Khan, the son of Dost Mohammed, the leader the British had deposed in Kabul, came down from the mountains to lead the rebellion.

The Afghans killed the British commander, General MacNaghten, dragged his body through the streets of Kabul, and put it on display. His deputy, General Elphinstone, negotiated with Akbar Khan for passage to Jalalabad for officials and their families.

On January 6, 1842, 700 British troops, 3,800 Indian troops, and 12,000 civilians set out for Jalajabad, 90 miles away. At every pass through the mountains, they were greeted by Afghan tribespeople waiting in ambush. They were massacred (some froze to death) long before they reached Jalalabad. The sole survivor, assistant surgeon William Brydon, rode into Jalalabad with a piece of his skull sheared off by a sword after being rescued by an Afghan shepherd. Asked for news of the British army from Kabul, he replied, "I am the army."

The British sent another expedition to rescue some prisoners and take revenge on the people of Kabul, but they abandoned the effort to occupy or control Afghanistan. The Afghans had established their independence and neither Britain, Russia, nor Persia occupied Afghan territory for the next 36 years. Mohammed Akbar Khan died, but Dost Mohammed and his other sons united Afghanistan and established relations with the British. Ironically, a truly independent Afghanistan served as a very effective buffer between the British and Russian Empires, and the British helped the Afghans to repel more Persian attacks on Herat in 1852 and 1856.

The Treaty of Gandamak

The second Afghan war began after Sher Ali Khan, Dost Mohammed's third son, accepted a Russian diplomatic mission to Kabul in 1878, but then rebuffed a British one. This resurrected the recurring specter of British insecurity over Afghanistan. Britain invaded again and occupied much of the country. Sher Ali died in February 1879 and the British persuaded his son Mohammad Yaqub Khan to sign the Treaty of Gandamak, which ceded Quetta and the Khyber Pass to Britain and gave Britain control over Afghan foreign policy in exchange for financial support.

The British army withdrew, but it left behind a diplomatic mission in Kabul. A few months later, the remaining British officials were all killed during a local rebellion. The British invaded again. After ten months of savage fighting, they defeated an Afghan army under Yaqub's brother, Ayub Khan, at Kandahar. The British installed Yaqub and Ayub's cousin Abdur Rahman Khan as Amir and he agreed to the terms of the Treaty of Gandamak. The British finally withdrew—though this time they did not leave a diplomatic mission behind in Kabul to be killed. Afghanistan became fully independent from Britain as a result of the third Afghan war in 1919, which was an Afghan invasion of the North West Frontier province of British India.

Throughout the 20th century, Afghanistan's people confronted the same existential questions as people in other non-Western countries. What aspects of modern Western technology and culture could they adopt without losing what they valued in their own way of life? As elsewhere, different classes within Afghan society answered this question according to their own interests and the resulting divisions left Afghanistan vulnerable to opportunistic exploitation and intervention by foreign powers, including Pakistan, Saudi Arabia, the Soviet Union, and the United States.

USSR Independence and Aid

Amanullah Khan, the king of Afghanistan, who won independence from Britain in 1919, admired the modernist regime of Kemal Ataturk in Turkey. He mandated compulsory elementary education, opened co-educational schools, and abolished the burqa for women. But conservative tribal and religious leaders rebelled and forced him to abdicate in 1929. The last king of Afghanistan, Zahir Shah, ruled for 40 years (1933-1973) by pursuing a more gradual approach to modernization.

Afghanistan was still in the same position geographically, but the world around it had changed. Instead of being sandwiched between the Russian and British Empires, it was now wedged between the Soviet Union and independent Pakistan. Mohammed Daoud Khan, the king's cousin, was his prime minister from 1953 until 1963 and Daoud envisioned a reunification of the Pashtun territories on either side of the British colonial border between Afghanistan and what was now Pakistan. After this initiative was rebuffed by Pakistan, Daoud increasingly turned northward to the USSR for both military and development aid.

In 1973, Daoud seized power from his cousin, but instead of declaring himself king, he abolished the monarchy and became Afghanistan's first president. He began by renewing Afghanistan's relationship with the USSR and used Soviet aid to build up the Afghan

> *The U.S., Pakistani, and Saudi governments began to provide funds, training, and weapons to the mujahideen and a new version of the "great game" was under way*

army. But he soon broke with his Marxist allies in the Peoples Democratic Party of Afghanistan (PDPA), distanced Afghanistan from the Soviet Union, and began to improve relations with Pakistan, Egypt, and other Western-oriented Muslim countries.

In 1978, a leading PDPA politician was murdered, causing the other PDPA leaders to believe that Daoud was planning to have them all killed. They staged a coup, killed Daoud and his family, and formed the new Democratic Republic of Afghanistan. They launched a radical secular reform program, banning burqas and forced marriages, closing mosques, redistributing land, and abolishing farmers' debts. Anehita Ratebzad, a female member of the Revolutionary Council, wrote in a *New Kabul Times* editorial, "Privileges which women, by right, must have are equal education, job security, health services, and free time to rear a healthy generation for building the future of the country.... Educating and enlightening women is now the subject of close government attention."

The USSR quickly provided $1.2 billion to build roads, schools, hospitals, and wells. The relatively small urban population welcomed the reforms and new development, but the interests of rural landowners and tribal and religious leaders were seriously threatened and they began to fund and support muja- hideen to commit terrorism and resist government forces. The U.S., Pakistani, and Saudi governments began to provide funds, training, and weapons to the mujahideen and a new version of the "great game" was under way.

For the Soviets, Afghanistan had lost none of its value since the 19th century. Their empire extended from Europe to Siberia, but nowhere did it reach southward to ports and the sea-routes to South Asia and Africa. The United States controlled those sea-lanes and had the same interest as Britain in the 19th century in keeping a buffer between the Russians and the ports of Pakistan. The establishment of a Soviet client state in Afghanistan offered the USSR the tantalizing promise of fulfilling historic ambitions. In funding, supplying, supporting, and training the mujahideen, U.S. policymakers believed they had found a low-cost means to neutralize a serious geostrategic challenge.

Presidents Carter and Brezhnev began this new "great game" as a proxy war to be fought mainly by Afghans against other Afghans. Soviet forces eventually lost 13,000 lives, but killed at least a million Afghans. The United States and its allies have so far lost only 1,500 dead, but have likewise killed tens of thousands of Afghans. Both the United States and the Soviet Union became engaged in Afghanistan because they had important strategic interests at stake, long before the emergence of the Taliban or al-Qaeda.

The New Great Game

Since the end of the Cold War, the two main thrusts of U.S. foreign policy have been to impose military control over every part of the world where oil is produced or shipped and to encircle Russia with a ring of U.S. allies and military bases from Poland to Georgia to Central Asia. Afghanistan's position between Iran, Central Asia, and Pakistan makes it a critical part of the pipeline map, potentially supplying Pakistan and India with oil and gas from Western operations in the Caspian Sea via Unocal (now Chevron) pipeline through Afghanistan. A U.S. ally and bases in strategically located Afghanistan would add an important link in the military encirclement of Russia, China, and Iran.

On the other hand, if Afghanistan was aligned with Russia, it could equally well serve as a route for a pipeline to transport Russian oil and gas to Pakistan and beyond and place Russian military or intelligence bases on the borders of Pakistan and Iran. The United States' interest in denying the Russians a pipeline route to the Arabian Sea and a client state on the border of Pakistan corresponds closely to Britain's fears of Russian expansion into Afghanistan in the 19th century. Even an independent Afghanistan free from U.S. or Russian influence could link Iran to China via yet another pipeline route.

As in the mid-19th century, a genuinely independent Afghanistan could actually be a stable and effective buffer between the great powers. As the Maliki government in Iraq gradually slipped the American leash, it has awarded oil contracts to Russian, Chinese, and South Korean companies as well as to Western ones. A future Afghan government could ultimately do likewise, playing suitors for pipeline deals against each other in the traditional fashion. In Iraq, Western oil companies have welcomed partnerships with Asian companies that can supply cheaper labor and equipment and are not tainted by a role in the invasion and destruction of the country.

In fact, as commerce of all kinds began to flow again in Iraq, the United States delivered a powerful message that aggression and mili-tary occupation do not pay. Total Iraqi imports grew from $25.7 billion in 2007 to $43.5 billion in 2008. But even as other countries' trade with Iraq has grown, exports from the United States to Iraq have remained a meager $2 billion per year, most of that stemming from existing contracts with the U.S.-backed government.

By contrast, Turkey, which refused to support the U.S. invasion, has become one of Iraq's largest trading partners, with exports of $10 billion to Iraq in 2008. At a recent trade fair in Baghdad, an Iraqi executive explained that his construction company preferred to do business with Turkish firms because costs were lower and the Turks "are not an occupier." Other countries that opposed the invasion—in particular Iran, France, and Brazil—have likewise become major trading partners.

On condition of anonymity, a European ambassador to Baghdad told the *New York Times* that his country's business relations with Iraq improved greatly once it withdrew its troops. "Being considered an occupier handicapped us extremely," he said. "The farther we are away from that the more our companies can be accepted on their own merits."

In some of the largest government contracts awarded since the invasion, the Iraqi transportation ministry recently awarded $30 billion to rebuild Iraq's railroads to a combination of British, Italian, and Czech companies. The Russian company RusAir won an exclusive air cargo contract that forced FedEx to terminate its operations in Iraq.

As in other parts of the world, the U.S. effort to control events by the (illegal) threat and use of military force is the central obstacle to a peaceful resolution for Afghanistan. The escalation of the war in Afghanistan since 2006 can be directly traced to a massive escalation of U.S. air strikes that year, even as numbers of U.S. casualties remained flat. Only 98 American troops were killed in Afghanistan in 2006, one less than the 99 killed in 2005. Yet the number of air strikes exploded from 176 in 2005 to 1,770 in 2006—a ten-fold increase. The flat casualty figures make it clear that this was an escalation initiated by U.S. forces, not by the Afghan resistance (2007 saw a further escalation to 2,926 air strikes).

The successful response of the Afghan resistance to the American escalation was entirely predictable, but it appears to have surprised U.S. planners. As in Iraq, the U.S. reacted to the failure of its puppet government to establish any legitimacy or control over most of the country with a massive escalation of military force, launching a desperate and bloody campaign to bomb and terrorize the population into submission. This brutal escalation was an abysmal failure, leading directly to the brink of defeat, where U.S. forces find themselves. The so-called "surge" in Iraq provided cover for a similar escalation of aerial bombardment, from 229 air strikes in 2006 to 1,119 in 2007, and 110 per month through most of 2008.

In Afghanistan, as in Iraq (and Vietnam), despite endless lip-service to phrases like "winning hearts and minds" and "clear, hold, and build," U.S. military strategists cling to the core belief that their virtually unlimited capacity for violence can ultimately carry the day if enough legal and political constraints are removed. Instead, the failures of U.S. military force and the success of "Anti-Coalition Forces" everywhere have confirmed Richard Barnet's Vietnam-era judgment that "at the very moment the number one nation has perfected the science of killing, it has become an impractical instrument of political domination."

Afghans believe that it was they who brought down the Safavids and the Soviets. While the Afghans definitely did their part, the forces that led to the collapse of those empires were really much closer to home in both cases. The real graveyard of the Soviet empire lay in the Kremlin where absolute power insulated

its leaders from the forces at work in the real world beyond its walls. The Afghan war was only one of many causes of discontent and dissolution within the Soviet political and economic system. A quiet underground movement of non-violent popular opposition grew steadily beneath the surface.

Since the 1970s, America's leaders have consolidated their political and economic power into effective monopolies. Most industries are dominated by two or three huge firms and the political system is controlled by a similar duopoly. Research on economic competition has established that such near-monopolies take on many of the characteristics of actual monopolies, stifling innovation and competition, destroying smaller businesses, exploiting employees, building inefficient bureaucracies, and spending more on marketing than on research and development. The U.S. health insurance industry employs 30 times as many administrative staff as it did in 1970. American firms spend $290 billion per year on advertising, almost $1,000 for every person in the country. And corporate control of politics has systematically dismantled every mechanism that could restore effective management or halt the system's relentless drive to devour everything, including itself. Looking for solutions from any of the leaders promoted by such a dysfunctional system is pure folly.

It is the policy of the United States, not that of Afghanistan, that is filling the graveyards and the great game that can stop the funerals will not be played out in Afghanistan, but in Washington and in local communities all over the United States as Americans organize for a post-imperial, post-corporate, and more democratic future.

From Z Magazine, *January 2010*
Volume 23, Number 1

16.

Anthropology's Colonial Legacy

By Maresi Starzmann

ANTHROPOLOGY FOR ACADEMIA has long proven unable to outright deny its colonialist legacy. This inheritance is well documented. The search for knowledge about an exoticized Other—the paradigmatic "noble savage" in numerous anthropological publications, museum displays, and other kinds of archives—has set the parameters

Musing over the events in Egypt this spring, public statements and commentaries released by anthropological organizations in Europe and the U.S. reflect the interests of empire

for scientific explanations of what it means to be human. Extremely exclusivist in terms of both its definition of humanity and its academic practice, the discipline of anthropology resides within and reproduces larger structures of rule established in the West that depend on the production of knowledge about the Other in order to control him/her. Unfortunately, efforts at coming to terms with the past more often perpetuate the tradition of imperialism, aligning its interests once again with those of empire.

Musing over the political events in Egypt this spring, public statements and commentaries released by anthropological organizations in Europe and the U.S. reflect the interests of empire. A Statement of Support for Egypt issued in February 2011 by the American Anthropological Association (AAA), considered an authority by policymakers and the public, first and foremost expresses concern about the losses to cultural heritage. Similarly, the self-proclaimed presidents of an imagined international community of archaeologists speak out for a "prioritization for the protection of Egypt's cultural heritage and the preservation of Egypt's invaluable and irreplaceable archaeological history."

While presuming to speak for a large number of anthropologists, the statement of the American Anthropological Association clearly reflects the class interests of the upper echelons of Western society in the context of a vast and expanding industry of cultural imperialism. After all, the discipline of anthropology (as many other academic disciplines) is situated in power structures that guarantee its representatives unequal access to symbolic and

> *If we look at this closely, it is specific class and racial interests that play out in the context of imperialist relations that put academia in place to stress concern for vanishing cultures, near-extinct species and threatened antiquities over concern for the lives and dignity of people*

economic capital, not only within their own society, but also against other societies. If we look at this closely, it is specific class and racial interests that play out in the context of imperialist relations that put academia in place to stress concern for vanishing cultures, near-extinct species and threatened antiquities over concern for the lives and dignity of people. As a consequence, major anthropological organizations were able to ignore in their statements the expressions of self-determination by the Egyptian people or the transformative meaning of the revolution not only for Egypt, but for Northern Africa and the Middle East.

The statements cited here clearly establish the value that the cultural heritage of Egypt holds for human history by referring to the World Heritage List of UNESCO, which assigns outstanding universal value to seven sites in Egypt. This value is, of course, defined in purely economic terms, meaning that: "The richness of this heritage is integral to the country's economic well-being, particularly in terms

of heritage tourism." Such constructs conceal not only the linked matrices of race, class, and culture that undergird tourist industries, but they also reveal the motives underlying the concern for protecting cultural heritage in the wake of imperial encounters. Followed by commercialization in an ever-expanding tourism industrial complex, antiquities have found their way into the global economy where they serve the interests of those who can afford to excavate, collect, curate, sell, buy, study, and display these objects.

This emphasis on cultural heritage with archaeological artifacts as invaluable and irreplaceable, reflects to some extent the events surrounding the U.S. invasion of Iraq in 2003, which involved the destruction and looting of major archaeological sites and museums, most notably the Iraq Museum in Baghdad. Famous antiquities stolen from the museum were soon put on international "Most Wanted" lists, while black market and public websites like ebay flourished. At the same time, U.S. soldiers received a crash course in ancient history and heritage management when the U.S. Department of Defense issued decks of playing cards depicting many of Iraq's archaeological sites and artifacts. Ironically, but not surprisingly, these cards complemented the already existing card games showing the heads of the most wanted officials of Saddam Hussein's regime.

In 2003, the concern that archaeologists working in the area expressed was very much in line with the Defense Department's phrasing of cultural history, which was written with the help of a cultural resource specialist, who was, not surprisingly, an anthropologist by training. In articles, public statements, and online publications, anthropologists called for the protection of the "universal" and "irreplaceable" cultural heritage of Iraq. In many cases, their concern for Iraq's material culture either outweighed or was completely divorced from the deeply felt emotional and political despair over an illegal war shared by millions of protesters in major cities all over the world.

The same scholars who worried over the loss of cultural heritage refrained from analyzing the structural meaning not only of the looting, but also of the ethical concerns that were expressed over it. More specifically, they refused to recognize how the destruction and international trafficking of artifacts from Iraq is economic appropriation in the context of neoliberal globalization—all this happening under the guise of cultural intervention. As antiquities move through spheres of exchange from the black market to auction houses and finally to museums or private collections in Europe or North America, they acquire market values that exceed the objects' original use-value. As valuable material culture, the artifacts and antiquities are claimed for the West's own purposes of producing knowledge about our "shared human past." Thus appropriated, the objects turn into commodities—indeed, fetishized commodities—that are essential to structuring the political and economic relations between "the West and the Rest."

As valuable material culture, the artifacts and antiquities are claimed for the West's own purposes of producing knowledge about our "shared human past." Thus appropriated, the objects turn into commodities...

Conquering Hearts & Minds

In Iraq, much of the damage done to archaeological sites resulted from U.S. bombs and not always from looters. As a result, anthropologists demonstrated at least some degree of self-criticism when they expressed their fear over the destruction of cultural heritage. Egypt, by contrast, where events appeared to take place independent from Western intervention, is not conducive to such anthropological reflectivity, which turns the country into the perfect site for reinventing Euro-America's superiority. This undertaking

is, however, not an easy task because the participants in Egypt's revolution have voiced a desire for democracy. Indeed, the democratization of civil society is a process that should immediately appeal to the middle and upper class of academics in Europe and North America, who frequently embrace freedom, liberty, and democracy as universal values. Therefore, in order for anthropology to be able to claim Egypt as the essential Other —the very "Orient" against which Europe's enlightened self-fashioning emerges—it had to ignore the meaning and content of the revolution and focus entirely on the looting of cultural heritage, framing these instances as the "barbaric" acts of an uneducated and inherently corrupt populace. At the same time, the reports of looting that reached Europe and the U.S. were highly controversial and could often not be verified. Many of the reports cited by anthropologists came from the blog and website of Zahi Hawass, former Minister of Antiquities in Mubarak's cabinet. Someone like Hawass, for whom much was at stake before Mubarak's resignation, would have been well aware of Western interest in Egypt's cultural heritage and would use this interest to appeal to Western academics and forge political ties.

The decision to dismiss the voices of the Egyptian people collapsed them into what some anthropologists perceived as a populist mass engaged in undifferentiated political agitation. This mass was, whether implicitly or explicitly, brought into contrast with the intelligentsia of professionals and academics trained in the West, such as Hawass himself. In doing so, Western academics dismissed the fact that Egyptians largely acted collectively in calling for the restoration of their dignity. While protesters in Tahrir Square and beyond focused on political change, risking their lives for a better future, anthropologists managed to erase the symbolic meaning of the revolution for the so-called post-colonial world. Egyptians wanted self-determination, but received, in the statement by the "International Archaeological Community," only a destroyed and lost heritage.

Despite the fact that the people in Egypt exercised autonomous political action to bring them one step closer to a truly decolonial position, anthropological organizations such as the American Anthropological Association continue to speak on behalf of cultural imperialism. The aforementioned statements express a distressing commitment to recreating an Orientalist fantasy in which Egypt serves as the "primitive" mirror image of the Western metropole. Essential to this invigorated Orientalism is a contradictory vision that keeps expressing claims of Euro-American ownership over history, materialized in military interventions and aggressive missions of heritage protection. This vision consists of the idea that the

> *Historically speaking, the protection of cultural heritage is almost always embedded in a larger framework of imperialist encounters*

human past has universal value as a "shared" past, exclusively managed by Euro-American academic and military industrial institutions. The ancient cultures of Egypt (or Iraq, Afghanistan, Iran, and so forth) are for Euro-America merely the proverbial "cradle of (our) civilization," kept in perpetual political-economic dependency by the West.

Similar examples can be found everywhere in colonialist and imperialist encounters. The United States justified its invasion of Afghanistan, in part, by explaining that the Afghan cultural heritage must be saved from its destruction by the Taliban. The fact that the timeline

is somewhat skewed, with Operation Enduring Freedom (the government name for the U.S. war in Afghanistan) commencing half a year after the destruction of the Bamiyan Statues, is not crucial. The political context of the invasion was, of course, grander than any mission of heritage protection could ever be. The West supposedly embarked on a humanitarian mission that was characterized by a rhetorical push to frame the war in Afghanistan as centering on women's rights. As a result, the U.S. military mission in Afghanistan was cast as one where white men went off supposedly to save brown women from brown men.

In misrecognition of its own practices, the West reserves labels such as "fundamentalist" and "violent" for all others, while the Western mission is imagined as one of democratization and liberation. This narrative is, of course, ideology at its purest, serving as cover for policies dictated by economic imperatives. For its greater goal, the Western civilizing mission obviously employs means that destroy people, decimate families, kill mothers and fathers, children, and elderly people. The preferred phrase that describes the victims of this violence has become "collateral damage," thus relegating killing to the realm of unintended consequences.

Historically speaking, the protection of cultural heritage is almost always embedded in a larger framework of imperialist encounters. The logic of cultural imperialism illustrates how missions of heritage protection are about more than preserving an "authentic culture" or an "irreplaceable heritage," which are part and parcel of humanitarian-military interventions. Claiming the universality of history, these encounters reach deep into the intimate aspects of political life.

Cultural heritage management in the context of war and conflict seeks to win hearts and minds under the pretense of protecting ancient sites and artifacts. One of the playing cards for U.S. soldiers in Iraq boldly states "showing respect wins hearts and minds," recalling a long-standing history of U.S. imperialism. The phrase "hearts and minds" was President Lyndon Johnson's euphemism for a brutal and violent military process of oppression, submission, and destruction during the Vietnam War.

Complicity in Structural Violence

Statements such as the one issued by the American Anthropological Association, if spun further, make clear that there is obviously no contradiction in "supporting (the people of) Egypt," on the one hand, and in turning to U.S. government forces to intercept purported activities of looting and the illegal trafficking in antiquities, on the other. These antiquities are, of course, mainly the paraphernalia of great kings and queens—their monuments and treasures, pyramids and palaces. Forgotten are those in slavery and bondage, who helped create the ancient treasures that wealthy tourists admire in Egyptian museums today. Similarly forgotten is the fact that a modern form of slavery exists in present-day Egypt where the brutal Mubarak regime created a vast population of political prisoners. For the American Anthropological Association, however, just as for Zahi Hawass, this merely creates more concern about antiquities. The fear is that "as the prisons are opened, the potential for greater loss [of cultural heritage] is created." While anthropologists worry about protecting antiquities from attacks by "hoodlums and criminals" (the choice of words on academic listservs), there is no such concern for assault on the political integrity of the imprisoned.

It is not surprising that practices of looting, neglect, and damage of objects of cultural heritage are most often documented in those areas of the world that are supposedly characterized by a lesser degree of "civilization" or "democratization." The classic anthropological idea of a failed modernity still legitimizes Western intervention—or what Slavoj Žižek calls "humanitarian militarism"—in all kinds of affairs, including the safeguarding of heritage. As such, this call for intervention employs the kind of psuedo-urgency that is otherwise only encountered in humanitarian work.

Žižek highlights the paradox that lies at the heart of humanitarianism and makes Western violence its necessary precondition. Only by participating in the structural violence that results in humanitarian intervention can we afford to partake in this discourse of fake urgency. This formulation also applies to an-

> *The classic anthropological idea of a failed modernity still legitimizes Western intervention—or what Slavoj Žižek calls "humanitarian militarism"—in all kinds of affairs, including the safeguarding of heritage*

thropologists who call for intervention for the sake of heritage protection. Western academia is essential to the functioning of structural violence, which creates the kinds of political situations that apparently require interference by Euro-American military and economic powers. As academics, we are complicit in this process when our work defends the interests of the state, of capital, of empire. While this complicity is not always discernible, certain situations are quite demonstrative of this process. Recently, the presence of military personnel in civilian attire or in combat fatigues has become a familiar sight at major anthropological conferences, such as the annual meetings of the American Anthropological Association.

In spite of this, the discipline of anthropology as a whole does not seem to perceive itself as complicit in neo-imperialist encounters. A North American anthropologist—who, in all sincerity, claims American innocence by calling the U.S. a former imperial power—blatantly ignores continued Western interests in Egypt (among countless other places). While this viewpoint is certainly not shared by all an-

> *This complicity of silence has for many years been a convenient placeholder for U.S. economic interests, for keeping the so-called post-colonial status quo in Northern Africa as oppressive and disenfranchising as was intended by its initial colonizers*

thropologists or all academics, the structural, and even direct, complicity of the U.S. government in the brutal politics of the Mubarak regime—Egypt is after all the second-largest recipient of U.S. military and economic aid, after Israel—is not a point that is opened up to analysis by the American Anthropological Association, which is first and foremost an academic organization. This complicity of silence has for many years been a convenient placeholder for U.S. economic interests, for keeping the so-called post-colonial status quo in Northern Africa as oppressive and disenfranchising as was intended by its initial colonizers.

The Post-Political

The statement by the American Anthropological Association shows something else: the fact that it is possible as an anthropologist to sever issues of heritage management from political culture. It is indeed considered methodologically rigorous and analytically sound to fashion oneself as the post-political anthropologist who merely collects and protects traits of a shared human past. Yet, any slight disapproval of the values associated with an imagined universal heritage triggers moral anxiety among those very anthropologists. The "post-political being" is, after all, an ideological illusion with no foundation in the real world. Under the pretense of being completely apolitical, the post-political anthropologist (or academic in the wider sense) simply commits to politics that do not "dwell on issues and will never ask

the question, 'who has power and why'." Being post-political, of course, also means having "absolutely no interest in class, whose very acknowledgment [is] the bases of all real politics and whose acknowledgment would only lead to an existential crisis in its ranks."

In response, anxious anthropologists present only a psychological mechanism of self-defense. We are not to blame, they cry, because our expertise is after all not in politics, but in (material) culture. Our "scientific" interests are entirely dispassionate. Is this just a case of Freudian moral anxiety over the internalized belief in Western universalisms? If that was so, it would not be the individual scholar who was to blame, but his/her "superego." More likely, we suffer from a severe case of what Sloterdijk has called "cynical reason." This suggests that we are not only aware of our ideologically-warped beliefs, but we consciously accept that these constructs constitute reality as we pursue our interests as privileged academics. For Žižek this paradox reflects an enlightened false consciousness in which those who partake in the ruling culture "know very well what they are doing, but still, they are doing it."

As anthropologists and academics we should really know that our disciplines are oftentimes essential to colonial missions and imperialist encounters. To ignore this is to ignore countless texts written about the colonial entanglements of anthropology and other academic disciplines and it is also to ignore the endless protests staged in opposition to it. From their seat of power, anthropologists, in particular, have mapped language groups and kinship systems, collected cultural artifacts, and named territories and peoples.

Further, the discipline is crucial in assisting the desire for ever-increasing cultural domination for the ultimate purpose of economic expansion that is founded upon and perpetuated by capitalism, of which academia as a whole is a constituent part. What started in the 18th century with early European explorers found its continuation in the anthropology of counterinsurgency, probably most often associated with the prominent figures of U.S. anthropologists Margaret Mead and Ruth Benedict. Today the so-called "embedded anthropologists" continue these practices in the context of the Human Terrain System (HTS) Project and other U.S. military programs worldwide.

While this direct involvement of anthropologists with military missions, and their often clear ideological and economic alignment, has led to major controversies in academia and beyond. The cynical reason that features so prominently in dominant anthropological discourses on popular culture and everyday politics is difficult to unmask. Similarly difficult to unmask is the very fact that the cynical anthropologist is not so different from the embedded anthropologist. Cynical reason is after all not naïveté and anthropologists who work in the service of the military industrial complex can-

not be called uninformed. They know all too well what they are doing and what the real interests are behind humanitarian missions in the name of universal principles. If these anthropologists have struggled against moral anxiety, their efforts have long been rendered meaningless in the face of a wholly altered reality. Fear of (self-)punishment and guilt are Freudian remnants that may affect our private lives, but they are irrelevant in a world where values of white Euro-America want to be defended once more in the name of exceptional power. At a particularly important and politically meaningful junction in Egypt's recent history, anthropology has chosen to side with empire rather than with the people of Egypt, for whom anthropology has no solidarity left.

From Z Magazine, *February 2012*
Volume 25, Number 2

Part 3

Expanding
An
Empire

17.

America's Death Squads

By Nicolas J.S. Davies

W HEN THE OBAMA administration took office in 2009, it was confronted with an extraordinary problem: what to do about the crimes of the previous administration, in particular its illegal global campaign of kidnapping, torture, and indefinite detention

Obama, predictably, went back on his promise to close Guantanamo where indefinite detention, unfair trials, beatings, and abuse continue unchecked

without trial of mostly innocent terrorism suspects. On taking office, President Obama announced that he would close the U.S. concentration camp at Guantanamo Bay within a year and he formally recommitted the U.S. military to legal prohibitions against torture and abuse of prisoners. But he rejected any effort to investigate his predecessor's crimes, claiming that he wanted to "look forward."

Obama, predictably, went back on his promise to close Guantanamo where indefinite detention, unfair trials, beatings, and abuse continue unchecked. Amnesty International lamented in November 2010 that the United States remains "an accountability-free zone" for war crimes. The Obama administration has not just provided "continuity" with Bush and Cheney's illegal policies, it has vastly expanded the illegal worldwide campaign of "targeted killings" or "manhunts" that were first approved by Donald Rumsfeld in 2003.

American Exceptionalism

American exceptionalism was conceived as a vision of America for the rest of the world to look up to. Instead, it has come to describe the systematic American violation of otherwise binding international laws. Today the U.S. rejects the international rule of law on basic issues. When U.S. officials say, "All options are on the table," it is well understood that they mean something quite different from, "All legal options are on the table."

Escaping international accountability has been critical to freeing U.S. military doctrine from otherwise binding legal constraints. Article 94 of the UN Charter states that, "by signing the Charter, a State Member of the United Nations undertakes to comply with any decision of the International Court of Justice in a case to which it is a party."

In 1984, the ICJ ordered the U.S. "to cease and to refrain" from its "unlawful use of force" against Nicaragua and to pay war reparations. The U.S. refused, declaring that it would no longer accept the binding jurisdiction of the court. Nicaragua asked the Security Council to enforce the judgment, but this was met with a U.S. veto. The U.S. likewise rejects the jurisdiction of the new International Criminal Court (ICC).

The doctrinal rejection of legal constraints set the stage for the systematic violations of the UN Charter and the Geneva Conventions that are essential to America's post-2001 war policy. With no fear that they will be forced to answer to impartial international courts, U.S. government legal advisers craft increasingly "bold" (meaning legally indefensible) rulings to provide cover for serious crimes, from torture to aggression to murder.

By contrast, in the UK, which is a party to both the ICJ and the ICC, the government's legal advisers warned repeatedly that invading Iraq would be a "crime of aggression" for which British officials could face prosecution. The Iraq Inquiry in London spent two years wrestling with the fact that the government ignored these warnings from its legal advisers.

A Policy of Cold-Blooded Murder

As the Obama administration took office in 2009, an Eminent Jurists Panel appointed by the International Commission of Jurists (ICJ) and chaired by Mary Robinson, the former President of Ireland, published a report on America's so-called "war on terror." It concluded that U.S. violations of international law were neither an appropriate nor an effective response to terrorism and that American leaders had confused the public by framing their counter-terrorism campaign in a "war paradigm." The panel insisted that established principles of international law "were intended to withstand crises and they provide a robust and effective framework from which to tackle terrorism."

Barack Obama has halted the macabre parade of hooded, shackled suspects in orange jumpsuits stumbling off American planes into the tropical sunshine at Guantanamo, but he has not done so by restoring the rule of law. Instead, to a great extent, he has replaced Bush's policy with a global campaign to kill a wide range of people in cold blood—terrorism suspects, resistance fighters, and anyone else added to secret lists for secret reasons.

From a uniquely American "exceptionalist" point of view, killing suspects instead of capturing them is a convenient way to avoid the embarrassment of sweeping up hundreds of mostly innocent people in an indiscriminate global dragnet and then not knowing what to do with them. The dead tell no tales. Public outrage is contained within the faraway countries where the killings take place and does not cause domestic political problems.

Without real accountability under established law, previously binding legal standards have been quickly dispensed with. U.S. officials have been formally prohibited from conducting assassinations since 1976 under President Ford's executive order 11905. U.S. legal advisers have subverted this prohibition by ruling that "targeted killings" are not assassinations, but acts of self-defense. This ignores established rules of international law, in this case the Caroline principle formulated by U.S. Secretary of State Daniel Webster in 1841 and now universally accepted, which limits the right of cross-border self-defense to a proportionate response to an imminent threat.

The U.S. forces committing these cold-blooded murders systematically count most of the innocent civilians they kill as "false positives." When U.S. forces in Afghanistan killed Zabet Amanullah in a case of mistaken identity, they also killed nine campaign staff who worked for his nephew, a candidate for the Afghan parliament, based only on "guilt by proximity." U.S. Special Operations officers explained to former BBC reporter Kate Clark that they operate under a general rule that proximity to a "target" is all the evidence they need to treat someone else as a target too. This helps to explain why U.S. body counts always claim more "insurgents" killed than civilians, despite illegal rules of engagement that routinely lead to excessive and indiscriminate killing.

U.S. "targeted killings" are conducted under the authority of both the CIA and U.S. Joint Special Operations Command (JSOC). The methods of killing generally fall into three categories: air strikes by planes or helicopters; air strikes by unmanned drones; and assassinations by JSOC forces on the ground.

The genesis of JSOC's assassination operations was an open-ended "execute order" written by Donald Rumsfeld in September 2003 as widespread resistance to the illegal U.S. invasion took hold in Iraq. In addition to authorizing assassinations in Iraq, Afghanistan, and Somalia under military command, Rumsfeld's order also authorized them in Algeria, Iran, Malaysia, Mali, Nigeria, Pakistan, the Philippines, Syria, and Yemen—subject to presidential approval. Whatever role the

United States is or isn't playing in the murders of Iranian scientists, Defense Secretary Panetta's sweeping statement—"That's not what the United States does"—was a disingenuous lie.

The Obama administration expanded U.S. special operations deployments from 60 countries to about 80 since it took office, but how many of these are JSOC operations that include "targeted killings" is a secret. Special Operations Command has 58,000 personnel under its command and up to 25,000 of them operate under JSOC on a flexible basis. As of June 2010, JSOC had 9,000 troops in Iraq and Afghanistan and 4,000 more deployed in other countries.

At least three units are permanently assigned to JSOC: the Army's Delta Force, the Navy's DEVGRU (formerly SEAL Team 6), and the Air Force's 24th Special Tactics Squadron. Other units that routinely operate under JSOC include the 75th Ranger Regiment and the 160th Special Operations Aviation Regiment (SOAR), known as the "Nightstalkers." The 160th SOAR operates attack and transport helicopters to support Special Forces operations. A "Special Police Transition Team" from the 160th, SOAR was also assigned to the Iraqi Interior Ministry's Wolf Brigade as it detained, tortured, and murdered thousands of civilians in Baghdad in 2005 and 2006.

Killing The Wrong People

Seymour Hersh reported in the *New Yorker* in December 2003 that JSOC forces were being trained by Israeli assassins or Mista'aravim, in Israel and North Carolina to conduct assassination operations in Iraq. "It is bonkers, insane," a U.S. intelligence official told the *Guardian*, "Here we are—we're already being compared to Sharon in the Arab world and we've just confirmed it by bringing in the Israelis and setting up assassination teams." Other officials explained that the targets of the campaign would not be limited to actual resistance fighters, but would include much of the Iraqi middle class, who they believed were supporting and funding the Iraqi Resistance. "The Sunni population is paying no price for the support it is giving to the terrorists," a U.S. officer told *Newsweek*. "From their point of view, it is cost-free. We have to change that equation."

The American death squads in Iraq were widely credited with a critical role in the so-called "surge" or escalation of the war in 2007. A retired U.S. officer told PBS's "Frontline" that they had become "so good at using electronic means of identifying, tracking, and finding" targets that they had created an "industrial strength counterterrorism killing machine." The "killing" part is true, but JSOC's "social network analysis" is a crude way to compile target lists based on numbers retrieved from captured cell-phones, with no effort to corroborate the data with real-world "human intelligence" as legitimate intelligence operations would require.

Two senior commanders made the extraordinary admission to Dana Priest of the *Washington Post* that JSOC raids have a less than 50 percent record of targeting the right person or house. The systematic failure to positively confirm the identities of the targets—who are mostly civilians not engaged in military operations at the time they are killed—makes the assassination campaign a very serious war crime, arguably even a crime against humanity, as it expands to kill more and more people in a growing number of countries.

Under President Obama, the number of night raids in Afghanistan expanded from 20 raids per month in May 2009 to over 1,000 per month by April 2011, using "social network analysis" of cell-phones captured in previous raids or confiscated in prisons to create ever-expanding target lists. Gareth Porter of Inter Press Service reviewed the records of 4,100 people captured in night raids in Afghanistan during a 6-month period in 2010 and

2011. He found that 86 percent were released immediately or on the first review of the evidence against them. U.S. officials only had real evidence against 14 percent of their prisoners. The same methods are used to generate target lists for "kill" as for "capture" operations. So were 86 percent of the people killed in night raids innocent as well?

The UN reported that only 80 civilians were killed in Afghanistan in "search and seizure" operations in 2010, along with about 2,000 so-called "insurgents." But the 80 civilian deaths were the result of only 13 incidents the UN had fully investigated, while 60 more incidents were still waiting investigation. Nader Nadery, of the Afghanistan Independent Human Rights Commission, estimated that the UN would eventually revise its count to about 420 civilian deaths if and when it resolved this backlog of cases.

But this would still be a low estimate of civilian deaths in night raids. The UN has no access to the resistance-held areas where most night raids occur, so it receives no reports at all from those areas. Even a complete analysis of all the incidents reported to the UN would yield only a fraction of the actual number of civilians killed. With at least 50 percent of raids targeting the wrong person or house, it is safe to say that more than half the 2,000 Afghans killed in night raids in 2010 were probably innocent civilians and that the escalation of the campaign in 2011 probably led to an even higher pro-portion of "false positives."

Indiscriminate Massacre

When assassinations are conducted by air strikes, they are even more likely to kill innocent people. In the case of Zabet Amanullah, he was targeted based entirely on "social network analysis" of cell-phone records, which misidentified him as Muhammad Amin, the Taliban shadow governor of Takhar province. U.S. officials thought that Amin was using "Amanullah" as an alias, but they didn't even bother to find out whether a real person called Zabet Amanullah existed. This would have been quite easy, as Amanullah was a commander who quit the Taliban in 2001 and became a well-known human rights activist in Kabul.

But "social network analysis" does not include asking people questions in the real world. If your cell-phone records match certain criteria, you are condemned to death, along with anyone else who is "guilty by proximity."

William Arkin was given rare access to the U.S. Combined Air and Space Operations Center in Qatar and was allowed to watch an air strike that targeted an alleged resistance leader named Baz Mohammed Faizan in Afghanistan. A team in Qatar went to some lengths to order up a strike by two A-10 Warthog warplanes with 500 pound bombs from Bagram Airbase. Officials explained that the 1,000 pound bomb on a nearby plane was too big and would kill too many civilians, while the 150 pound Hellfire missiles on the Predator drone that had been tracking Faizan could easily miss—so much for "precision" drone strikes.

The U.S. Air Force's A-10s were designed and built in the 1970s and early 1980s for use against Soviet tanks. Their main weapon is a cannon made by General Electric that fires armor-piercing shells at a rate of 65 per second. Watching the A-10s in action on TV monitors in Qatar, Arkin saw one of them drop its bomb and then come around for a second pass and strafe the whole area with a torrent of fire from its tank-busting cannon.

Arkin expressed shock that this "precision" strike had suddenly turned into an indiscriminate massacre. A U.S. official quickly told him that the strafing "was not unauthorized" and that, once an attack is under way, JSOC air controllers on the ground take full control of the operation. Arkin had discovered a dirty little secret of JSOC operations. All the precautions taken by analysts, JAG officers, and senior officials to use proportionate force in

When assassinations are conducted by air strikes, they are even more likely to kill innocent people. In the case of Zabet Amanullah, he was targeted based entirely on "social network analysis" of cell-phone records, which misidentified him as Muhammad Amin, the Taliban shadow governor of Takhar province.

planning operations no longer apply once the operations are under way.

Despite this excessive and indiscriminate use of force, an officer later showed Arkin a memo from the CIA, which concluded that Faizan had walked away alive at the end of the attack. Apparently he did not tell Arkin how many other people it had killed and wounded or how many of them were innocent civilians.

License To Kill

But the most indiscriminate weapon used in U.S. assassinations is the drone. In 10 years, Predator and Reaper drone operations have mushroomed from an experimental program at Nellis Air Force Base in Las Vegas and a few take-off sites in Iraq and Afghanistan to 60 locations around the United States and the world where hundreds of missile- and bomb-laden drones are operated by CIA, U.S. Air Force, and Air National Guard personnel and "contractors."

The Obama administration has expanded the CIA's drone campaign in Pakistan from 42 strikes under Bush to 241 strikes since 2009. They have killed between 1,700 and 2,700 people, of whom at least 90 percent were civilians, according to Pakistani journalists and human rights groups. U.S. claims of fewer civilian deaths are undoubtedly tainted by "false positives."

On June 2, 2010, the UN Special Rapporteur for Extrajudicial Executions, Philip

Alston, issued this diplomatic but damning statement: "Targeted killings pose a rapidly growing challenge to the international rule of law, as they are increasingly used in circumstances which violate the relevant rules of international law.... The most prolific user of targeted killings today is the United States, which primarily uses drones for attacks...this strongly asserted but ill-defined license to kill without accountability is not an entitlement which the United States or other states can have without doing grave damage to the rules designed to protect the right to life and prevent extra-judicial executions...

"...the United States has put forward a novel theory that there is a 'law of 9/11' that enables it to legally use force in the territory of other states as part of its inherent right to self-defense on the basis that it is in an armed conflict with al-Qaeda, the Taliban and 'associated forces,' although the latter group is fluid and undefined. This expansive and open-ended interpretation of the right to self-defense goes a long way towards destroying the prohibition on the use of armed force contained in the UN Charter."

> *Under cover of a UN mandate to protect civilians, NATO besieged, starved, bombed, and shelled Sirte and Bani Walid for over a month, leaving them and other towns in ruins. NATO's war killed far more Libyans in 8 months than Colonel Gaddafi had in 42 years*

But drones fulfill important political objectives for U.S. policymakers. U.S. war policy since 1945 has been driven by a never-ending quest to inflict death and destruction in other countries without a political backlash from large numbers of American casualties. Foreign casualties, even of innocent civilians, are politically less damaging than even small numbers of U.S. casualties.

Illegal U.S. rules of engagement reflect these priorities, authorizing excessive and indiscriminate use of force in the interest of "force protection." As a result, the 6,400 U.S. deaths in Iraq and Afghanistan are hardly one-tenth the number of Americans lost in Vietnam, even though more than a million Iraqis and Afghans have been killed. In the bloody calculus of American politics, the reduced American death toll has minimized the political cost of war and made it a safer option for policymakers. The use of unmanned drones provides an even more politically attractive way to wage war, with no immediate danger of American casualties. Drone manufacturers currently have orders for another 730 armed drones.

A Revised U.S. War Policy

The U.S. "targeted killing" campaign and NATO's campaign in Libya are two tracks of a revised U.S. war policy following its failed occupations of Afghanistan and Iraq. In Libya, NATO conducted 9,700 air strikes in 8 months, the most concentrated bombing campaign anywhere since Iraq in 2003. The U.S. role was "disguised, quiet, and media-free," even though it supplied two-thirds of the NATO personnel, half the planes, nearly all the drones and cruise-missiles, and officially spent more on the war than the UK did.

Public credit was reserved for the Libyan rebels. The role of British, French, Jordanian, and Qatari Special Forces on the ground was shrouded in secrecy. When Qatari Special Forces blasted their way into Gaddafi's compound in Tripoli, the world saw only jubilant Libyans. Under cover of a UN mandate to protect civilians, NATO besieged, starved, bombed, and shelled Sirte and Bani Walid for over a month, leaving them and other towns in ruins. NATO's war killed far more Libyans in 8 months than Colonel Gaddafi had in 42 years. The new government estimates that 25,000 people were killed in the war. Other estimates run as high as 50,000. This is a far higher death toll than in all the other Arab Spring revolutions combined, a good reason for people everywhere to choose non-violent revolution over U.S. or NATO intervention if they have any choice in the matter. The Obama administration conducted the entire war without authorization from Congress in open violation of U.S. law.

The Obama administration bases its aggressive and global use of force on the Authorization for the Use of Military Force (AUMF) passed by Congress in 2001. The AUMF gave the president the authority to use "all necessary and appropriate force against those nations, organizations, or persons" who he determined to have "planned, authorized, committed, or aided" the terrorist crimes of September 11, 2001 in the U.S.

As John Bellinger, the Bush administration's State Department Legal Adviser, explained to the *Washington Post* in June 2010, most of the people the Obama administration is targeting had nothing to do with the 9/11 crimes, so Obama had no authority under U.S. law for most of these operations.

Because President Obama did not act firmly to stop his government's violations of U.S. and international law and to hold U.S. officials accountable, America's descent into systematic international crime has continued on his watch, leading to new war crimes for which he and his subordinates are criminally accountable. Far from a "shining city on a hill," American exceptionalism has led to a graveyard in a dark valley. Americans must accept the same international laws, treaties, and standards of accountability as our "unexceptional" neighbors if we are ever to break the death spiral of American neo-imperialism and begin the conversion to a sustainable and peaceful society.

From Z Magazine, *March 2012*
Volume 25, Number 3

18

The Manufactured Threat

By M.L. Rantala

THE BUSH ADMINISTRATION has floated several reasons for going to war with Saddam Hussein. The one that seems to have the most currency is that we need to stop Saddam before he strikes us or someone else. Saddam has been so thoroughly demonized by American politicians, the media, and your local coffee vendor that nearly any claim

The CIA's most recent assessment of Iraq, parts of which were declassified in October, is striking for its puny, yet highly indignant account of a slender arsenal. But it does tell us two vitally important things. First, Iraq does not have a nuclear weapon and, unless it gets whopping big help from someone, won't have one for years.

about him is accepted by a large number of people without burdening themselves with issues of proof. Is there evidence that Saddam Hussein has and will use weapons of mass destruction (WMDs) against others anytime in the near future?

The CIA's most recent assessment of Iraq, parts of which were declassified in October, is striking for its puny, yet highly indignant account of a slender arsenal ("Iraq's Weapons of Mass Destruction Programs," CIA: October 2002). But it does tell us two vitally important things. First, Iraq does not have a nuclear weapon and, unless it gets whopping big help from someone, won't have one for years. Second, although we have no idea what chemical and biological stockpiles exist in Iraq, the CIA tells us there are no missiles that come even close to being able to deliver such weapons to the U.S. There is no imminent danger or grave risk to any American apartment or farmhouse, grocery store or baseball diamond from putative Iraqi weapons, and this according to the Administration's main source of information about Iraq.

The Blair Dossier, issued to rally the world behind an immediate attack on Iraq, is interesting for its recounting of Iraq's repeated failure to make significant progress in producing nuclear weapons. Iraq has been pursuing nuclear weapons since the 1950s, receiving considerable assistance from the Soviet Union beginning in 1959. In the 1980s Iraq commenced an electromagnetic isotope separation (EMIS) program, but could never get the technology to work and abandoned it by 1991. In August 1990, Iraq initiated a crash program to build a single nuclear weapon within a year, contemplating rapid development of a small 50 ma-

> *The Blair Dossier, issued to rally the world behind an immediate attack on Iraq, is interesting for its recounting of Iraq's repeated failure to make significant progress in producing nuclear weapons*

chine gas centrifuge cascade to produce weapons-grade highly enriched uranium using fuel from their Soviet research reactor, but the program had evinced little success by the time of the Gulf War ("Iraq's Weapons of Mass Destruction: The Assessment of the British Government").

So we know that Iraq has repeatedly tried and failed to produce a nuclear weapon. We know that it had been at it for nearly four decades at the time the UN weapons inspectors went and dismantled it all. It's true that a soufflé requires know-how as much as eggs and a hot oven. And the one thing the UN inspectors could not destroy was the human capital invested in Iraq's nuclear program. But is that enough to make the nuclear threat credible? We are asked to believe that unsuccessful work conducted over 40 years and with help from the Soviet Union and others might now be successfully conducted in some 46 months when Iraq's resources are monumentally constrained and every possible weapon compo-

nent or tool—from test tube to centrifuge rotor—must be procured covertly with most developed nations refusing to offer the least assistance. What about chemical and biological weapons? What both the CIA Assessment and the Blair Dossier make clear is that no one knows what Iraq has. (What they don't make clear is just how much of it, in the 1970s and 1980s, came from Anglo-American sources. This would be useful, as we could gauge a lot from it.)

These government briefs go to great lengths to list chemical and biological stocks that could possibly have remained after the UN inspections ended in 1998, yet remarkably the Blair Dossier, an unabashed manifesto for war, doesn't hide how speculative a proposition this is. It quotes a report prepared by Richard Butler, the last head of the UN weapons inspectors and a man incapable of hiding his rabid anti-Iraq sentiments. Butler's UN Security Council brief importantly, even surprisingly, acknowledges, "Iraq undertook extensive, unilateral and secret destruction of large quantities of proscribed weapons and items." Then, the British government concluded, "Without U.N. weapons inspectors, it is very difficult therefore to be sure about the true nature of many of Iraq's facilities."

The problem when the UN inspectors were there, and the problem now, is that some people will forego any rules of honest proof: if we find the weapons, then they exist; and if we don't find the weapons, they exist, too, but are hidden.

Sure, Iraq has some (and perhaps very few) chemical and biological weapons. But what Iraq lacks, and both the CIA Assessment and the Blair Dossier go into this in great detail, is the means of propelling these poisons any great distance outside of Iraq. The British government maintains that Saddam has the delivery mechanisms to threaten only "Cyprus, Eastern Turkey, Tehran, and Israel" and that this is not bound to change anytime soon as the "development of new longer-range missiles is likely to be a slow process" because various restrictions on Iraq have been very successful, including those on the use of foreign experts, the conduct of test flights in ranges greater than 150 km, and the acquisition of guidance and control technology.

Some people fear an attack not on the U.S., but on Israel. But whatever actual weapons Saddam has, if he can't deliver them, they mean little. According to the Blair Dossier, he has no more than 20 al-Hussein (SCUD) missiles (probably far fewer), that are limited in range to 650 km. UN agreements limit Iraq to missiles that cannot reach beyond 150 km. Notably, there is no evidence in the Blair Dossier or the CIA assessment of any activity since 1998 on the part of the Iraqi government to test a missile that can travel farther than 150 km. This is hardly surprising. Such activity is easily monitored by American, British, and Israeli intelligence.

This means that whatever chemical or biological weapons we may guess or insist he possesses can't effectively be delivered very far. This also limits the cursedness of the mobile units purported to contain biological weapons, so often invoked as uninspectable. If Saddam can't deliver his weapons, they are not much threat outside his own country or those contiguous to Iraq.

The idea that chemical or biological weapons might be indiscriminately scattered well outside of Iraq after having been transported in a suitcase or some other innocuous device by a terrorist verges on the preposterous. Iraqi borders are elaborately policed, as anyone who tries to bring shoes or foodstuffs into the country can attest. Even if the substances should find their way across the border, the technological difficulties of dispersing the agent effectively are immense. U.S. experi-

menters, who have far more weapons of mass destruction at their fingertips, as well as the resources to hone their lethal delivery and effects, have worked for decades to create a truly effective dispersal mechanism and failed.

Dead Man Bombing

Although the two governments most raucously calling for war have provided nothing in the way of proof of a grave and imminent threat from Saddam Hussein, let's assume that things are worse than the U.S. and UK have outlined. Assume numerous nasty

The idea that chemical or biological weapons might be indiscriminately scattered well outside of Iraq after having been transported in a suitcase or some other innocuous device by a terrorist verges on the preposterous. Iraqi borders are elaborately policed, as anyone who tries to bring shoes or foodstuffs into the country can attest.

weapons poised for an attack. Is this a valid justification for going to war with Iraq? Bush maintains that a regime change in Iraq is necessary because Saddam might unleash his weapons. In a speech in Cincinnati, the president invoked the specter of an Iraqi-generated mushroom cloud and, demonstrating that he doesn't understand the effective use of metaphor, described this as a smoking gun.

The CIA's assessment is quite different. Recently, George Tenet declassified some material concerning Iraq after pressure from the Senate Intelligence Committee. In his letter of October 7, 2002 to Senator Bob Graham, Tenet wrote: "Baghdad for now appears to be drawing a line short of conducting terrorist attacks with conventional or C.B.W. (chemical and biological weapons) against the United States.

"Should Saddam conclude that a U.S.-led attack could no longer be deterred, he probably would become much less constrained in adopting terrorist actions. Such terrorism might involve conventional means, as with Iraq's unsuccessful attempt at a terrorist offensive in 1991, or C.B.W.

"Saddam might decide that the extreme step of assisting Islamist terrorists in conducting a W.M.D. attack against the United States would be his last chance to exact vengeance by taking a large number of victims with him" (Letter dated October 7, 2002 to Senator Bob Graham, Democrat of Florida and Chairman of the Intelligence Committee, by George J. Tenet, Director of Central Intelligence, about decisions to declassify material related to the debate about Iraq).

There was also a closed hearing and Tenet declassified a portion of testimony offered: "Senator Carl Levin, Democrat of Michigan: ...[If Saddam] did not feel threatened, is it likely that he would initiate an attack using a weapon of mass destruction?

"Senior Intelligence Witness: My judgment would be that the probability of him initiating an attack—let me put a time frame on it—in the foreseeable future, given the conditions we understand now, the likelihood I think would be low.

"Senator Levin: But what about his use of weapons of mass destruction? If we initiate an attack and he thought he was in extremis or otherwise, what's the likelihood in response to our attack that he would use chemical or biological weapons?

"Senior Intelligence Witness: Pretty high, in my view" (Tenet letter, October 7, 2002).

The Blair Dossier doesn't offer the discordance with government policy displayed in the differences between Bush and Tenet. But it also does not make a case that Saddam is itching to use his weapons. Nor does the Blair government so grandiosely assume that it might be in Saddam's sights when the weapons are prepped for use (although there is one patriotic reference to UK Sovereign Base Areas in Cyprus that are within Iraqi range). The British government's psychologizing over Saddam maintains that he has a fetish for toxic weapons in order to strike fear in his neighbors: "... chemical and biological weapons play an important role in Iraqi military thinking: intelligence shows that Saddam attaches great importance to the possession of chemical and biological weapons which he regards as being the basis for Iraqi regional power. He believes that respect for Iraq rests on its possession of these weapons and the missiles capable of delivering them."

There's a lot that's interesting in this assessment, including the fact that the British maintain that chemical and biological weapons are only in his quiver to make others in the region shiver. But even more interestingly, the British never show that he's likely to use them. Their tacit conclusion is that Saddam sees the threat as more powerful than the execution. It's a reasonable assessment, since Saddam hasn't used any weapon outside of Iraq in over a decade, yet has managed to remain a source of concern and tension in the region.

Why hasn't Saddam used his weapons? Why is he unlikely to? The same reason he didn't use chemical or biological weapons against Americans in the Gulf War: he wants to stay in power. He may be a bully and a murderous tyrant, but he knows that America can crush him should it decide to. The frightening irony of the War to Stop Weapons of Mass Destruction is that if Bush prosecutes this war, then and only then do we put Saddam in a position where there is absolutely no reason for reason for him not to use everything he's got. Regime change is a euphemism for a military campaign that doesn't cease until Saddam is dead. He might decide that his place in history will be assured by hurling every last gram from the Iraqi weapons apothecary at the enemy.

Ironically, Saddam can't deploy these weapons (if they exist) to the U.S., but Bush's proposed war would put Americans conveniently within his grasp. American ground troops seem more likely at risk than Israel—often cited as in danger from Saddam—since what missiles Iraq's got are neither modern nor stealthy and Israel must surely be aware of the risks attendant on Bush's proposed war and be planning appropriate, very likely disproportionate, measures. Saddam's got nothing to lose in deploying his weapons if the United States wages an all-out attack against Iraq aimed at his destruction. He's a dead man bombing.

A Viable Alternative

The obvious policy worth pursuing with more vigor and honesty than either the U.S. or UK governments have attempted is to get the weapons inspectors back into Iraq. In a summary report to the Security Council, the Director General of the International Atomic Energy Agency (who conducted the nuclear weapons aspect of the UN inspections) wrote: "Document GOV/INF/827 reported that there were no indications that Iraq had achieved its programme objective of producing nuclear weapons nor were there indications that Iraq had produced more than a few grams of weapon-usable nuclear material or had otherwise acquired such material. It also reported that there were no indications that there remains in Iraq any physical capability for the production of weapon-usable nuclear material of any practical significance and that all weapon-usable nuclear material (research reactor fuel) has been removed from Iraq." Several other reports were similarly summarized, indicating how thoroughly the nuclear weapons program of Iraq was dismantled.

Why did the inspectors leave? Richard Butler, head of the UN inspectors in 1998, ex-

plained to the Security Council why he decided to remove all inspectors from Iraq: "On 16 December 1998, the Executive Chairman [sic] wrote to the President of the Council, confirming his previous evening's conversation with the President, during which he told the President that he had decided to remove all the Commission's personnel from Iraq. IAEA personnel also departed. This decision was taken in consultation with IAEA. The executive chair's letter noted that the prime considerations in his decision were to ensure the safety and security of the Commission's personnel and the need to act immediately" (Report of the Executive Chair on the activities of the Special Commission established by the Secretary-General pursuant to paragraph 9 (b) (i) of resolution 687 (1991), United Nations Security Council document S/1999/401, 9 April 1999, paragraph 24).

Butler acknowledges that on the very day the inspectors withdrew, the U.S. and the UK proceeded to bomb Iraq, "On 16 December

> *Butler acknowledges that on the very day the inspectors withdrew, the U.S. and the UK proceeded to bomb Iraq*

1998, military action was initiated against Iraq by the United States and the United Kingdom (S/1998/1181 and S/1998/1182)."

Even though we pulled the inspectors out, can't we send them back in? Of course we can, but the coverage of the wrangling over inspections has repeatedly failed to report one of the main reasons Baghdad prevaricates and is so distrustful of the process: United Nations Security Council Resolution 1284. Up to December 1999, Security Council Resolutions linked a successful weapons inspection and eradication program with the lifting of sanctions. But SCR 1284 made a significant change, deciding that full compliance with UN weapons inspections would lead only to a suspension, and not a lifting, of economic sanctions, and that sanctions could be re-imposed every 120 days on the wishes of any one permanent member of the Security Council (United Nations Security Council Resolution 1284, December 17, 1999).

Saddam knows that Bush and Blair want him out and believes that either one of them could use his Security Council vote to keep sanctions in place indefinitely. The Iraqis, not unreasonably, wonder whether sanctions will ever be lifted as long as Saddam remains in power. Iraqi Foreign Minister Naji Sabri asked the Security Council this very question earlier this year and received no answer.

Additionally, to be successful, weapons inspectors can't be allowed to conduct military spying. The existence of U.S. spies among the inspectors may not be universally acknowledged, but earlier this month the *New York Times* took it for granted, writing, "The reform followed the disclosure that a United States spy on the United Nations team had planted an electronic eavesdropping device in Baghdad that helped guide allied bombing in December 1998" (*New York Times,* October 2, 2002). The head of UNMOVIC (the successor to UNSCOM) is reportedly aware that the integrity of the weapon inspections system has been damaged by this spying, especially since Iraq learned that the survival of the regime was put at risk when they cooperated.

What we need is a plan that puts teeth in the inspections, preferably one that doesn't perpetuate the brutal sanctions that notably fail to punish Saddam Hussein, but that have caused enormous suffering and inexcusable deaths in the hundreds of thousands. What we don't need is for the U.S. and UK to become increasingly belligerent, leaving Saddam convinced that he must react with deadly vengeance.

When an all-stick, no-carrot policy fails to work, it is dimwitted to propose as the only alternative a much bigger stick. This is a hysterical approach, utterly devoid of any sense of proportion or justice. It urges us to rain bombs down on innocent heads in order to stop a hypothetical future attack based on flimsy evidence. We need effective weapons eradication conducted under the auspices of the UN, not a cruel unilateral policy that leaves in its wake the tragedy of unnecessary death.

From Z Magazine, *December 2002*
Volume 15, Number 12

19.

The Great Iraq Heist

By A.K. Gupta

FORGET FOR A MOMENT about quagmire, the growing heaps of U.S. and Iraqi dead, and the rebellious population. George Bush, Paul Bremer, and gang have pulled off the biggest heist in history. They and no one else own 100 billion barrels of crude oil—a windfall of at least $3 trillion —along with the entire assets and resources of Iraq.

> *Since March 2003, a series of executive orders by Bush, UN documents, and regulations and orders issued by Iraqi Proconsol Paul Bremer have put the U.S. in absolute control of the state of Iraq, its oil industry and monies, all while lifting barriers to repatriating profits*

Since March 2003, a series of executive orders by Bush, UN documents, and regulations and orders issued by Iraqi Proconsol Bremer have put the U.S. in absolute control of the state of Iraq, its oil industry and monies, all while lifting barriers to repatriating profits. In the name of reconstruction and security, the Bush administration has essentially granted itself the power to use the wealth of the Iraqi people as it sees fit. Never mind that the new "fiscal matrix" in Iraq violates international law—a fact of little concern to the White House when the war was illegal to begin with.

The largest contracts have gone to corporations like Halliburton, Bechtel, and Fluor, which are big contributors to the Republicans and now enjoy oversight of their Iraq activities by former executives who now sit in the Bush administration. Furthermore, Bush has given the corporate victors the ultimate protection: indemnifying them from liability for any and all activities related to Iraqi oil.

To top it all off, the Coalition Provisional Authority in Iraq is using money from oil sales to help pay for the counterinsurgency campaign. So not only are U.S. corporations reaping billions off the conflict in sweetheart deals with legal impunity, but Iraqis are being forced to pay for the very war being waged against them. The story begins in February 2003 when the U.S. Agency for International Development secretly asked six companies to bid on a reconstruction contract worth, at minimum, $900 million. The six—Bechtel, Fluor, Halliburton subsidiary Kellogg, Brown & Root, Louis Berger Group, Parsons, and Washington Group International—were all generous supporters of Republicans, having given them a combined $2.3 million between 1999 and 2002.

As the war was launched, Bush issued Executive Order 13290 on March 20. It mandates the confiscation of "certain property of the Government of Iraq and its agencies, instrumentalities, or controlled entities, and that all right, title, and interest in any property so confiscated should vest in the Department of the Treasury." Practically, this means the Bush administration seized $1.7 billion in Iraqi funds.

On March 24, the Army Corps of Engineers awarded a no-bid contract to Kellogg Brown & Root to fight oil fires and assess and repair Iraq's oil infrastructure. Two days after U.S. forces toppled Saddam Hussein's statue in Baghdad, the Corps mentions KBR's contract has a ceiling of $7 billion.

To pay for the war, Congress passed a $78.5 billion bill on April 14, setting aside $2.5 billion for the creation of an Iraq Relief and Reconstruction Fund.

On April 17, USAID awarded Bechtel a $680 million contract to rebuild everything in Iraq—power plants, water and sewage systems, airports, seaports, hospitals, schools, government buildings, irrigation structures, and transport links.

On May 8, one week after Bush's carrier landing that marked the end of "combat operations," UN ambassadors from the United Kingdom and the United States sent a letter to the Security Council establishing their governments' authority over Iraq. They listed among their many tasks "deterring hostilities [and] maintaining civil law and order."

The battered United Nations passed Resolution 1483 on May 22, endorsing the "specific authorities, responsibilities, and obligations" of the United States and United Kingdom as "occupying powers," and specifically citing the May 8 letter. The Resolution notes the "establishment of a Development Fund for Iraq to be held by the Central Bank of Iraq" and decides that 95 percent of "all export sales of petroleum, petroleum products, and natural gas from Iraq...shall be deposited into the Development Fund for Iraq." For start-up, the UN bequeaths the Fund with $1 billion from the Oil-for-Food program.

As for the Fund, Resolution 1483 notes the monies "shall be disbursed at the direction of the Authority," meaning Paul Bremer, who had been appointed Administrator 16 days earlier.

Bremer, for his part, is perched in Baghdad's Republican Palace issuing regulations, "instruments that define the institutions and authorities of the Coalition Provisional Authority," and Orders, "binding instructions or directives to the Iraqi people that create penal consequences or have a direct bearing on the way Iraqis are regulated."

Regulation One established Bremer's absolute authority in Iraq as CPA Administrator effective May 16, 2003. Regulation Two concerns the Development Fund. It defined the Administrator as the one who "Oversees and controls the establishment, administration and control of the Fund for and on behalf of the Iraqi people, and directs disburse- ments from the Fund."

It cited Resolution 1483 in noting, "The Development Fund for Iraq shall be used in a transparent manner to meet the humanitarian needs of the Iraqi people, for the economic reconstruction and repair of Iraq's infrastructure, for the continued disarmament of Iraq, and for the costs of Iraqi civilian administration." In direction violation of UN Resolution 1483, Bremer mandated that the Fund "shall be held in an account…in the [U.S.] Federal Reserve Bank." The United Nations had intended that the money go directly to the Central Bank of Iraq.

The order unleashed a flood of imported goods that left Iraq's worn-out manufacturers unable to compete, pushing them to the brink of insolvency

Bremer signed Regulation Three on June 15, setting up the Program Review Board. It states: "The Board shall be responsible for recommending expenditures of resources from the Development Fund for Iraq" and all the other funds provided to the CPA, such as the various monies from Iraq seized by the Bush administration and funds provided for by Congress.

On May 22, the same day UN resolution 1483 passed, Bush signed Executive Order 13303 granting blanket immunity to any U.S. corporation dealing with Iraqi oil through 2007. Researcher Jim Vallette, who stumbled across the order in the Federal Register, says it "unilaterally declares Iraqi oil to be the unassailable province of U.S. corporations.... In other words, if ExxonMobil or Chevron-Texaco touch Iraqi oil, it will be immune from legal proceedings in the United States."

On May 25, Bremer issued Order Four. After "recognizing that the assets and property of the Iraqi Baath Party constitute State assets," Bremer ordered that Baath Party assets and property "are subject to seizure by the CPA."

So in a little more than two months, the Bush administration staked claim to and received UN approval to every significant asset and resource Iraq has in the world, established sole power over how to spend Iraq's oil money, and indemnified its corporate cronies from liability. But the work had just begun. During the next few months, as the resistance heated up, Bremer fulfilled the wildest dreams of every capitalist by eliminating virtually all barriers to the flow of capital and throwing in a flat tax to boot.

The plan was actually outlined in a secret USAID document issued February 21 and later leaked to the media. Entitled, "Moving the Iraqi Economy from Recovery to Sustainable Growth," it calls for "mass privatization" of state-owned enterprises, trade liberalization, changing laws to favor the "repatriation of capital" and foreign investment in Iraq, and shifting the tax burden from business to consumers. In a move that hardly bodes well for sustainable growth, Bremer issued CPA Order 12 on June 8, which lifts "All tariffs, custom duties, import taxes, licensing fees, and similar surcharges for goods entering or leaving Iraq."

The order unleashed a flood of imported goods that left Iraq's worn-out manufacturers unable to compete, pushing them to the brink of insolvency. As for state-owned enterprises, which employed about 100,000 workers, Bremer decided it was better to pay the workers to sit around and do nothing than breed more anti-American sentiment by eliminating their jobs. Even then, in a guide for the 2004 budget, the CPA warned the enterprises that their budgets "should be prepared on the basis that the salaries of employees of SOEs will not be funded from January 1, 2004."

On June 19, the Export-Import Bank of the United States announced it is "prepared to immediately start processing applications for exports to Iraq," including "subcontractors providing goods and services to Iraq under USAID contracts." The Ex-Im Bank (as it's called) went on to explain "support may be available for transactions where…the primary source of repayment is the Development Fund for Iraq or another entity established under the auspices of the Coalition Provisional Authority."

The sole purpose of the Ex-Im Bank is to help "finance the sales of U.S. exports, primarily to developing markets, by providing guarantees, export credit insurance, and loans." Thus, in the case of Iraq, the Bank will provide credit for purchases for goods and services authorized by Bremer—including all of Bechtel and Halliburton's contracts.

This is amplified by CPA Order 20 from July 17, establishing the Trade Bank of Iraq. Its purpose was to provide "financial and related services to facilitate the importation and exportation of goods and services to and from Iraq." Money to support the trade bank comes from Iraq's oil money, yet another instance of public monies being used unaccountably for private profit.

In the same order, Bremer bestowed upon himself the power to "promulgate additional regulations, orders, memoranda, or other doc-

Precisely what were Paul Bremer and the Coalition Provisional Authority doing with all the money they'd been allocated? That's a $160 billion question.

umentation that further define the purpose of the DFI." This is legalese for Bremer saying he can do whatever he wants with the fund.

Bush issued Executive Order 13315 on August 28, deeming "that it is in the interest of the United States to confiscate certain additional property of the former Iraqi regime, certain senior officials of the former regime, immediate family members of those officials, and controlled entities." Essentially this allows the Bush administration to nab whatever Iraqi money it hasn't already laid its hands on.

Bremer gave corporations another gift in Order 37 by instituting a flat tax. He decreed on September 15, "The highest individual and corporate income tax rates for 2004 and subse-

quent years shall not exceed 15 percent." This also implies that the tax could be set much lower as 15 percent is just the ceiling.

On September 19, Bremer issued Order 39 on Foreign Investment. Bremer wrote, "This Order replaces all existing foreign investment law." All sectors of the economy apart from oil and gas are opened to foreigners "on terms no less favorable than those applicable to an Iraqi investor."

Iraq went from having one of the most closed economies in the world to one of the most open. A press release, dated September 21 from Iraqi Minister of Finance Kamel al-Gailani, enthusiastically lists among the law's new provisions the "full and immediate remittance of profits, dividends, interest, and royalties."

The neoliberal wish list was now complete. Even as U.S. forces struggled to establish a security matrix to contain the growing Iraqi insurgency, Bush and Bremer put in place a fiscal matrix to extract Iraq's enormous riches unhindered.

Precisely what were Paul Bremer and the Coalition Provisional Authority doing with all the money they'd been allocated? That's a $160 billion question. Congress appropriated around $150 billion for the war and reconstruction in Iraq. Of that, the CPA received some $3 billion in two separate funds—the Relief and Reconstruction Fund and a Natural Resource Fund. Another $20 billion is on the way for 2004.

On its website, the CPA has released bits of information on expenditures (and even less on how decisions were made). This lack of transparency led to widespread criticism. In a scathing report dated October 23, British NGO Christian Aid charged, "The billions of dollars of oil money that has already been transferred to the U.S.-controlled Coalition Provisional Authority has effectively disappeared into a financial black hole."

The CPA has so far received $5 billion in Iraqi money and is expected to add another $4 billion by the end of the year. Bremer released a budget on July 7 for July to December 2003 that called for $6.1 billion in expenditures and forecasted a $2.2 billion deficit. By October, the deficit was up to $3 billion due to the shortfall in oil revenues from resistance attacks. But only $2.6 billion of the budget will be channeled through the Iraqi ministries.

The budget lumps together the U.S. and Iraqi funds as revenue sources. The CPA also subtracts out $1.2 billion for prior expenditures without ever explaining what they were. It mentions in a footnote that some $900 million will be funded off line. All told, $5.5 billion remains unaccounted for.

Nonetheless, revealing information can be gleaned from official documents and media reports. An examination of expenditures reveals Bremer is lavish to foreign contractors while miserly to Iraqis. Since coming under fire, the CPA has released some data on what it's doing with Iraq's oil money, but it has refused to establish proper auditing oversight as mandated in UN Resolution 1483, so it's still unknown how decisions are being made.

> $120 million was spent on a new Iraqi currency, despite the fact that Iraq has a currency press. This decision is typical of the CPA process. Rather than repair the dilapidated and looted Baghdad mint so the country can retain valuable infrastructure and jobs, the job is outsourced to British security company De La Rue, which prints the currency of 125 nations. It also happens to be one of the largest owners of electronic voting machines in the United States and is linked to the Carlyle Group, which is thick with former officials from the Reagan and first Bush administration.

> $105 million has been given to U.S. military commanders under the "Commanders Emergency Response Program." Officially, the program is part of the "reconstruction" effort, but it's being used as an integral component in the guerrilla war. A commander in the volatile town of Ramadi says "Contracts are our No. 1 method of control." Lt. Col. Hector Mirabile explained to *Newsweek* that after a resistance attack, he'll pressure local leaders to provide information or he'll reduce their contracts. The commander of the 101st Airborne, echoes this sentiment, saying, "Money is the most powerful ammunition we have." But numerous criticisms are being raised. For one there is little oversight and most of the contracts are no-bid.

> Second, few of the military commanders have the technical skills to evaluate bids.

> Third, it blurs the line between combat and humanitarian aid, which many NGOs say put aid organizations at greater risk of attack—something that has been devastatingly true in Iraq. Most troubling, it seems U.S. forces are using Iraqis' own money to pressure them into collaborating with the occupation.

> $51 million is approved for a program called Toward a Cleaner & Brighter Iraq —a public works project to employ 300,000 people at $3 a day to clean streets and haul away debris. The money goes to local subcontractors, however, who skim $1 off the top and fire those workers who complain.

> $51 million is approved to ship the new currency to and distribute it within Iraq. It's unclear why so much money is needed to distribute the bills to 250 "centers," mainly banks. Even though the media report heavily armed U.S. troops guarding the exchanges, other security guards are also present delivering the bills. It turns out millions are being spent on foreign mercenaries, many of them former British and American soldiers, to guard the money.

> The foreign guns in Iraq cost up to $1,500 a day whereas Iraqi forces being trained by the U.S. receive as little as $5 a day. Even the $51 million is not enough; CPA officials

approved another $9 million on October 21 to cover "additional transportation and support costs." (Adding insult to irony, CPA officials decided on October 28 to use Iraq's oil fund to pay the cost of shipping Iraq's money back to Iraq after having deposited the oil money in the Federal Reserve Bank of New York—in violation of UN Resolution 1483.)

> $2.4 million has been set aside for new Kalishnakovs. U.S. forces have seized huge caches of assault rifles, including tens of thousands of new AK-47s in Tikrit alone, according to a report in the *LA Times*. But the CPA decided to purchase 40,000 rifles anyway. It's suspected that the winner is a Polish company as a way to reward Poland for leading a multinational division in Iraq.

> $250 million a month is allocated to import fuels into oil-rich Iraq. The failure of the CPA to reconstruct Iraq has led to fuel shortages—gasoline, diesel, and cooking gas. Congressperson Henry Waxman accused Halliburton of price gouging for charging up to $2.62 a gallon, whereas Iraqis pay less than $.15 a gallon for the same gas.

> $23 million has been budgeted to rebuild a cement factory. Instead, Iraqis did it for barely 1 percent of the cost, about $250,000. The CPA also budgeted more than $1 million to rebuild another cement factory that was fixed by Iraqis for just $80,000. (The interest in cement is for huge blast barriers to ring occupation facilities.)

It's estimated there are 20,000 private contractors in Iraq supporting the occupation, including thousands of former Special Forces soldiers. Some are guarding Baghdad Airport under a $17 million contract. Others from the British mercenary company Erinys are training members of the Facilities Protection Services to protect oil pipelines under a $45 million Contract. The biggest mercenary contract was landed by DynCorp, worth $480 million for training a new police force. Even the moribund Iraqi Governing Council was outraged when it was revealed that training will occur in Jordan, ensuring Iraq receives no economic benefits from the funds. Huge sums of money are also being spent to equip new Iraqi militias:

> $8 million was approved just for emergency equipment for the new border patrol by the CPA on October 18. In the 2003 budget $81 million was allocated for "Security equipment for operating new prisons." This doesn't include tens of millions in "life support" or recruiting costs for the militias as well as millions for the repair and reconstruction of prison facilities, one of the few boom industries in the new Iraq.

> $90 million has been set aside for police equipment, including millions for 9mm Glocks. Yet the months-long process in shipping and distributing goods in Iraq means that many Iraqi police remain unarmed even as the country is awash with weapons.

> $12 million was allotted to purchase 10,000 police radios at a princely $1,200 per unit approved by the CPA on October 11.

As for projects that might truly benefit Iraqis, the allocations are peanuts in many cases, such as $118,200 for housing and construction in Basrah; $3,500 to pay the stipends for a Baghdad theater festival; and $400,000 for the Ministry of Youth and Sports.

What makes Iraqis especially indignant is that theirs is a nation of engineers and scientists who are left to watch as the billions in reconstruction funds go outside their country. During Iraq's heyday in the 1970s, Iraqis were known as the Germans of the Middle East for their technical prowess.

Bechtel, for example, has an omnibus contract for reconstruction, but has only provided jobs for 40,000 Iraqis through subcontractors. This doesn't even make the barest dent in the 70 percent unemployment rate, which has left about 5 million Iraqis unemployed. Rather than rebuild Iraq's infrastructure so it can be independent (and likely an economic powerhouse in the region), the Bush plan is to sell Iraq's assets off like a fire sale.

Iraqis can see that their country is being divided among the victors and that the only reconstruction taking place is projects that serve U.S. security interests. That's what's fueling the resistance, not Saddam loyalists or tribal codes of honor.

From Z Magazine, *January 2004*
Volume 17, Number 1

20.

The Global War on Tribes

By Zoltan Grossman

THE SO-CALLED GLOBAL War on Terror is quickly growing outside the borders of Iraq and Afghanistan into new battle-grounds in Pakistan, Yemen, Somalia, and beyond. The Pentagon is increasing missile and gunship attacks, Special Forces raids, and proxy invasions—all in the name of combating

> *Modern counterinsurgency doctrine views tribal regions as festering cauldrons of lawlessness and "breeding grounds" for terrorism, unless the tribes themselves are turned against the West's enemies*

"Islamist terrorism." Yet within all five countries, the main targets of the wars are predominantly "tribal regions" and the old frontier language of Indian fighting is becoming the lexicon of 21st-century counterinsurgency. The Global War on Terror is fast morphing into a Global War on Tribes.

Local areas where tribes are the dominant form of social organization, where tribal identities often trump state, ethnic, and even religious identities, are identified as tribal areas. Tribal peoples' traditional societies are based on a common culture, dialect, and kinship ties (through single or multiple clans). Nearly all tribal communities in the Middle East and Central Asia have been Islamicized or Christianized, but still retain their ancient social bonds.

Modern counterinsurgency doctrine views tribal regions as festering cauldrons of lawlessness and "breeding grounds" for terrorism, unless the tribes themselves are turned against the West's enemies. The *London Times* (1/5/10), for example, asserts that Yemen's "mountainous terrain, poverty and lawless tribal society make it...a close match for Afghanistan as a new terrorist haven." This threatening view of tribal regions is, of course, as old as European colonialism.

Tribes and Ethnic Nations

Tribes are distinct from ethnic groups. Ethnic group identity is based largely on language, such as Pashtun, Kurdish, Somali, Tajik, and so on. Many ethnic groups also assert a territorial nationhood, whether or not they have their own independent state. Tribal group identity is based on smaller and older regional clans and dialects, such as Zubaydi and Jibbur (Iraq), Durrani and Ghilzai (Afghanistan), Wazir and Mehsud (Pakistan), Wahidi and Zaydi (Yemen), and Darod and Hawiye (Somalia). These internal divisions are familiar to anyone who has studied ethnic nationhood. The Lakota Nation, for example, contains seven bands, such as the Oglala, Hunkpapa, and Sicangu. In most other countries, these "bands" would be termed tribes and the Lakota Nation would not be called a tribe.

Tribes can be viewed as the building blocks for ethnic nations, but in many countries the cement has never really dried. (In Europe, different local dialect regions were only recently absorbed into modern states, as Eugèn Weber demonstrates in his *Peasants into Frenchmen).* Tribal regions in the Middle East and Central Asia function as a layer below ethnic and religious territories, which in turn function as a layer below modern states and their 19th century colonial boundaries. Contemporary armed conflicts in the region can be best understood not as struggles between political ideologies, but between these different layers of collective identity.

Western society tends to portray tribes as primitive, backward people and views "tribalism" as ignorant villagers acting brutally in their narrow self-interest. Colonial authorities often diminish the status of ethnic nations by defining them as "tribes," and employ divide-and-conquer strategies to pit them against each other. Yet, in some regions, a local tribal identity may be more inclusive of human differences than larger-scale ethnic or religious identities. For example, some Iraqi tribes include both Sunni and Shi'a Muslims and help to transcend the tense sectarian divide. Within some tribes around the world, more than one language or dialect may be spoken. Tribal identities and boundaries are not simply fixed in the past—they can be fluid and dynamic.

AFGHANISTAN. In southern and eastern Afghanistan, Pashtun tribes have existed for millennia and have only nominal loyalty to the modern state. Because Pashtun tribes straddle the colonial "Durand Line" boundary between Afghanistan and Pakistan, they do not recognize the authority of either country and exhibit their traditional hospitality to Taliban insurgents. Although tribal stature has been weakened somewhat by Soviet occupation, civil war, and pan-Islamic ideologies, the NATO occupation has—perhaps inadvertently—resurrected a role for some tribal leaders. The U.S. has been paying and arming them to turn against the Taliban, with only limited success.

The *New York Times* (1/29/10) reports that "American civilian and military leaders are turning to some of these tribes as potentially their best hope for success.... Led by councils of elders, tribes provided their members with protection, financial support, a means to resolve disputes.... Successfully turning Pashtun tribes against the Taliban...could deliver a serious blow to the insurgency." The Council on Foreign Relations report, "A Tribal Strategy for Afghanistan" (11/7/08), admits that "Ahmed Rashid, a Pakistani journalist...predicted that arming Pashtun militias in the south would renew tribal rivalries that had been dormant for years; some analysts believe that has happened."

PAKISTAN. In northwestern Pakistan, U.S. drones and Special Forces raids have attacked insurgents in the Pashto-speaking North-West Frontier Province (recently renamed Khyber

Pukhtoonkhwa) and the Federally Adminis-tered Tribal Areas, particularly in Waziristan. President Bush evoked American frontier im-agery when he stated in the *New York Times* (2/18/07), "Taliban and Al Qaeda figures do hide in remote regions of Pakistan. This is wild country; this is wilder than the Wild West."

The U.S. media consistently refers to Pakistan's Northwest as a "lawless" tribal region. In its article "Waziri-stan: The Last Frontier," the *Econo-mist* (12/30/09) clarified that, "The tribes are mostly free to decide…matters among them-selves, which they do, remarkably harmoniously, through jirgas and riwaj—tribal customary law. In Waziristan, as in most of the tribal areas, there is no written land register. Nor, until 2001, was there much crime. 'The tribal area was law-less only in the sense that there are no laws. But they have a certain way of going about things there,' says Major Geoffrey Langlands, a British colonial officer who stayed on."

IRAQ. In central Iraq, tribal traditions and ter-ritories are somewhat more critical to Sunni Arabs than to religious Shi'a Arabs in the south or ethnonationalist Kurds in the north. Tribal sheiks serve as community leaders, me-diators, intermediaries, and regional power-players. Their support has become critical to both insurgent and occupation force. The British and Saddam Hussein tried to exercise control over tribes (and larger tribal confeder-ations)—and also attempted to curry their fa-vor—but ended up alienating them from state power.

An article in *Military Review* (9/10/07) re-ports that for U.S. operations in Iraq, "Tribal engagement has played a particularly promi-nent role…. This reflects the enduring strength of the tribes in many of Iraq's rural areas and some of its urban neighborhoods. Tribal engagement has been key to recent ef-forts to drive a wedge between tribally-based Sunni Arab insurgents and al-Qaeda in Iraq in Anbar province and elsewhere." This Sunni "awakening" did more to weaken al-Qaeda than the U.S. "surge," but now it appears the tribes are dissatisfied with the weak support shown by Baghdad and Washington.

> *The British and Saddam Hussein tried to exercise control over tribes (and larger tribal confederations)—and also attempted to curry their favor—but ended up alienating them from state power*

YEMEN. In southern Yemen, the U.S. has launched missile attacks against what it de-scribes as al-Qaeda targets, and assists, Ye-meni military raids against separatist rebels in the tribal region. As in central Iraq, instead of the tribes giving haven to Islamist "terrorists," their sense of independence may end up be-ing directed against both the Pentagon and al-Qaeda.

In the Carnegie Endowment for Interna-tional Peace report, "What Comes Next in Yemen?" Sarah Phillips explains, "al-Qaeda operatives have found safe haven in some of Yemen's tribal regions, but their goal of estab-lishing an international caliphate conflicts with many local political realities, potentially limit-ing this hospitality. Tribal society in Yemen is regulated by complex rules that bind its mem-bers to one another. Much of Yemen's pe-riphery is without effective formal, state-ad-ministered governance, but this does not mean that these regions are ungoverned—or there for the taking, particularly by outsiders to the area."

SOMALIA. In southern Somalia, virtually all Somalis hold the same customs, speak the same language, and practice the same reli-gion. Nevertheless, since 1991 the region was torn by civil war along clan (tribal) lines. When, in 1992, U.S. forces intervened osten-sibly as "peacekeepers," they failed to consult with tribal elders, who are the traditional de-cision-makers in Somali society. Instead, the

U.S. took the side of some militia warlords against other clan warlords and paid the price in the infamous "Black Hawk Down" battle.

In 2006, an Islamist front took control of the capital of Mogadishu and brought a relative calm to the country, which was shattered when the U.S. backed an Ethiopian invasion. The renewed war stimulated a nationalist backlash, offshore "piracy," and the growth of

> *The renewed war stimulated a nationalist backlash, offshore "piracy," and the growth of the small ultra-Islamist Al Shabaab militia.*

the small ultra-Islamist Al Shabaab militia. The Pentagon is now using missile strikes, Special Forces raids, and AC-130 aerial gunship attacks to help a new government retake Mogadishu from Al Shabaab rebels. The *New York Times* (3/5/10) reported that, "Even though there is a new religious overlay to Somalia's civil war...clan connections still matter and could spell success—or disaster."

If the Global War on Tribes is as old as European colonialism, in the United States it is as old as the doctrine of Manifest Destiny. In U.S. foreign policy, we can trace it to the Vietnam War (including the tribal highlands of South Vietnam and Laos) and farther back to the Philippine-American War and the Indian Wars. In his classic *Facing West: the Metaphysics of Indian-Hating and Empire Building,* Richard Drinnon connects the colonization of Native American nations in the West to U.S. overseas expansion into the Philippines and Vietnam, which used the identical rhetoric of insurgent territory as hostile "Indian Country."

Drinnon concluded, "In each and every West, place itself was infinitely less important...than what the white settlers brought in their heads and hearts to that particular place. At each magic margin, their metaphysics of Indian-hating underwent a seemingly confirmatory 'perennial rebirth.' Rooted in fears and prejudices buried deep in the Western psyche, their metaphysics became a time-tested doctrine, an ideology, and an integral component of U.S. nationalism....

All along, the obverse of Indian-hating had been the metaphysics of empire-building.... Winning the West amoun- ted to no less than winning the world."

One of the hallmarks of American colonization is to pit favored tribes and ethnic nations against the national security threat of the moment—Crow against Lakota, Igorot against Filipino, Montagnard against Vietnamese, Hmong against Lao, Miskito against Nicaraguan, Kurd against Arab. When the minority tribal allies (with their very real grievances) were no longer needed, Washington quickly abandoned its defense of their "human rights." These divide-and-conquer strategies are being revived from Pakistan to Yemen, as the Pentagon arms tribal militias to do its bidding—often against other tribes.

The Global War on Tribes can be traced even farther back in history to its roots in Europe—including the English colonization of Celtic tribal lands, the mass burning of women who kept tribal healing practices alive, and the suppression of peasant rebellions emerging from local clan resistance (as shown by Carolyn Merchant in *The Death of Nature: Women, Ecology and the Scientific Revolution*). Perhaps the ultimate model is the Roman Empire, which emerged from three early tribes in Rome (the word "tribe" comes from the Latin for "three"), and waged wars against numerous so-called "barbarian" tribes.

Updating the War

Proponents of the Global War on Tribes are seemingly unafraid to connect it to past campaigns. Analyst and author Robert D. Kaplan wrote in the *Wall Street Journal* (9/24/04) that "...the American military is back to the days of fighting the Indians. The red Indian metaphor is one with which a liberal policy nomenklatura may be uncomfortable, but Army and Marine field officers have embraced it because it captures perfectly the combat challenge of the early 21st century.... The range of Indian groups, numbering in their hundreds, that the U.S. Cavalry...had to confront was no less varied than that of the warring ethnic and religious militias spread throughout Eurasia, Africa, and South America in the early 21st century."

Kaplan brazenly compared Iraq to Indian Country: "When the Cavalry invaded Indian encampments, they periodically encountered warrior braves beside women and children, much like Fallujah.... Indian Country has been expanding in recent years because of the security vacuum created by the collapse of traditional dictatorships.... Iraq is but a microcosm of the Earth in this regard."

Tribal resistance against Western intervention and corporate globalization takes different forms in different countries. In Pakistan and Iraq, tribes may fight under the green banner of political Islamism. In India and Peru, some tribal peoples have fought under the red flag of Maoist rural insurgent armies. In Bolivia, Ecuador, and Mexico, they have coalesced in self-defined indigenist movements, which have effectively intersected with socialist and environmental movements.

But to U.S. counterinsurgency tacticians, the ideology is secondary. The primary threat is that people retain a tribal identity and allegiance—an identity that has not been formed or encouraged by capitalism. The goal of the Pentagon and CIA is either to harness tribal loyalties to weaken their enemies or to destroy tribal identity. Even in supporting tribal allies for their own ends, they may end up destroying the tribes in the process.

In central and northeastern India, the Indian Army has launched a counterinsurgency war against Naxalite rebels to open up the tribal forest regions to mining and timber companies. The Naxalites are usually described as Maoists, but as the writer Arundhati Roy observed in *Outlook India* (3/29/10),

> *In the Americas, powerful and growing indigenous tribal movements are increasingly being targeted by U.S. military and intelligence agencies as a potential national security threat to U.S. interests*

"It's convenient to forget that tribal people in Central India have a history of resistance that predates Mao by centuries.... Naxalite politics has been inextricably entwined with tribal uprisings."

On "Democracy Now!" (3/22/10), Roy further explained, "If you look at Afghanistan, Waziristan...the northeast states of India...the entire thing is a tribal uprising. In Afghanistan, obviously, it's taken the form of a radical Islamist uprising. And here [in India], it's a radical left uprising. But the attack is the same. It's a corporate attack...on these people. The resistance has taken different forms."

In the Americas, powerful and growing indigenous tribal movements are increasingly being targeted by U.S. military and intelligence agencies as a potential national security threat to U.S. interests, as explained by Naomi Klein in the *Nation* (11/4/05). The National Intelligence Council projected in its 2005 report, "Mapping the Global Future 2020," that "the failure of elites to adapt to the evolving demands of free markets and democracy probably will fuel a revival in populism and drive indigenous movements, which so far have sought change through democratic means, to consider more drastic means."

The Army's Foreign Military Studies Office (FMSO), headquartered at Fort Leavenworth, Kansas, has applied this emerging doctrine to Latin America. In a *Military Review* bibliography (7-8/99), the FMSO lumped together "Insurgencies, Terrorist Groups and

Indigenous Movements," and in another article warned of indigenous rebellions and other "insurgencies" in Mexico (5-6/97). FMSO official Lt. Col. Geoffrey Demarest stated in his book *Geoproperty: Foreign Affairs, National Security and Property Rights* that, "The coming center of gravity of armed political struggles may be indigenous populations, youth gangs...or insurgents" and that the Internet is increasingly being used by "Indigenous rebels, feminists, troublemakers...." Counterinsurgency planners are no longer simply targeting "Communists" or "narco-guerrillas" in Latin America, but also indigenous-led movement alliances.

Reasons for War

Whether in Mexico, India, Iraq, the United States, and Canada, the Global War on Tribes has some common characteristics. First, the war is most blatantly being waged to steal the natural resources under tribal lands. The rugged, inaccessible terrain that prevented colonial powers from eliminating tribal societies also made accessing minerals, oil, timber, and other resources more difficult. Acre for acre, more of the resources are now left on tribal lands than on more accessible lands.

Resources are not always the underlying explanation for war, but they're a pretty good start at an explanation. In the case of indigenous tribal peoples, their historic attention to biodiversity has also enabled natural areas to be relatively protected until now, as corporations seek out the last remaining pockets of natural resources to extract. Look no further than the Alberta Tar Sands, for instance, to see the exploitation of native lands by modern oil barons.

Native peoples often resist the militarization brought by corporate invaders seeking to mine "unobtainium" (as in the film *Avatar*) and they don't need a white messiah riding a red dragon to guide them to victory. In his book *Resource Rebels: Native Challenges to Mining and Oil Corporations,* Al Gedicks notes, "Up until recently, the tendency in the mass media has been to stereotype native people as fighting a losing battle against the onslaught of industrial civilization. But after two decades of organizing local, national, regional, and international alliances, assisted by...the Internet, native voices can no longer be ignored in powerful places."

Second, the Global War on Tribes is a campaign against the very existence of tribal regions that are not under centralized state control. The tribal regions still retain forms of social organization that have not been solely determined by capitalism. In her anthology, *Paradigm Wars*, Victoria Tauli-Corpuz, chair of the United Nations Permanent Forum on Indigenous Issues, comments that "promoters of economic globalization, the neocolonizers, use the overwhelming pressure of homogenization to teach us that indigenous political, economic, and cultural systems are obstacles to their 'progress'."

The point is not that all tribal peoples pose an egalitarian alternative to neoliberal capitalism. Some (such as indigenous peoples) certainly do have strong egalitarian principles, but many other tribal peoples—such as in the new conflict zones—certainly do not (particularly toward women). The salient point is not that all tribal cultures are paradise, but that they are not capitalist and neoliberal capitalism cannot stand anything other than total control.

Third, the collective form of organization enables tribal people to fight against state control and corporate globalization. When I asked Arundhati Roy at a recent forum why counterinsurgency wars seem to be focused on tribal regions, she answered that "resistance is possible in those areas because they have an imagination outside this bar-coded capitalist society that everybody else lives in...that's why there's huge resistance there...a whole bandwidth of resistance that has actually managed for quite a few years now to stall the corporate onslaught." Tribes still have the social networks to defend their lands and ways of life—networks of trust anchored in deeply held values that citizens of urban industrial societies generally lack.

That is why the "lawless tribal regions" have to be "tamed," so as not to become a "festering sore," and a source of resistance to the corporate state. The only way for tribal leaders not to be crushed by the counterinsurgency campaign is to accept its aims, its money, and its weapons. Tauli-Corpuz concludes that indigenous peoples "believe they already constitute a viable alternative to globalization, underpinned by the fundamental values of reciprocity...community solidarity and collectivity."

During European colonial expansion, tribal peoples who could not muster large military alliances were vulnerable to conquest and occupation. In most countries, the colonization process left them divided and fighting each other. In the 21st century—just as remaining pockets of exploitable resources are located in tribal regions—the most successful pockets of resistance may be found in the mountains, deserts, and forests where tribal peoples refuse to die.

From Z Magazine, *June 2010*
Volume 23, Number 6

21.

AFRICOM: Washington's New Imperial Weapon

By Stephen Roblin

THE LEADING SCHOLAR on the new U.S. Africa Unified Command (AFRICOM), Daniel Volman, summarizes the Obama administration's foreign policy towards Africa as continuing "the expansion of U.S. military activity on the continent initiated by President Bill Clinton in the late 1990s and dramatically esca-

> *Already the Obama administration has made significant increases in funding in the Fiscal Year 2010 budget for U.S. military programs concerning Africa (expected to grow more the following year). It has also expanded direct U.S. military operations on the continent, particularly in Nigeria, Mali, and Somalia.*

lated by President George W. Bush from 2001 to 2009." Already the Obama administration has made significant increases in funding in the Fiscal Year 2010 budget for U.S. military programs concerning Africa (expected to grow more the following year). It has also expanded direct U.S. military operations on the continent, particularly in Nigeria, Mali, and Somalia. These developments qualify as additional evidence for "Obama's continuity with George W. Bush's foreign policy," as described recently by Edward S. Herman in *Z Magazine* ("Obama and the Steady Drift to the Right," March 2010).

The current direction of U.S.-Africa relations is by no means unexpected, given one of the more significant changes to the U.S. military structure implemented during the Bush II administration—the October 2008 addition of the sixth U.S. unified command, AFRICOM. Prior to its establishment, five unified commands coordinated, integrated, and managed all U.S. defense assets and operations for their respective regions. Africa fell under the responsibility of three different commands: European Command (EUCOM), Central Command (CENTOCM), and Pacific Command (PACOM). Each viewed the continent, particularly sub-Saharan Africa, as a "secondary or even tertiary concern." Thus, as "Africa's position in the U.S. strategic spectrum...moved from peripheral to central," AFRICOM was established to take over all U.S. military assets and operations conducted on the continent (with the exception of Egypt) in order to achieve a "unity of focus throughout Africa."

Foreign policy scholars identified three principal reasons for increased U.S. military focus in Africa: securing key natural resource bases, responding to China's growing influence, and acquiring a strategic position to continue the so-called "war on terror." AFRICOM planners, however, dismissed these strategic interests as "myths." They instead promoted the command through "the language and aims of humanitarianism" while pursuing a diplomatic campaign in 2007 for African countries to host its headquarters.

Despite these attempts, citizens and civil society organizations responded to the plan with hostility and, with the exception of Liberia, all target governments declined to host the new command. In responding to the "image problem" surrounding the campaign for AFRICOM, one State Department official said, "[p]ublic opinion is really against getting into bed with the U.S. They just don't trust the U.S." (In a prudent PR maneuver, AFRICOM planners decided to establish the new command's headquarters in Stuttgart, Germany for the time being.)

Africa's shift from "peripheral to central" on Washington's strategic radar was a key component of the changing landscape of U.S.-Africa relations, which should also be understood in terms of geopolitical developments occurring outside of Africa, such as Latin America's increasing internal integration and

independence. Accompanying the changing landscape are historical continuities. These continuities run counter to declarations from AFRICOM planners about it being a "different kind of command" that represents a new "paradigm" in U.S. military engagement.

Two continuities explored in this article are: (1) the consistency of AFRICOM's overall strategy of "sustained security engagement" with established U.S. military doctrine, specifically the "counterinsurgency" and "low-intensity conflict" doctrines, and (2) Obama's continuation of interventionist policies in response to conflicts on the continent, as in the case of Somalia, a nation driven deeper into crisis as a result of the U.S.-backed Ethiopian invasion and occupation during Bush II's tenure. These continuities demonstrate clearly that the U.S. global military system is advancing significantly on African soil.

A Different Kind of Command?

AFRICOM planners cite two reasons why the new command is "different": first, the command's overall strategy, "sustained security engagement," and, second, the "interagency coordination" built into the command's structure. AFRICOM's commander, General William Ward, provided a detailed description of the strategy in three testimonies before Congress (2008, 2009, and 2010). According to General Ward, sustained security engagement is a strategy that emphasizes "building African security capability and capacity" with a primary focus on "conflict and crisis prevention rather than reaction." As part of this so-called "preventive strategy," AFRICOM enhances conventional military and security forces of client governments through a wide-range of "security assistance" programs. Such programs include training military and security forces, providing them with weaponry and military equipment, and improving their logistical and intelligence capacity. In addition, AFRICOM conducts and helps coordinate military operations on the continent, particularly in the area of naval operations which have undergone a "significant expansion."

According to the general, sustained security engagement will enable "partner" nations to counter "the greatest security threats facing Africa," which he identifies as "enduring conflicts, illicit trafficking, territorial disputes, rebel insurgencies, violent extremists, piracy, and illegal immigration." AFRICOM would also pursue objectives that included: ensuring "access and freedom of movement" throughout the continent for the U.S. military; developing "en-route infrastructure" to better enable the "rapid deployment" of troops from U.S. bases positioned around the world to anywhere in Africa (and vice versa); and preventing the "unsanctioned possession and proliferation of WMD capabilities and expertise." The first two objectives are addressed later in this article. As for the third, it is important to recall that the African Union (AU) established the African nuclear-weapons free zone, but with only one minor glitch: U.S. and UK defiance over a small island included in the treaty, Diego Garcia, "one of the most valuable (and secretive) U.S. military bases overseas," in part because of the "nuclear material and nuclear weaponry regularly transiting...the base." So when General Ward says "unsanctioned," he means unauthorized specifically by the U.S, not by law or an AU unanimous decision.

The new command is intended to be heavily involved in peacekeeping operations and civic military initiatives, such as humanitarian and disaster relief programs, all of which are to be facilitated by interagency coordination. Given the hostility towards AFRICOM from African citizens, civil society organizations, and governments, these programs and operations offer important entry points for the command to operate on African soil, as well as opportunities to shape public opinion. For example, forces that receive peacekeeping training are often the same forces that AFRICOM trains to engage in more aggressive military action, enabling peacekeeping training to serve more interventionist

> *So when General Ward says "unsanctioned," he means unauthorized specifically by the U.S, not by law or an AU unanimous decision*

ends. In fact, peacekeeping training in general is being transferred from the State Department to the Pentagon, thereby freeing it from the mild "human rights and democracy conditionalities under congressional supervision" that were "at least a deterrent to some of the worst abuses" (Noam Chomsky, "Coups, UNASUR, and the U.S.," *Z Magazine*, October 2009).

The Pentagon is also increasingly contracting out military functions, such as training military and peacekeeping forces, to private military contractors (PMCs), despite their poor human rights record. According to experts, because PMCs "are contracted by the U.S. government, they are answerable only to them and not the host government.

"African states can only deal with them through U.S. diplomatic missions ("The Role of Private Military Companies in US-Africa Policy," *Review of African Political Economy*, December 2008). Hence, relying on PMCs is one method of limiting the control African governments have over the training their militaries receive. U.S. planners are, in turn, able to alter African militaries and security forces to become "more geared towards protecting U.S. geo strategic interests."

This form of "capacity building" can potentially render these same forces less capable of addressing "the real security threats facing their respective countries." Thus, seemingly benign operations and programs, which in some cases can benefit the target populations, help lay the groundwork for Washington to pursue more interventionist policies. It grants the U.S. military and its private subsidiaries leverage and access on the ground, unfettered by the minimal constraints placed on civilian agencies, namely the Department of State and USAID.

The developments described here are not the qualities attributed to AFRICOM's uniqueness. Instead, AFRICOM planners have heralded the "visionary concept" of integrating civilian personnel into the command's organizational structure, ostensibly as a means to advance collaboration between the Defense (War) Department and civilian agencies. However, due to difficulties in recruiting civilian personnel, efforts at building interagency coordination have been largely unsuccessful as nearly all of AFRICOM's personnel are from the military. The opportunity for civilian agencies to play a significant role in planning AFRICOM's programs and operations is further undermined by the steep decline in funding for these branches (particularly USAID) since the end of the Cold War. As M. J. Williams puts it in a 2008 International Affairs article, "The State Department and USAID have been rotting financially for almost 20 years." Also, PMCs are integral to programs coordinated by AFRICOM and are taking over roles, "that were formerly the exclusive reserve of civilian organizations." These developments run counter to claims of interagency "cooperation," and instead represent a significant achievement by the Defense Department: its increased independence from civilian branches of government in the areas of implementing foreign aid and development programs and peacekeeping operations, which naturally have been altered to meet more militaristic ends.

Doctrinal Antecedents

Immediately after entering office, the Kennedy administration initiated an unprecedented "shift in strategic focus from conventional and nuclear warfare to unconventional forms of conflict" in order to crush the revolutionary movements sweeping the Third World during the early post-war era. This shift was the "first comprehensive effort of the U.S. government to devise a politicomilitary strategic program to deal with guerilla and counter-guerilla warfare." The result was the "counterinsurgency doctrine," which utilizes indigenous military and security forces to carry out Washington's orders, as in the case of South Vietnam.

The significance of the doctrine was at least twofold. First, it elevated unconventional warfare to a level "equal in importance to conventional warfare." Second, it emphasized employing the full-arsenal of state power (military, economic, diplomatic, etc.) to shape Third World affairs.

In Low Intensity Warfare: Counterinsurgency, Proinsurgency, and Antiterrorism in the Eighties, Michael Klare outlines the tactics of the counterinsurgency doctrine:

> direct combat operations: destroying or neutralizing enemy tactical forces and bases, particularly through special operations forces

> military civic action: using military forces in development projects, particularly in rural areas, in order to win popular support for the established government

> psychological operations: enhancing the popular image of client governments and isolating and discrediting insurgent movements, largely through the use of propaganda as well as military civic actions

> military intelligence: obtaining information on the enemy's organizational structure, command and control systems, communications systems, and logistical support, and on the mass civil organizations supporting to the enemy cause

In addition to these tactics, counterinsurgency includes a key feature of U.S. foreign policy: arming, training, and financing client forces with the condition that they obey commands from Washington. Following the withdrawal of U.S. troops from Vietnam, foreign policy planners were well aware of the "pervasive reluctance of American citizens to support overt U.S. intervention in local Third World conflicts." The Reagan administration responded to what is called the "Vietnam syndrome" by initiating its own "strategic reorientation of the U.S. military establishment." What ensued was a new military doctrine called "low intensity conflict" (LIC).

The LIC doctrine proved useful in circumventing the lack of domestic support for U.S. interventions by placing central significance to propaganda campaigns waged at home and a reliance on Special Operations forces to engage in a form of unconventional warfare, sometimes called "clandestine warfare." The purpose was to keep Americans ignorant of their government's application of the doctrine, while convincing them that Communists were out to get them. Reagan made good use of the doctrine in his terror campaigns in Central America, which devastated the region for decades to come. According to Klare in the study cited above, LIC maintained all the tactics of counterinsurgency, but distinguished itself through the addition of the following:

> PROINSURGENCY: sponsoring and supporting anti-Communist insurgencies fighting against enemy governments

> PEACETIME CONTINGENCY OPERATIONS: engaging in short-term military activities, such as show-of-force operations, punitive strikes, assassinations, and rescue missions

> TERRORISM COUNTERACTION: taking defensive and offensive measures to prevent or counter international terrorists

> ANTIDRUG OPERATIONS: destroying foreign sources of illegal narcotics and curbing the flow into the U.S.

> PEACEKEEPING OPERATIONS: using U.S. forces to police cease-fire agreements or serve as a buffer between enemy armies

In addition, LIC emphasized the rapid introduction of U.S. forces to achieve "fast victories through overwhelming strength and firepower" and the ability of U.S. forces to "shift rapidly from one type of LIC activity to another" across great geographical distances, referred to respectively as rapid deployment and rapid mobility.

AFRICOM's strategy of sustained security engagement is largely consistent with the tactics of the full LIC "spectrum" highlighted by Klare above. But before comparing the LIC doctrine with AFRICOM's command strategy, it is important to make two points. First, we must distinguish between the pretexts for intervention and the tactics of intervention. In the case of AFRICOM, the "war on terror" and the other "security threats" identified by General Ward serve as justifications for interventions, as opposed to the Cold War pretext central to LIC articulations.

Second, the tactical categories identified above are by no means employed in a discrete fashion. Instead, they often overlap as many programs and operations engage in multiple tactics, such as training forces to engage in peacekeeping and direct combat operations. With this said, AFRICOM's programs and operations closely adhere to LIC and counterinsurgency tactics as follows:

Weapons Transfers and Training: AFRICOM provides military and security training through a variety of programs, such as the Africa Contingency Operations Training and Assistance (ACOTA) and International Military Education and Training (IMET) programs. Weapons and military/security equipment are being transferred to governments through the Foreign Military Sales (FMS), Foreign Military Financing (FMF), and other programs. For the FMF alone, Obama's budget is set to increase its funding for sub-Saharan African countries from just over $8.2 million to more than $25.5 million.

Psychological Operations: Psychological operations are conducted on the continent through Operation Objective Voice, one of AFRICOM's "information operations" that leverages "media capabilities" to disseminate propaganda in order to shape public opinion in accordance with U.S. strategic objectives.

Direct Combat Operations: AFRICOM has already coordinated direct combat operations on the continent. The Combined Joint Task Force-Horn of Africa (CJTF-HOA), now under the command authority of AFRICOM, has conducted operations in Somalia killing numerous individuals with alleged links to al-Qaeda. For example, in August 2009, the Obama administration authorized a U.S. Special Forces operation where an alleged al-Qaeda operative, Ali Saleh Nabhan, was assassinated in Somalia.

Civic Military Initiatives: One example of a civic military initiative currently being performed through AFRICOM is its HIV/AIDS program. This program aims to prevent the escalation of HIV/AIDS infection rates within African military and security forces. Another civic military initiative was the MEDFLAG program where the U.S. Army Africa and U.S. Air Forces Africa designed a mass casualty scenario to exercise the Swaziland Defense Force's "response capabilities and its interoperability with civilian first-responders."

Military Intelligence: AFRICOM conducts programs and operations in order to "collect, analyze, and synthesize information." An example of an intelligence program is AFRICOM's Intelligence Security Cooperation and Engagement (ISCE), which "seeks to build sustainable military intelligence capacity in designated partner nations and regional organizations." Intelligence operations are crucial components of other operations (highlighting how multiple tactics are employed in single programs). For example, airborne surveillance and intelligence gathering is included in the African Coastal and Border Security Program (ACBS), which provides equipment to im-

prove border and costal patrol operations, particularly in strategic waterways like the oil-rich Gulf of Guinea.

Peacekeeping Operations: AFRICOM offers training to indigenous forces for peacekeeping operations. For example, through the Africa Contingency Operations Training and Assistance program (ACOTA), training is provided to African military and security forces in order to improve police, counterinsurgency, and conventional military operations as part of a peacekeeping initiative (highlighting again tactical overlap). PMCs are "an intrinsic part" of ACOTA and other peacekeeping operations, such as the Global Peace Operation Initiative (GPOI).

Anti-drug Operations: In expanding the "war on drugs" to the continent, the Obama administration increased funding for antidrug opera-

> *For example, airborne surveillance and intelligence gathering is included in the African Coastal and Border Security Program (ACBS), which provides equipment to improve border and costal patrol operations*

tions in Africa, such as the International Narcotics Control and Law Enforcement (INCLE) programs. INCLE and other counter-narcotics programs "train, equip, and support partner nation law enforcement, paramilitary, and military units" so that forces can conduct "the full range of counter-drug activities," which includes interdicting and seizing vessels.

Peacetime Contingency Operations: Maritime security operations is one area where the U.S. engages in peacetime contingency operations in Africa. U.S. ships are increasingly being deployed off the coast of the oil-rich Gulf of Guinea. A goal of these operations is to prevent oil theft and the sabotage of oil exploitation facilities owned by Shell, ExxonMobil, and other multinational oil companies operating in Nigeria's Niger Delta region, which provides 10 percent of U.S. oil imports.

Proinsurgency: While to my knowledge AFRICOM has not engaged in any pro-insurgency campaign, its programs enable it to arm, train, and finance insurgent movements fighting against enemy governments at a moment's notice. Any government deemed to have links to al-Qaeda or any other terrorist group will be particularly susceptible to pro-insurgency (with a virtually non-existent factual threshold to justify the intervention, as many cases demonstrate).

Terrorism Counteraction: AFRICOM conducts a variety of programs and operations through the Anti-Terrorism Assistance program (ATA) established in 1983 during the first "war on terror." These programs include: Operation Enduring Freedom—Trans Sahara (OEF-TS), a program conducted by special operations forces to deny "safe havens to terrorists"; the Kenyan Anti-terrorism Police Unit (KAPU); the East Africa Counter-Terrorism Initiative (EACTI); and the Global Equip and Train program, which permits the Pentagon to provide training and equipment to foreign military, police, and other security forces to combat terrorism with minimal congressional oversight. Funding for anti-terrorism programs in Africa have increased significantly in Obama's FY 2010 budget.

Rapid Deployment and Mobility: A primary objective for the new command is to develop "en-route infrastructure" to better enable rapid deployment of U.S. troops from the homeland to anywhere the Pentagon wants them. In fact, the Air Mobility Command released a document in March 2009 that proposes a "global en route strategy" with the goal of achieving "global access" for the U.S. military, particularly in "key areas" such as Africa. The document describes AFRICOM as instrumental in achieving "significant mobility capability" in Africa and states that U.S. bases in South America will assist with "the mobility routing to Africa," thereby designating the

continent as a possible "launching pad for airlift into Africa."

According to Daniel Volman, these base access agreements grant U.S. "access to local military bases and other facilities so that they can be used by American forces as transit bases or as forward operating bases for combat, surveillance, and other military operations." In addition to these agreements, military personal are being transferred to all U.S. embassies in Africa, creating "mini-AFRICOM headquarters in every single country." Moreover, the CJTF-HOA base at Camp Lemonnier, Djibouti has been identified as AFRICOM's "main operational presence in

> *According to Daniel Volman, these base access agreements grant U.S. "access to local military bases and other facilities so that they can be used by American forces as transit bases or as forward operating bases for combat, surveillance, and other military operations"*

Africa," a de facto headquarters on the continent currently undergoing expansion. In light of these developments, the decision to keep the new command's official headquarters in Stuttgart, Germany after all African governments (except Liberia) declined to host it was hardly a set-back in achieving direct military access on African soil.

Though not an exhaustive comparison, we can see that there are significant historical continuities of military doctrine and strategy, which can be traced back further than the contributions made by Kennedy and Reagan. These continuities challenge official declarations describing AFRICOM as a "different kind of command" or a radical post-Cold War "experiment." Instead, such declarations should be viewed more as a response to the "image problem" the U.S. military faces in Africa, with the ultimate aim of obscuring that AFRICOM is instrumental in Washington's quest to subordinate African states to U.S. imperial dominance by employing the full arsenal of state power, including direct military intervention when the need arises. While maintaining the character of established military doctrine, there is one innovation in AFRICOM's strategy worth noting: the enhancement of what is being called "counter-piracy." This innovation comes as a response to incidents of piracy off the coast of Somalia, a nation pointed to as justification for the recent increased militarization of U.S. foreign policy towards Africa.

Momentum Gains, Conflicts Persist

Two prominent scholars of Africa, William Minter and Daniel Volman, warned a year ago of AFRICOM's developing "institutional momentum," which they argued could induce the Obama administration to initiate interventionist policies in response to Africa's various conflicts and crises ("Making Peace or Fueling War in Africa," *FPIF*, March 13, 2009"; "Somalia Crossroads," *In These Times*, June 29, 2009). Key factors galvanizing AFRICOM's "momentum" are the strategic interests driving the expansion of U.S. militarism on the continent—securing natural resource bases, competing with China and other growing powers, waging the "war on terror," etc.

Stimulating additional momentum is the fact that U.S. foreign policy planners are now equipped with a comprehensive strategy that improves the prospects of achieving these strategic interests. Another crucial factor is the ability of the new command's high-ranking staff to more effectively compete for the ever-growing pool of military funds. In fact, the U.S. Government Accountability Office recently recommended that CJTF-HOA receive increased long-term funding.

Minter and Volman go on to identify the "fundamental alternatives" for the Obama administration's security policy towards Africa: (1) continue waging counterterrorism and counterinsurgency campaigns and reinforce oppressive regimes in the process or (2) prioritize building multilateral capacity to respond to conflicts more diplomatically while addressing the root causes of instability on the continent (poverty, unemployment, lack of access to education and health care, violence against women, global warming, and so on).

The first alternative moves in the direction of AFRICOM's growing momentum, while the latter cuts against it. From the Obama administration's significant budget increases for AFRICOM and its handling of one of Africa's most enduring crises in Somalia, there are signs that U.S. foreign policy towards Africa is taking the predictable path of moving with the momentum.

A recent Human Rights Watch report describes the current humanitarian crisis in Somalia: "About 1.5 million Somalis are displaced from their homes and half the population is in urgent need of humanitarian aid. More than half-a-million people have sought shelter in other countries as refugees. As of this writing the UN World Food Program (WFP) had to suspend food aid to a huge swath of southern Somalia."

The mainstream press has largely stuck with the U.S. official position that "Somalia has collapsed in on itself," attributing the crisis to internal factors. But the historical record reveals that it is directly linked to Bush II era policies, key features of which are being continued by Obama. Like Bush II, Obama is arming, training, financing, and providing diplomatic cover for allies as they hunt "radical Islamists," killing significant numbers of civilians in the process.

The U.S. is also conducting direct military operations on Somali soil. In response to the recent "7/11" terrorist attacks in Uganda, Obama has pledged to "redouble" U.S. efforts to crush the militant group al Shabaab, which took credit for attacks that killed 76 civilians. Respected analysts, however, have continually warned that Obama's militarized response will only exacerbate the crisis, as well as the threat of terrorism.

The Bush II policy towards Somalia began immediately after 9/11 when the Administration led an international effort to shut down Al-Barakaat, the Dubai-based Somali remittance network responsible for bolstering the fragile economy to the amount of some $250 million. This action was initially justified on grounds that Al-Barakaat was financing terror, a charge Washington withdrew a year later. In another policy of combating fictional terrorism, Bush II, in 2006, supported a coalition of warlords in their campaign against a popular coalition.

The Islamic coalition had liberated Somalia's capital Mogadishu and the southern region from U.S.-backed warlords, who had long terrorized the region and formed the Union of the Islamic Courts (UIC). The UIC immediately gained widespread support from Somalis across the country for offering an alternative to 16 years of warlord terror and failed attempts to provide basic security and government services by the "corrupt and feeble" Transitional Federal Government (TFG), Somalia's internationally recognized government since 2004. UIC control, however, only lasted from June to December 2006, during which time Somalia experienced "a degree of peace and security unknown to the south for more than fifteen years," according to an International Crisis Group report.

Confronted with the so-called UIC threat, Washington's regional client, Ethiopia, began preparing for its overthrow by immediately sending troops and military supplies across the border to bolster the TFG (whose only stronghold was a small city north of Mogadishu). By November, thousands of troops were positioned in Somalia. Ethiopia prevented a peaceful settlement by refusing to respect Somalia's autonomy and withdraw its over 7,000 troops from Somali soil—a direct violation of longstanding UN Resolution 733, which called on all states to refrain from any action that might increase tension and impede "a peaceful and negotiated outcome to the conflict in Somalia."

U.S. officials provided diplomatic support for Ethiopia's looming assault by declaring that the UIC was "controlled" by al Qaeda, notwithstanding expert opinion that found the pretext to be a gross "exaggeration" and "unfounded." The Administration then sponsored UN Security Council Resolution 1725 on December 6, which authorized the deployment of African "peacekeeping" forces, but omitted a demand for the withdrawal of Ethiopian troops.

Later that month, the U.S.-backed Ethiopian invasion took full force. The CJTF-HOA, now considered a "model" "critical to

> *By the time Ethiopia pulled out of Somalia in January 2009, the horror unleashed from "saving Somalia from terror" amounted to thousands of murdered civilians, over one million displaced and over three million in desperate need of humanitarian assistance*

accomplishing U.S. Africa Command's mission," played an active role through training Ethiopian troops, providing U.S. military advisors, offering intelligence on the positions of UIC fighters, and carrying out airstrikes. The invasion ended the six-month period of relative peace and security ushered in by the popular UIC and drove the nation back into a familiar state of war, terror, and repression. By the time Ethiopia pulled out of Somalia in January 2009, the horror unleashed from "saving Somalia from terror" amounted to thousands of murdered civilians, over one million displaced and over three million in desperate need of humanitarian assistance. The Bush II response was to refuse to "confront or even publicly acknowledge the extent of Ethiopian military and TFG abuses" (much less its own), thereby continuing the recurrent U.S. policy of "not counting bodies" when saving the world from fictional terrorism by unleashing real terror and aggression.

The U.S.-backed Ethiopian invasion drove the moderate elements of the UIC out of the country, leaving the more militant to fight the occupation. They formed al Shabaab, the "radical offshoot" of the UIC. Bush's policy of sponsoring warlord terror and foreign aggression had the predictable consequence of engendering terrorism. According to Human Rights Watch, while by no means a "proxy" of al-Qaeda, as has been described by Washington, some of al Shabaab's leaders have declared ties to al-Qaeda, whereas others are resistant to the external influence. Moreover, foreign fighters from Afghanistan and Pakistan have reportedly been traveling to Somalia to fight with al Shabaab, a development referred to as the "internationalization of the conflict," having now reached inside Uganda with the recent terrorist attacks. Meanwhile, the U.S. is currently backing previously designated "extremists" and "terrorists," such as the former UIC leader Sheik Shariff who now heads TFG.

Currently, the TFG controls only a "sliver" of territory in Mogadishu and would collapse were it not for the protection of the 6,000-strong African Union Mission in Somalia

Somalis have responded to the incessant violence, which has claimed over 21,000 lives since 2007, by fleeing in droves to neighboring countries, mainly Kenya, a nation whose police welcome Somali refugees by routinely beating and raping them

(AMISOM), controlled by Uganda and Burundi, both loyal U.S. clients. The majority of southern Somalia is instead controlled by armed opposition groups, the most powerful being al Shabaab, which subjects the population under its control to "targeted killings and assaults, repressive forms of social control, and brutal punishments under its draconian interpretation of Sharia." Since Ethiopia's January 2009 withdrawal from Somalia, the population

has been caught in the middle of clashes between the AMISOM-backed TFG, al Shabaab, and other armed groups. Human Rights Watch reports that "[a]ll sides have violated the laws of war by conducting indiscriminate attacks," the majority of which have occurred when TFG and AMISON forces responded to al Shabaab attacks by launching mortars into civilian dense areas.

Additional crimes include both TFG and al Shabaab forces impeding the flow of aid convoys, a charge routinely attributed to only al Shabaab, relying significantly on child soldiers. Somalis have responded to the incessant violence, which has claimed over 21,000 lives since 2007, by fleeing in droves to neighboring countries, mainly Kenya, a nation whose police welcome Somali refugees by routinely beating and raping them.

The Somali Crisis

The July 11 terrorist attacks in Uganda placed the Somalia crisis at the top of the agenda during the recent AU summit (July 24-27). African leaders attending the summit agreed to authorize a more aggressive "peacekeeping" mandate and increased the AMISOM mission to 8,000 soldiers, a number expected to rise above 10,000. Joining Uganda and Burundi in contributing troops are Djibouti and Guinea, the latter's armed forces notorious for their gross human rights abuses, "including the massacre of over 150 opposition supporters in 2009 and several gang rapes." There are several factors that fail to elicit confidence in AMISOM and the TFG's ability and willingness to take measures to ensure Somali civilians do not bear the burden of the more aggressive mandate with their lives, as has been the case with the recent heightened attacks on al Shabaab from AMISOM, following the Uganda terrorist attacks.

Two factors include the regular crimes committed by TFG and AMISOM and TFG incompetence—exemplified by reported incidents of "fierce fighting" between its army and police, its high rate of defections, the fact that its troops lacked a "physical headquarters," and its overall inability to demonstrate itself as a viable political option to Somalis. Also, there were reports of tensions between AMISOM and the TFG, with a few TFG officials speaking out against the spike in casualties resulting from the decision by Uganda's president, Museveni, to intensify AMISOM shelling in retaliation for the Uganda terrorist attacks. An additional factor is the role of regional powers, mainly Ethiopia and Uganda, in shaping the AMISOM mandate. Museveni, in particular, had considerable influence over the AU mission, given that most of its troops were provided by Uganda, the site for the majority of U.S. training coordinated through AFRICOM (some of which was contracted out to PMCs). Both are calling for more resources from its paymaster for the looming "intervention," but with no plans to clean up AMISOM's pitiful human rights record.

Turning to the paymaster, the U.S., of course, is capable of exerting significant influence given its position as primary financier to the mission. Following the 7/11 terrorist attacks, the Obama administration exerted its influence by pledging to "redouble" support in the "same fashion" it has done thus far. This amounted to employing key tactics of AFRICOM's strategy of sustained security engagement by training, arming, and providing intelligence, logistical support, and transportation to TFG and AMISOM forces, while refusing to take even the smallest measures to reduce U.S.-sponsored crimes—for example, by establishing a minimal adherence to international humanitarian law as a prerequisite for military assistance, as recommended recently by Human Rights Watch. Though clearly the Administration does not want to become invested in any full-scale U.S.-led intervention in Africa, direct combat operations, particularly through the use of Special Operations Forces, remain an option, such as the operation that killed an alleged al-Qaeda operative last year, a fact that evidently slipped General Ward's mind when he said recently that the U.S. is not interested in "direct foreign involvement" as it often becomes "an irritant and a distraction."

In short, key factors point to an escalation of the bloodbath in Somalia, which will likely be in domains controlled by al Shabaab and other armed groups. An alternative to this potential scenario, however, is to call for dialogues with the armed groups, as proposed recently by the International Crisis Group. Unfortunately, the Obama administration is pursuing interventionist policies in response to Africa's conflicts and crises and ignoring their root causes. In fact, the Administration is reportedly considering creating a Marine rapid deployment force composed of 1,000 troops to "intervene in African hot spots."

Now that AFRICOM is operational, Africa and all of its "hot spots" are subject to the new command's so-called revolutionary strategy, equipped with tactics fine-tuned through a long history of subordinating weaker states to imperial dominance by conventional and unconventional means. And with AFRICOM's growing momentum, driven primarily by the movement of Africa's strategic importance from "peripheral to central," we should expect ample opportunities for Washington to exercise its new imperial weapon, even with a "son of Africa" now calling the shots.

From Z **Magazine**, *September 2010*
Volume 23, Volume 9

22.

The World of Drones

By Tim Coles

FEBRUARY 2012 WILL mark the 15th anniversary of the U.S. Space Command's declaration of war on the world, namely its quest to achieve Full Spectrum Dominance of land, sea, air, and outer space by 2020, "to close the ever-widening gap between diminishing resources and in-

> *One of the many dangerous aspects of Full Spectrum Dominance is the U.S. Air Force's Prompt Global Strike doctrine, which will give the United States, "the capability to rapidly attack fleeting or emerging high-value targets without warning, anywhere on the globe"*

creasing military commitments." Commenting on the Space Command's announcement, Rebecca Johnson of the UN Disarmament Commission observed that, "Notions of full spectrum dominance...are perceived as a security threat by countries that have no political desire or intention to threaten the United States, but which would be expected by their own citizens and militaries to develop countermeasures to deter the United States nevertheless."

One of the many dangerous aspects of Full Spectrum Dominance is the U.S. Air Force's Prompt Global Strike doctrine, which will give the United States, "the capability to rapidly attack fleeting or emerging high-value targets without warning, anywhere on the globe"—in the words of the U.S. Air Force (USAF). The British company BAE Systems is developing the Taranis unmanned aerial vehicle (drone), which is being designed to "test the possibility of developing the first ever autonomous stealthy Unmanned Combat Air Vehicle (UCAV) that would ultimately be capable of precisely striking targets at long range, even in another continent," the company boasted, indicating the drone's potential for Prompt Global Strike.

Following the exploitation of 9/11, the Pentagon and Whitehall succeeded in securing two of the world's major energy regions—the Middle East and Central Asia. Under the pretext of a self-appointed Responsibility to Protect, they are developing the means to control a third—North Africa (in lieu of the NATO assault on Libya). War planners envisage key energy areas and, eventually, the world in general, patrolled by drones in order "to close the ever-widening gap," about which the Space Command is concerned.

In 2009, it was reported, erroneously, that U.S. Defense Secretary Robert Gates had cancelled a Bush-era $340 billion-dollar Future Combat Systems program, which was designed to "build an entirely new army, reconfigured to perform the global policing mission."

It transpired that the system was not only going ahead, but it was being expanded (just the Unmanned Ground Vehicle component was being cut). Renamed the Army's Brigade Combat Team Modernization Initiative, the program involved the acquisition of more drones than previously anticipated—as P.W. Singer noted in *Wired For War*, his enthusiastic study of robotic warfare. Furthermore, the principal contracts have been awarded to the Boeing corporation.

These, and other drones, allowed the USAF to achieve its ultimate goal, "to find, fix, track, target, and engage any moving ground target anywhere on the surface of the Earth."

Civilian Deaths

Ever since a Boeing-co-produced Hellfire missile was launched from a Predator drone in 2002, the human cost of drones has been exponential. "[A]long the mountainous eastern border of Afghanistan, a Predator reportedly followed and killed three suspicious Afghans, including a tall man in robes who was thought to be Bin Laden. The victims turned out to be innocent villagers gathering scrap metal," the *New Yorker* reported. In November of that year, six people, each of them alleged to be suspected al-Qaeda militants, were also killed at the push of a button as they travelled through Yemen in a car.

The U.S. is currently running two drone operations: the military's and the CIA's. The latter is classified and assassination orders come directly from the president. During George W. Bush's tenure, the CIA conducted 45 known drone attacks. In the first year of Obama's tenure, the CIA conducted 53 known drone attacks.

According to the *Foreign Policy Journal*, the CIA's program "extends further [than the military's], reaching countries such as Pakistan, Yemen, and Somalia." The drone strikes in Somalia and elsewhere, "anger the population and make the Islamic insurgents more popular." In its public letter to Obama, Human Rights Watch noted that, "The U.S. government says [the terrorist sympathizer, Anwar] al-Awlaki is linked to the Yemen-based al Qaeda in the Arabian Peninsula, but has not brought formal charges against him," concluding that targeting individuals for death without due process of law "will inevitably violate international law and set a dangerous precedent for abusive regimes around the globe." Obama's repeal of Executive Order 12333 gave the president the self-appointed right to assassinate U.S. nationals (al-Awlaki) on the basis of their beliefs.

In 2009, Kathy Kelly reported that 30 schools in Afghanistan had closed because the children were too afraid of the drones to attend and those who did could not concentrate. *Foreign Policy Journal* reported that, "Since January 2008, more than 1,000 Predator sorties were flown out of Balad," a U.S.-occupied Air Base in Iraq, "lasting more than 20,000 hours." The *New York Times* claimed that in 2007, the U.S. launched 46 drone strikes in Iraq, 77 in 2008, and 6 in 2009. As the strikes apparently decreased in Iraq, they increased exponentially in Pakistan and Afghanistan.

In January 2010, Bloomberg reported that the Pakistani government "said it doesn't support U.S. drone attacks in its territory as they are counterproductive, after reports that raids…killed 17 [alleged, suspected] militants in a northwest region bordering Afghanistan." In 2010, it was reported that, since the start of drone operations in Pakistan in 2004, operators had killed 1,200 people. Of that number, 32 percent were civilians, according to an organization which supports drone attacks, the New America Foundation.

This would appear to be a gross underestimate when we consider that General Petraeus's military advisor, Lt. Col. David Kilcullen, informed the *New York Times* that 714 people had been killed by drone operators in Pakistan from mid-2008 to mid-2009 alone, of whom 14 were "al-Qaeda" and/or Taliban suspects—meaning that 98 percent of the victims in that one period were civilians. (Kil- cullen's figure is compounded by other factors present in the New America Foundation study.)

In the first two months of 2010, at least 140 people had been killed in drone attacks. In that year, the U.S. launched 118 strikes. According to Channel 4 News Online, the New America Foundation estimated that between 607 to 993 people had been killed by drone operators in 2010 and "the foundation [sic] suggests that only two percent were senior Taliban or al-Qaeda figures," a figure which corresponds to Kilcullen's estimate for the previous year. In the Afghanistan-Pakistan region, "the number of attacks has increased from one per week to one per day," *Foreign Policy Journal* noted. On March 17, 2011, the Associated Press reported that "Pakistan's army chief [Ashfaq Kayani] strongly condemned a U.S. drone attack that killed more than three dozen people, saying the missiles struck a peaceful meeting of tribal elders near the Afghan border.… Kayani's condemnation

contradicted statements provided by Pakistani intelligence officials," whom, the AP reported, had originally claimed that the "38 people killed and 7 wounded in the attack were militants meeting to discuss sending additional

> *In the first two months of 2010, at least 140 people had been killed in drone attacks. In that year, the U.S. launched 118 strikes.*

fighters into Afghanistan."

Drone attacks seem to be linked to a frightening new development in military/secret service assassinations: "nanotags" or Radiofrequency Identification (RFID) chips. "I was given $122 to drop chips wrapped in a cigarette paper at al-Qaeda and Taliban houses. If I was successful, I was told, I would be given thousands of dollars," a young man from Wiziristan confessed to the Taliban before being shot for treason. "I thought this was a very easy job. The money was good so I started throwing the chips all over. I knew people were dying because of what I was doing, but I needed the money." The U.S. historian and investigator, Gareth Porter, reported that "residents of Waziristan, including one student identified as Taj Muhammad Wazir, had confirmed that tribesman have been paid to lay the electronic devices to target drone strikes."

The *New Yorker* also reported "rumors that paid C.I.A. informants have been planting tiny silicon-chip homing devices for the drones in the tribal areas." There are long-standing U.S. military plans to "nanotag" everything.

Britain's Prince Harry exemplified the undying colonial-era racism of the UK establishment when he referred to one of his Army colleagues, Ahmed Raza Khan, as "our little Paki friend"—which was "just a joke," of course. Contempt for people of another age, ethnicity, gender, nation, religion, etc., is a necessary part of the dehumanization process, which is itself necessary in order to attempt to justify the killing and torture of others—especially to oneself. When it comes to drones, however, there seems to be a new form of psychological distancing between the action and the consequence. In 2009, the UN Rapporteur on Extrajudicial, Summary or Arbitrary Executions, Philip Alston, cautioned that operators risk developing "a Playstation [sic] mentality" to killing. Indeed, many drone and robot control panels are modelled on PlayStation and Xbox joypads.

The grainy, monochrome, low-resolution images of buildings being vaporized seems to be part of the propaganda process of dissociation in the era of "clean wars." The media rarely report who was in the given building and, when doing so, usually cite unchallenged military allegations that the victims were "al-Qaeda" militants or Taliban fighters. This is not surprising. USAF's 46-year drone expansion plan stated in 2009 that the Air Force would seek to monopolize all the information released to the media regarding drone attacks.

"In order to conduct a successful communication campaign, public affairs activities focus on three main areas of operation—Media Relations, Internal Information and Community Relations," according to the detailed plan. "Additionally, communication strategies are executed at the senior levels of government by appropriate Air Force leadership to enhance leaders' and lawmakers' understanding of UAS [unmanned aerial systems'] current and future role."

"You'd be hard pressed to find a Pakistani anywhere in the world, regardless of class, education, or citizenship, who does not object to the U.S. drone strikes that have killed hundreds of innocent civilians in Pakistan since President Barack Obama took office," *Business Week* reported, adding that, "It would also be difficult to find a Pakistani who does not object to the government in Islamabad allowing the strikes to continue."

Liaquat Ali Khan reported in CounterPunch that, "In a case filed with the Pakistan Supreme Court," a petition read: "The Americans, like in [former Pakistani President] Musharraf's time, have also been given a free hand by President Zardari and fundamental rights of the (indigenous) people are being violated daily in tribal areas and (in northern areas of) Dir, Swat, and Chitral. A large number of (indigenous) people have migrated from these areas and suffered tremendous losses with no hope of returning to their homes because of U.S. drone attacks, but the government is sitting as a silent spectator."

"Presuming that Pakistan is secretly supporting drone strikes," Ali Khan continued, "the vengeful militants have begun to attack the citadel cities of Lahore and Islamabad. As drone attacks continue to kill and generate the IDPs [internally displaced persons] among the indigenous population and as militants undertake retaliatory measures in major cities, the nuclear-armed Pakistan is predicted to plunge into uncontrollable chaos and carnage threatening international peace and security."

In their analysis of the overall death toll in Pakistan from drone strikes between early—to mid-2009, BBC South Asia—tellingly, not BBC UK—highlighted the corollary between drone attacks and terrorist reprisals. Between 2009 and 2010, "nearly 2,500 people have been killed in Pakistan as a result of U.S. drones and Islamic militant attacks.... Islamic militant strongholds in the border area close to Afghanistan have been targeted by U.S. drone aircraft, while, at the same time, Islamic militants have carried out attacks across Pakistan."

The BBC went on to explain how, "Missile attacks by U.S. drones in Pakistan's tribal areas have more than trebled under the Obama administration.... Compared with 25 drone strikes between January 2008 and January 2009, there were at least 87 such attacks between President Obama taking office on January 20, 2009 and the end of June 2010. More than 700 people have been killed in such attacks under Mr. Obama, compared with slightly fewer than 200 from under his predecessor, George W Bush. The militant backlash over the same period has been even more violent. Extremists have struck more than 140 times in various Pakistani locations, killing more than 1,700 people and injuring hundreds more."

The BBC concluded that, "Pakistan has consistently argued that drone attacks are hindering rather than helping with the battle against extremism, saying they fuel public anger against the government and the U.S. and boost support for militants." The information on drone cause and effect in terms of how such civilian murders radicalize populations is very rarely reported by mainstream, Western television news networks, making Muslim terrorism (which is always reported) seem unprovoked.

> *The BBC concluded that, "Pakistan has consistently argued that drone attacks are hindering rather than helping with the battle against extremism, saying they fuel public anger against the government and the U.S. and boost support for militants."*

More recently, Reuters reported "mounting resentment from Pakistanis who decry the government for bowing to U.S. wishes." Perhaps in an effort to appease the mounting civilian opposition to drone attacks, President Zardari did acknowledge that "drones are radicalizing more people to side with the Taliban," Arnaud de Borchgrave reported.

In 2009, Pakistan's Prime Minister, Yousuf Raza Gilani, "said missile strikes by U.S. drones on the northwestern tribal areas bordering Afghanistan were in fact strengthening the militants," the *Financial Times* (London) reported. Mehdi Hasan in the *Guardian* explained that Obama's "backing of indiscriminate slaughter in Pakistan can only encourage new waves of militancy." David Kilcullen recognized that "Every one of these dead noncombatants represents an alienated family, a new revenge feud, and more recruits for a militant movement that has grown exponentially even as drone strikes have increased."

Kathy Kelly reported in the *Huffington Post*, "The drones feed hourly intelligence information to U.S. war commanders, but the machinery can't inform people about the spiraling anger as the U.S. conducts assassination operations in countries throughout the 1.3 bil-

lion-strong Muslim world." Kelly cited Fred Branfman as saying that, "Sold as defending Americans…[it] is actually endangering us all. Those responsible for it, primarily General Petraeus, are recklessly seeking short-term tactical advantage while making an enormous long-term strategic error that could lead to countless American deaths in the years and decades to come."

Likewise, *Le Monde Diplomatique* confirmed that, "The drones worsen the resentment of Pakistan's people: Public opinion, which already views its government as corrupt, sees drones as an attack on the legitimacy of national power. While most of the world gives more credit to Obama than to his predecessor, his ratings in Pakistan are little higher than those of George Bush."

Furthermore, *Business Week* reported that the hometown of the failed Times Square bomber, Faisal Shahzad, "is close to the Pakistani region where the militants are now being targeted by U.S. drone attacks." Terrorism specialist Jerrold Post was quoted as saying, "There is intense anti-American sentiment in Pakistan. This has been magnified by some of the drone killings, [and] targeted assassination[s]." *Business Week* added that, "Shahzad felt let down when his home government failed to put a stop to the drone strikes carried out by the government of his host country. He seems to have experienced some sort of psychological break[down], after which he was no longer defined by family and career, but by what he felt was the failed policy of both countries."

Human Rights Watch noted in its annual global report that, "Anti-U.S. sentiment deepened markedly in Pakistan in 2009 due to perceived U.S. violations of Pakistani sovereignty through aerial drone strikes in the tribal areas that killed hundreds of civilians and persistent rumors, denied by Pakistani authorities, that personnel from the private military company Xe Services ([formerly] Blackwater) are conducting covert operations in Pakistan," concluding that "Substantial sections of Pakistani society, particularly opinion makers and the media, blamed U.S. behavior for the surge in militant attacks in the country, even as they expressed broad support for the government's fight against the Taliban and affiliated groups."

Drone resistance is proving difficult, with "a Pakistani court up[holding] the dismissal of a petition against U.S. drone attacks," the *Jurist* reported in 2009. Added to which, Kathy Kelly and three friends were arrested in the United States for trespassing, "when after a ten-day vigil outside the [Creech] air force base, we entered it with a letter we wanted to circulate among the base personnel, describing our opposition to a massive targeted assassination program."

Le Monde Diplomatique highlighted the "economic reality" of murdering people with robots. "It costs $2.6 million to train a U.S. fighter pilot and just $135,000 to train a drone pilot." Micah Zenko, of the Council on Foreign Relations, was quoted as saying that in 2008, "the Bush administration took the decision to turn the CIA into a counter-insurrection air force working in support of the Pakistani government.... The CIA attacks are secret, which rules out a public debate on their effectiveness."

There is something familiar to intelligence analysts, which does not seem to penetrate much mainstream or even anti-war analysis, namely that a destabilized Pakistan is in the Pentagon's interest because of its destabilizing effect on China. A National Intelligence Council (NIC) Study pointed out in 2008 that were Pakistan to "erupt," it would hamper the Sino-Iranian oil and gas ambition to construct a pipeline through Pakistan in order to supply China with cheap Iranian resources (China already having taken a loss on Iraqi oil due to the Anglo-American occupation, the Iraqis having taken an incomparably worse loss). "China's concerns about security in Pakistan...have dampened plans for a Pakistan-China oil pipeline," the NIC affirmed. By 2025, the NIC predicted in a futures study, "the long-delayed plans for the "peace pipeline" connecting Iran, Pakistan, and India (IPI) are back on track again and the IPI pipeline may be extended to China," hence the need to destabilize Pakistan. The only feasible routes for the pipeline are through Afghanistan and Pakistan—one of which is under an Anglo-American occupation and the other is being subjected to mounting drone attacks.

These "chessboard" games, as British colonialists used to refer to the ruining of people's lives, have an extra, potentially terminal, potency in today's nuclear weapons-armed world —as Liaquat Ali Khan, and others, have pointed out.

As trade barriers are lowered for nanotech and other highly dangerous technologies, the human race is pushed to what Martin Rees, one of the world's leading astrophysicists, cautioned in his book *Our Final Hour?*, namely humanity's "50-50" odds of surviving the next 90 years "without a serious setback."

Robot Ethics?

A few years after Rees's warning, a U.S. Navy-commissioned study into robot ethics noted parenthetically that "civilian computer systems have failed and raised worries that can carry over to military applications.... Thus, it is a concern that we also may not be able to halt some (potentially-fatal) chain of events caused by autonomous military systems that process information and can act at speeds incomprehensible to us, e.g., with high-speed unmanned aerial vehicles." Likewise, the UK

Ministry of Defense (MOD), a couple of years later, predicted that by 2040, "the increased complexity of networks are likely to increase the risk, and the impact of catastrophic systems failure."

These highly dangerous systems are due to become even more hazardous as human beings are put "out of the loop," to use the military parlance, by autonomous systems. According to USAF's drone expansion plan, "Increasingly humans will no longer be "in the loop," but rather "on the loop"—monitoring the execution of certain decisions." However, the U.S. Navy-commissioned study noted that, "One of the few near-certainties in the development of military robots is that keeping a human in the decision-making loop is going to seriously degrade battle efficiency," meaning that safety is an institutional flaw of the military.

Humanity's greatest challenges were perhaps best laid out in a futures study by the MOD, published a few years prior to the one cited above: "Many of the concerns over the development of new technologies lie in their safety, including the potential for disastrous outcomes, planned and unplanned." We may wish to take note of the word planned. "For example, it is argued that nanotechnology could have detrimental impacts on the environment, genetic modification could spiral out of control and that AI [artificial intelligence] could be superior to that of humans, but without the restraining effect of human social conditioning." The MOD concluded, "Various doomsday scenarios arising in relation to these and other areas of development present the possibility of catastrophic impacts, ultimately including the end of the world, or at least of humanity."

From Z **Magazine,** *October 2011*
Volume 24, Number 10

23.

Coups, UNASUR, and the U.S.

By Noam Chomsky

T HE LAST TIME I had the opportunity to speak in Caracas
was about a year ago, right after the UNASUR (Union of South
American Nations) meeting in Santiago in September 2008. That meeting
was called "with the purpose of considering the situation in the Republic
of Bolivia," after an uprising backed

These are the words of the final Declaration, which also warned that the participating governments— all of the South American Republics—"energetically reject and do not recognize any situation that implies an intent of civil coup d'etat, the rupture of institutional order, or that compromises the territorial integrity of the Republic of Bolivia"

by the traditional elites who had lost power in the impressive democratic elections of 2005.
UNASUR condemned the violence and the massacre of peasants by the quasi-secessionist elements and declared "Their fullest and decided support for the constitutional government of
President Evo Morales, whose mandate was ratified by a wide margin in the recent referendum."

These are the words of the final Declaration, which also warned that the participating governments—all of the South American Republics—"energetically reject and do not recognize any situation that implies an intent of civil coup d'etat, the rupture of institutional order, or that compromises the territorial integrity of the Republic of Bolivia." In response, President Morales
thanked UNASUR for its support and observed that, "For the first time in South America's his-

tory, the countries of our region are deciding how to resolve our problems, without the presence of the United States."

True, and a fact of historic significance. It is instructive to compare the Charter of the Organization of American States (OAS) with that of the African Union (AU). The latter permits intervention by African states within the Union itself in exceptional circumstances. In contrast, the Charter of the OAS bars intervention "for any reason whatever, in the internal or external affairs of any other state." The reasons for the difference are clear. The OAS Charter seeks to deter intervention, from the "colossus of the North"—and has failed to do so. That is an enduring problem in the Western hemisphere, nowhere near solution, though there has been significant progress. After the collapse of the apartheid states, the AU has faced no comparable problem.

South American Integration Process

Last year's UNASUR meeting in Santiago took a step forward in the difficult process of integration that is taking place in South America. This process has two aspects: external and internal. The external process establishes bonds among countries that had been largely separated from one another since the early European conquests, each one oriented towards the West. The internal process seeks to integrate the vast impoverished and oppressed majorities into the societies that took shape under colonial and neocolonial domination. These societies have typically been ruled by small Europeanized elites who had amassed enormous wealth and were linked to the imperial societies in many ways: export of capital, import of luxury goods, education, and many other dimensions. The ruling sectors assumed little responsibility for the fate of their own countries and their suffering people.

These critical factors sharply distinguish Latin America from the developmental states of East Asia. The processes of internal integra-

tion in South America, quite naturally, are arousing great concern among the traditional rulers at home and abroad, and strong opposition if they go beyond minor reforms of the worst abuses.

In early August, UNASUR met in Ecuador, which assumed the presidency of the organization. The announced goal of the meeting was to carry forward the process of integration, but the meeting took place under the shadow of renewed U.S. military intervention. Colombia did not attend, in reaction to broad concern in the region over its decision to accept U.S. military bases. The host of the meeting, President Correa of Ecuador, had announced that the U.S. military would no longer be permitted to use its Manta base, the last major U.S. base remaining in South America.

Bases and Coups

Establishing U.S. bases in Colombia is only one part of a much broader effort to restore Washington's capacity for military intervention. In recent years, total U.S. military and police aid in the hemisphere has come to exceed economic and social aid. That is a new phenomenon. Even at the height of the Cold War, economic aid far exceeded military aid. Predictably, these programs have "strengthened military forces at the expense of civilian authorities, exacerbated human rights problems and generated significant social conflict and even political instability," according to a study by the Washington Office on Latin America. By 2003, the number of Latin Americans troops trained by U.S. programs had increased by more than 50 percent. It has probably become higher since. Police are trained in light infantry tactics. The U.S. Southern Military Command (SOUTHCOM) has more personnel in Latin America than most key civilian federal agencies combined. That again is a new development. The focus now is on street gangs and "radical populism": I do not have to explain what that phrase means in the Latin

American context. Military training is being shifted from the State Department to the Pentagon. That shift is of some importance. It frees military training from human rights and democracy conditionalities under congressional supervision, which has always been weak, but was at least a deterrent to some of the worst abuses.

Military bases are also being established where possible to support what are called "forward operations"—meaning military intervention of one or another sort. In a related development, the U.S. Fourth Fleet, disbanded in 1950, was reactivated after Colombia's invasion of Ecuador in March 2008. With responsibility for the Caribbean, Central and South America, and the surrounding waters, the Fleet's "various operations...include counter-illicit trafficking, Theater Security Cooperation, military-to-military interaction and bilateral and multinational training," the official announcement says. Quite properly, these moves elicited protest and concern from the governments of Brazil, Venezuela, and others.

In past years the U.S. routinely helped carry out military coups in Latin America or invaded outright. Examples are too numerous and familiar to review and are awful to contemplate. That capacity has declined, but has not disappeared. In the new century there have already been three military coups: in Venezuela, Haiti, and Honduras.

Venezuela

The first, in Venezuela, was openly supported by Washington. After a popular uprising restored the elected government, Washington immediately turned to a second plan to undermine the elected government: by funding groups of its choice within Venezuela, while refusing to identify recipients. Funding after the failed coup reached $26 million by

2006. The facts were reported by wire services, but ignored by the mainstream media. Law professor Bill Monning of the Monterey Institute of International Studies in California said that, "We would scream bloody murder if any outside force were interfering in our internal political system." He is, of course, correct: such actions would never be tolerated for a moment. But the imperial mentality allows them to proceed, even with praise, when Washington is the agent.

> *In past years the U.S. routinely helped carry out military coups in Latin America or invaded outright. Examples are too numerous and familiar to review and are awful to contemplate.*

The pretext, invariably, is "supporting democracy." In the real world, the measures employed have been a standard device to undermine democracy. Examples are numerous. To mention just a few, that is how the ground was prepared for the U.S.-backed military coup in Haiti after its first democratic election in 1990, bitterly opposed by Washington. And in another part of the world, it is happening right now in Palestine where the outcome of a free election in January 2006 was counter to Washington's wishes.

At once, the U.S. and Israel, with Europe tagging politely along as usual, turned to severe punishment of the population for the crime of voting "the wrong way" in a free election, and also began to institute the standard devices to undermine an unwanted government: "democracy promotion" and military force. In this case, the military force is a collaborationist paramilitary army under the command of U.S. General Keith Dayton, trained in Jordan with Israeli participation. The Dayton army received great acclaim from liberals in the government and the press when it succeeded in suppressing protests in the West Bank during the murderous and destructive U.S.-backed Israeli military campaign in Gaza earlier in 2009. Senator John Kerry, chair of the Senate Foreign Relations committee, was one of many close to the Obama administration who saw in this success a sign that Israel may at last have a "legitimate negotiating partner" for its U.S.-backed programs of taking over what is of value in the occupied territories, under the guise of a "political settlement."

All of this is routine and very familiar in Latin America where U.S. invasions have regularly left what remains of the country under the rule of brutal National Guards and collaborationist elites. The policies were initially developed with considerable sophistication a century ago after the U.S. conquest of the Philippines, which left hundreds of thousands of corpses. And these measures have often been successful for long periods. In the original testing ground, the Philippines, the impact still remains a century later, one reason for the continuing ugly record of state violence, and the failure of the Philippines to join the remarkable economic development of East and Southeast Asia in recent years.

Haiti and Honduras

Returning to coups in Latin America in the new millennium, the first one, in Venezuela, was unsuccessful. The second was in Haiti two years later. The U.S. and France intervened to remove the elected president and dispatched him off to Central Africa, actions that precipitated yet another reign of terror in this tortured country, once the richest colony in the world and the source of much of France's wealth, destroyed over the centuries by France and then the U.S. I should add that the harrowing history, in Haiti and elsewhere, is almost unknown in the U.S.—worse, it is replaced by fairy tales of noble missions that have sometimes failed because of the unworthiness of the beneficiaries. These are among the prerogatives of power and facts that cannot be ignored by the traditional victims.

The third coup is, of course, the one taking place right now in Honduras where an openly class-based military coup ousted left-leaning President Zelaya. This coup was unusual in that the U.S. did not carry it out or directly support it, but rather joined the Organization of American States in criticizing it, though weakly. Washington did not withdraw its ambassador in protest as Latin American and Eu-

> *All of this is routine and very familiar in Latin America where U.S. invasions have regularly left what remains of the country under the rule of brutal National Guards and collaborationist elites.*

ropean countries did, and made only limited use of its enormous military and economic influence, as it could easily have done by simple means—for example, by canceling all U.S. visas and freezing U.S. bank accounts of leaders of the coup regime. A group of leading U.S. Latin American scholars recently reported that "not only does the administration continue to prop up the regime with aid money through the Millennium Challenge Account and other sources, but the U.S. continues to train Honduran military students at the Western Hemispheric Institute for Security Cooperation— the notorious institution formerly known as the School of the Americas," from which much of the top Honduran military has graduated. Amnesty International has just released a long and detailed account of extremely serious human rights violations by the coup regime. If such a report were issued concerning an official enemy, it would be front-page news. In this case, it was scarcely reported, consistent with the downplaying of coups to which U.S. political and economic power centers are basically sympathetic, as in this case.

The U.S. surely hopes to maintain and probably expand its military base at Soto Cano (Palmerola) in Honduras, a major base for the

U.S.-run terrorist war in Nicaragua in the 1980s. There are unconfirmed rumors of plans for other bases. (The best source of information and analysis is the consistently outstanding work by Mark Weisbrot at the Center for Economic and Policy Research, who also reviews the media's refusal to rise to minimal journalistic standards by reporting the basic facts.)

Imperial Mentality and Drug Wars

The justification offered for the new military bases in Colombia is the "war on drugs." The fact that the justification is even offered is remarkable. Suppose, for example, that Colombia, or China, or many others claimed the right to establish military bases in Mexico to implement their programs to eradicate tobacco in the U.S., by fumigation in North Carolina and Kentucky, interdiction by sea and air, and dispatch of inspectors to the U.S. to ensure it was eradicating this poison—which is, in fact, far more lethal even than alcohol, which in turn is far more lethal than cocaine or heroin, incomparably more than cannabis. The toll of tobacco use is truly fearsome, including "passive smokers" who are seriously affected though they do not use tobacco themselves. The death toll overwhelms the lethal effects of other dangerous substances.

The idea that outsiders should interfere with U.S. production and distribution of these murderous poisons is plainly unthinkable. Nevertheless, the U.S. justification for carrying out such policies in South America is accepted as plausible. The fact that it is even regarded as worthy of discussion is yet another illustration of the depth of the imperial mentality and the abiding truth of the doctrine of Thucydides that the strong do as they wish and the weak suffer as they must—while the intellectual classes spin tales about the nobility of power. Leading themes of history, to the present day.

Despite the outlandish assumptions, let us agree to adopt the imperial mentality that reigns in the West—virtually unchallenged, in fact, not even noticed. Even after this extreme concession, it requires real effort to take the "war on drugs" pretext seriously. The war has been waged for close to 40 years and intensively for a decade in Colombia. There has been no notable impact on drug use or even street prices. The reasons are reasonably well understood. Studies by official and quasi-official governmental organizations provide good evidence that prevention and treatment are far more effective than forceful measures in reducing drug abuse: one major study finds prevention and treatment to have been 10 times as effective as drug interdiction and 23

> *These and other facts leave us with only two credible hypotheses: either U.S. leaders have been systematically insane for the past 40 years or the purpose of the drug war is quite different from what is proclaimed*

times as effective as "supply-side" out-of-country operations, such as fumigation in Colombia, more accurately described as chemical warfare. The historical record supports these conclusions. There is ample evidence that changes in cultural attitudes and perceptions have been very effective in curtailing harmful practices. Nevertheless, despite what is known, policy is over-whelmingly directed to the least effective measures, with the support of the doctrinal institutions.

These and other facts leave us with only two credible hypotheses: either U.S. leaders have been systematically insane for the past 40 years or the purpose of the drug war is quite different from what is proclaimed. We can exclude the possibility of collective insanity. To determine the real reasons, we can follow the model of the legal system, which takes predictable outcome to be evidence of intent, particularly when practices persist over a long period and in the face of constant failure to approach the announced objectives. In this case, the predictable outcome is not obscure, both abroad and at home.

Abroad, the "supply-side approach" has been the basis for U.S.-backed counterinsurgency strategy in Colombia and elsewhere, with a fearful toll among victims of chemical warfare and militarization of conflicts, but enormous profits for domestic and foreign elites. Colombia has a shocking record of human rights violations, by far the worst in the hemisphere since the end of Reagan's Central American terror wars in the 1980s, and also the second-largest internal displacement of populations in the world, after Sudan. Meanwhile, domestic elites and multinationals profit from the forced displacement of peasants and indigenous people, which clears land for mining, agribusiness production and ranching, infrastructure development for industry, and much else.

At home, the drug war coincided with the neoliberal financialization of the economy and the attack on government social welfare systems. One immediate consequence of the war on drugs has been the extraordinary growth in scale and severity of incarceration in the past 30 years, placing the U.S. far in the lead worldwide. The victims are overwhelmingly African-American males and other minorities, a great many of them sentenced on victimless drug charges. Drug use is about the same as in privileged white sectors, which are mostly immune.

In short, while abroad the war on drugs is a thin cover for counterinsurgency, at home it functions as a civilized counterpart to Latin America limpieza social cleansing, removing a population that has become superfluous with the dismantling of the domestic productive system in the course of the neo-liberal financialization of the economy. A secondary gain is that, like the "war on crime," the "war on drugs" serves to frighten the population into obedience as domestic policies are implemented to benefit extreme wealth at the expense of the large majority, leading to staggering inequality that is breaking historical records, and stagnation of real wages for the majority while benefits decline and working hours increase.

These processes conform well to the history of prohibition, which has been well studied by legal scholars. I cannot go into the very interesting details here, but quite generally, prohibition has been aimed at control of what are called "the dangerous classes"—those who threaten the rights and well-being of the privileged dominant minorities. These observations hold worldwide where the topics have been studied. They have special meaning in the U.S. in the context of the history of African-Americans, much of which remains generally unknown. It is, of course, known that slaves were formally freed during the American Civil War, and that after ten years of relative freedom, by 1877 the gains were mostly obliterated as Reconstruction was brought to an end.

But the horrifying story is only now being researched seriously, most recently in a study called "Slavery by another name" by *Wall Street Journal* editor Douglas Blackmon. His work fills out the bare bones with shocking detail, showing how after Reconstruction African-American life was effectively criminalized, so that black males virtually became a permanent slave labor force. Conditions, however, were far worse than under slavery, for good capitalist reasons. Slaves were property, a capital investment, and were, therefore, cared for by their masters.

Those criminalized for existing are similar to wage laborers, in that the masters have no responsibility for them, except to make sure that enough are available. That was, in fact, one of the arguments used by slave owners to claim that they were more moral than those who hired labor. The argument was understood well enough by northern workers, who regarded wage labor as preferable to literal slavery only in that it was temporary, a position shared by Abraham Lincoln among others. Criminalized black slavery provided much of the basis for the American industrial revolution of the late 19th and early 20th century. It continued until World War II, when free labor was needed for war industry.

During the postwar boom, which relied substantially on the dynamic state sector that had been established under the highly successful semi-command economy of World War II, African-American workers gained a certain degree of freedom for the first time since post-Civil War Reconstruction. But since the 1970s, that process is being reversed, thanks in no small measure to the "war on drugs," which in some respects is a contemporary analogue to the criminalization of black life after the Civil War—and also provides a disciplined labor force, often in private prisons, in gross violation of international labor regulations.

For such reasons as these, we can expect that the "war on drugs" will continue until popular understanding and activism reach a point where the fundamental driving factors can be discerned and seriously addressed.

Last February, the Latin American Commission on Drugs and Democracy issued its analysis of the U.S. "war on drugs" in the past decades. The Commission, led by former Latin American presidents Cardoso, Zedillo, and Gavíria, concluded that the drug war had been a complete failure and urged a drastic change of policy, away from criminalization and "supply-side" operations towards much less costly and more effective measures of education, prevention, and treatment.

Their report had no detectable impact, just as earlier studies and the historical record have had none. That again reinforces the natural conclusion that the "drug war"—like the "war on crime" and "the war on terror"—has quite sensible goals, which are being achieved, and therefore continue in the face of a costly failure of announced goals.

Returning to the UNASUR meeting, a dose of realism and skepticism about propaganda would be helpful in evaluating the pretexts offered for the establishment of U.S. military bases in Colombia, retention of the base in Honduras, and the accompanying steps towards militarization. It is very much to be hoped that South America will bar moves towards militarization and intervention and will devote its energies to the programs of integration in both their external and internal aspects—establishing political and economic organizations, overcoming internal problems of deprivation and suffering, and strengthening varied links to the outside world.

Environmental Crises

But Latin America's problems go far beyond. The countries cannot hope to progress without overcoming their reliance on primary product exports, including crucially oil, but also minerals and food products. All these problems, challenging enough in themselves, are overshadowed by a critical global concern: the looming environmental crisis.

Current warnings by the best-informed investigators rely on the British Stern report, which is very highly regarded by leading scientists and numerous Nobel laureates in economics. On this basis, some have concluded, realistically, that "2009 may well turn out to be the decisive year in the human relationship with our home planet."

In December, a conference in Copenhagen is "to sign a new global accord on global warming," which will tell us "whether or not our political systems are up to the unprecedented challenge that climate change represents." I am quoting Bill McKibben, one of the most knowledgeable researchers. He is mildly hopeful, but that may be optimistic unless there are large-scale public campaigns to overcome the insistence of the managers of the state-corporate sector on privileging short-term gain for the few over the hope that their grandchildren will have a decent future.

At least some of the barriers are beginning to crumble, in part, because the business world perceives new opportunities for profit in alternative energy. Even the *Wall Street Journal*, one of the most stalwart deniers, has recently published a supplement with dire warnings about "climate disaster," urging that none of the options being considered may be sufficient and that it may be necessary to undertake more radical measures of geo-engineering, "cooling the planet" in some manner.

Meanwhile, the energy industries are vigorously pursuing their own agenda. They are organizing major propaganda campaigns to defeat even the mild proposals being considered in Congress. They are quite openly following the script of the corporate campaigns that have virtually destroyed the very limited health care reforms proposed by the Obama administration so effectively that the business press now exults that the insurance companies have won—and everyone else will suffer.

The picture might be much grimmer even than what the Stern report predicts. A group of MIT scientists have just released the results of what they describe as, "The most comprehensive modeling yet carried out on the likelihood of how much hotter the Earth's climate will get in this century, [showing] that without rapid and massive action, the problem will be about twice as severe as previously estimated six years ago—and could be even worse than that [because the model] does not fully incorporate other positive feedbacks that can occur, for example, if increased temperatures caused a large-scale melting of permafrost in arctic regions and subsequent release of large quantities of methane."

The leader of the project, a prominent earth scientist, says that, "There's no way the world can or should take these risks," and that, "The least-cost option to lower the risk is to start now and steadily transform the global energy system over the coming decades to low or zero greenhouse gas-emitting technologies." There is little sign of that.

While new technologies are essential, the problems go far beyond. It will be necessary to reverse the huge state-corporate social engineering projects of the post-World War II period—or at least severely ameliorate their harmful effects. These projects quite purposefully promoted an energy-wasting and environmentally destructive fossil fuel-based economy. The state-corporate programs, which included massive projects of suburbanization along with destruction and then gentrification of inner cities, began with a conspiracy by manufacturing and energy industries to buy up and destroy efficient electric public transportation systems in Los Angeles and dozens of other cities; they were convicted of criminal conspiracy and given a light tap on the wrist. The Federal government then joined in, relocating infrastructure and capital stock to suburban areas and creating the interstate highway system, under the usual pretext of "defense." Railroads were displaced by government-subsidized motor and air transport.

The public played almost no role, apart from choice within the narrowly structured framework of options designed by state-corporate managers. One result is atomization of society and entrapment of isolated individuals with self-destructive ambitions and crushing debt. A central component of these processes is the vigorous campaign of the business world to "fabricate consumers," in the words of the distinguished political economist Thorstein Veblen, and to direct people "to the superficial things of life, like fashionable consumption" (in the words of the business press). The campaign grew out of the recognition a century ago that it was no longer as easy as before to discipline the population by force and that it would, therefore, be necessary to resort to propaganda and indoctrination to curtail democratic achievements and to ensure that the "opulent minority" is protected from the "ignorant and meddlesome outsiders," the population.

These are crucial features of really existing democracy under contemporary state capitalism, a "democratic deficit" that is at the root of many of today's crises. While state-corporate power was promoting privatization of life and maximal waste of energy, it was also undermining the efficient choices that the market does not provide—another destructive built-in market inefficiency. To put it simply, if I want to get home from work, the market offers me a choice between a Ford and a Toyota, but not between a car and a subway. That's a social decision and in a democratic society would be the decision of an organized public. But that's just what the elite attack on democracy seeks to undermine.

The consequences are right before our eyes, in ways that are sometimes surreal—no less surreal than the huge resources being poured into militarization of the world while a billion people are going hungry and the rich countries are cutting back sharply on financing meager food aid. The business press recently reported that Obama's transportation secretary is in Europe seeking to contract with Spanish and other European manufacturers to build high-speed rail projects in the U.S., using federal funds that were authorized by Congress to stimulate the U.S. economy. Spain and other European countries are hoping to get U.S. taxpayer funding for the high-speed rail and related infrastructure that is badly needed in the U.S. At the same time, Washington is busy dismantling leading sectors of U.S. industry, ruining the lives of the workforce, families, and communities.

It is difficult to conjure up a more damning indictment of the economic system that has been constructed by state-corporate managers, particularly during the neoliberal era. Surely the auto industry could be reconstructed to produce what the country needs, using its highly skilled workforce—and what the world needs—and soon, if we are to have some hope of averting major catastrophe. It has been done before, after all. During World War II, the semi-command economy not only ended the Great Depression, but also initiated the most spectacular period of growth in economic history, virtually quadrupling industrial

production in four years as the economy was retooled for war, and laying the basis for the "golden age" that followed.

But all such matters are off the agenda and will continue to be until the severe democratic deficit is overcome. In a sane world, workers and communities would take over the abandoned factories, convert them to socially useful production, and run the factories themselves. That has been tried, but was blocked in the courts. To succeed, such efforts would require a level of popular support and working class consciousness that is not manifest in recent years, but that could be reawakened and could have large-scale effects.

These issues should be very prominent right here in Venezuela, as in other oil-producing countries. They were discussed by President Chavez at the meeting of the UN General Assembly in September 2005. I will quote his words, which unfortunately were not reported, at least in the U.S. press: "Ladies and gentlemen, we are facing an unprecedented energy crisis in which an unstoppable increase of energy is perilously reaching record highs, as well as the incapacity of increased oil supply and the perspective of a decline in the proven reserves of fuel worldwide…. It is unpractical and unethical to sacrifice the human race by appealing in an insane manner to the validity of a socioeconomic model that has a galloping destructive capacity. It would be suicidal to spread it and impose it as an infallible remedy for the evils which are caused precisely by them."

These words point in the right direction. To avoid the suicide of the species there must be coordinated efforts of producers and users, and radical changes in prevailing socioeconomic models and global organization. These are very large and urgent challenges. There can be no delay in understanding them, and acting decisively to address them.

From Z Magazine, *October 2009*
Volume 22, Number 10

24.

Reflections On Empire, Inequality, and Brand Obama

By Paul Street

HERE ARE 53 WORDS that might help situate President-elect Barack Obama in the world of power as it really is, not as many of us wish it to be: "As we understand it, Obama has been advised and agrees that there is no peace dividend.... In addition, we believe, based on discussions with industry sources, that Obama has agreed not to cut the defense budget at least until the first 18 months of his term as the national security situation becomes better understood." These two sentences come from a report issued by the leading Wall Street investment firm Morgan Stanley one day after the November 2008 elections.

"Defense" is in an interesting label for a giant military budget that pays for two occupations (in Iraq and Afghanistan) and 770 military bases located in more than 130 countries. The United States accounts for nearly half (48 percent) the military spending on the planet.

The company probably understates matters. We should not anticipate significant Pentagon expenditure reductions at any point under the new Administration, unless they are forced by popular pressure that the American power elite expects Obama to preempt. "The Democrats," Morgan Stanley's researchers note, "are sensitive about appearing weak on defense and we don't expect strong cuts."

"Defense" is in an interesting label for a giant military budget that pays for two occupations (in Iraq and Afghanistan) and 770 military bases located in more than 130 countries. The United

States accounts for nearly half (48 percent) the military spending on the planet. Coming in at $1 trillion (by the measure of the U.S. Office of Management and Budget's National Income and Product Accounts) in 2007, American "defense" spending outweighs domestic U.S federal expenditure on education by more than 8 to 1; income security by more than 4.5 to 1; nutrition by more than 11 to 1; housing by 14 to 1; and job training by 32 to 1. The military accounts for more than half of all discretionary federal spending.

The "peace dividend" refers to the notion of reversing these "perverted national priorities" (Dr. Martin Luther King's phrase) by taking money spent on war and the preparation for war and using it to address human problems like poverty, ecological crisis, crumbling infrastructure, joblessness, and inadequate education, health, housing, and schooling.

The idea of a "peace dividend" received some attention in the U.S. around the end of the Cold War, when many progressives hoped that the collapse of the Soviet Union would encourage a shift in public resources from militarism to social health.

For nearly half a century, the alleged (mythical) threat posed by Russian "communism" provided the core propagandistic justification for the expansion and use of U.S. military power. With the Soviet-specter eliminated, progressives dreamed the U.S. could now be realistically pressured to transfer significant public resources towards meeting social needs and away from the maintenance of the most spectacular and deadly military-imperial system in history.

The dream was ended by George Bush I's two wars of invasion (Panama, 1989 and Iraq, 1990-91), Bill Clinton's air war on Serbia (1999), and the dominant U.S. media throughout. The "military-industrial-media triangle" (John Bellamy Foster, Hannah Holeman, and Robert W. McChesney's term) and its many enablers and allies in church, school, academia, and other wings of so-called "civil society"

rapidly substituted new pretexts for the persistence of a permanently militarized U.S. economy and culture: purported protection and advance of "free markets" and "democracy" (falsely conflated), the U.S, right of "humanitarian intervention," and the grave dangers posed by terrorists, drug traffickers, and "weapons of mass destruction."

Still, a 2004 poll by the Chicago Council of Foreign Relations found that just 29 percent of Americans support the expansion of government spending on "defense." By contrast, 79 percent support increased spending on health care, 69 percent support increased spending on education, and 69 percent support increased spending on Social Security.

The American Moment

Obama's National Security cabinet picks were consistent with Morgan Stanley's judgment on the president-elect's likely policy direction. As *New York Times* political analyst David Sanger noted on his paper's front page in December, those appointments include "two veteran Cold Warriors [National Security Adviser and former NATO commander James L. Jones and current and future Defense Secretary Robert Gates] and a political rival [Secretary of State Hillary Clinton] whose records are all more hawkish than the new president."

Sanger's commentary left out other "hawkish" appointments, including Vice President Joe Biden (a major facilitator of George W. Bush's pre-Iraq invasion propaganda in the U.S. Senate), United Nations Ambassador Susan Rice (an eager promoter of the myth that Saddam Hussein possessed "weapons of mass destruction" and "need[ed] to be dealt with forcefully"), and White House Chief of Staff Rahm Emmanuel (a fierce opponent of anti-war sentiment inside the Democratic Party and a leading supporter of U.S.-sponsored Israeli militarism, occupation, and apartheid).

Sanger also deleted the critical fact that Obama's real foreign policy record is much more "hawkish" than the dovish imagery his marketers crafted for liberal and progressive voters during the presidential campaign. Beyond his longstanding stealth support for the occupation of Iraq, Obama has repeatedly announced his fierce devotion to the broader underlying American empire project in numerous statements meant to demonstrate his safety to the U.S. foreign policy establishment.

Declaring that "we can be [Kennedy's] America again," a 2007 Obama article (titled "Renewing American Leadership") in the Council of Foreign Relations journal *Foreign Affairs*, Obama essentially accused the Bush administration of dropping the ball of American world supremacy. "The American moment is not over, but it must be seized anew," Obama proclaimed, adding that "we must lead the world by deed and by example" and "must not rule out using military force" in pursuit of "our vital interests." The last three words a code phrase for other nations' oil, located primarily in the Middle East.

"A strong military," Obama wrote, "is, more than anything, necessary to sustain peace." We must "revitalize our military" to foster "peace," Obama added, partly by adding 65,000 soldiers to the Army and 27,000 to the Marines. "We must also become better prepared to put boots on the ground...on a global scale." Reassuring top militarists that he would not be hamstrung by international law and civilized norms when "our vital interests" are "at stake," Obama added that "I will not hesitate to use force unilaterally, if necessary.... We must also consider using military force in circumstances beyond self-defense in order to provide for the common security that underpins global stability."

Leading neoconservative foreign policy advisor Robert Kagan crowed after reading a typically imperial Obama speech to the Chicago Council on Global Affairs last year: "Obama talks about...maintaining 'a strong nuclear deterrent.' He talks about how we need to 'seize' the 'American moment.' We must 'begin the world anew.' This is realism? This is left-liberal foreign policy? Ask Noam Chomsky next time you see him" (*Washington Post*, April 29, 2007).

"Spiritual Death" Lives

According to Dr. Martin Luther King, Jr. in 1967, "A nation that continues year after year to spend more money on military defense than on programs of social uplift, is approaching spiritual death." Thirty-one years later, as the openly imperial Obama ascends to power draped (for many) in the rebel's clothing of Dr. King, the top 1 percent in the U.S. owns nearly 40 percent of the nation's wealth—a natural outcome of the so-called "free market capitalism" Obama repeatedly embraced during the presidential campaign.

A shocking 43 percent (equaling nearly 16 million) of those officially poor Americans live in what researchers call "deep poverty," at less than half the federal government's notoriously inadequate poverty

The privileged American "overclass" enjoys astonishing opulence while more than 37 million Americans live beneath the federal government's notoriously inadequate poverty level, even before the onset of full-blown economic crisis in the fall and winter of 2008-09. A shocking 43 percent (equaling nearly 16 million) of those officially poor Americans live in what researchers call "deep poverty," at less than half the federal government's notoriously inadequate poverty.

Deep poverty has been on the rise in the U.S. over recent years and decades, thanks in part to Bill Clinton and Newt Gingrich's elimination ("reform") of poor families' entitlement to federal family cash assistance. Currently at its highest rate since 1975, the "deep poverty" measure and other terrible socioeconomic indicators will only worsen as the U.S. heads into its worst recession since the 1970s and, perhaps, into a depression.

Even without recessions or depressions, the U.S. is the industrialized world's most unequal and wealth top-heavy society by far. Wealthy Americans have the benefit of the finest health care in history while 45 million Americans lacked health insurance even before the latest recession. Expect that number to hit 50 million any day if it hasn't already. African Americans are afflicted with a national median-house-

> *Numerous interrelated forms of institutional racism continue to saddle black America with a heavily disproportionate burden of poverty, injury, sickness, homelessness, unemployment, incarceration, and criminal marking even as the nation celebrates Obama's election as a symbol of its transcendence of racial bigotry*

hold-wealth gap of seven black cents on the white dollar. Numerous interrelated forms of institutional racism continue to saddle black America with a heavily disproportionate burden of poverty, injury, sickness, homelessness, unemployment, incarceration, and criminal marking even as the nation celebrates Obama's election as a symbol of its transcendence of racial bigotry.

Meanwhile, American corporations and wealthy elites get regular public assistance (corporate welfare) that belies the privileged few's ritual proclamations of faith in the mythical notion of free market capitalism. They profit from numerous powerful state-capitalist protections and subsidies while U.S. social programs are minimal compared to those of Western Europe and Canada.

The extravagant "defense" (empire) budget that Morgan Stanley expects Obama to keep funded at fantastic levels, even while deep poverty spreads at home and abroad, is itself a giant public subsidy to leading high-tech and energy corporations like Boeing, Raytheon, General Dynamics, Lockheed Martin, and the oil

majors, who have enjoyed record profits during the recent and continuing "wartime" period.

The need for a peace dividend is more urgent than ever in what John Bellamy Foster rightly calls "a period of imperialist development that is potentially the most dangerous in all of history"—one where "life on the planet as we know it can be destroyed either instantaneously through global nuclear holocaust, or in a matter of a few generations by climate change and other manifestations of environmental destruction." As Foster, Hannah Holleman, and Robert W. McChesney recently argued in *Monthly Review*: "A society that supports its global position and social order through $1 trillion a year in military spending, most likely far exceeding that of all the other countries in the world put together—unleashing untold destruction on the world, while faced with intractable problems of inequality, economic stagnation, financial crisis, poverty, waste, and environmental decline at home—is a society that is ripe for change."

Put less delicately, it is a society overdue for what the democratic socialist Dr. King called the "real issue to be faced" beyond "superficial" problems: "radical reconstruction of society itself."

Accommodate Existing Institutions

Obama would never have been permitted to make a serious presidential run if the U.S. ruling class believed he shared King's hopes for "radical reconstruction." The corporate and imperial gatekeepers of U.S. power are not in the business of handing over the world's most potent office to progressive opponents of empire and inequality. They began determining five years ago (as Obama was picked to run for the U.S. Senate) that Obama the politician was a privilege-friendly person of the state-capitalist, neoliberal center. As Larissa MacFarquhar noted last year in a carefully researched *New Yorker* essay: "In his view of history, in his respect for tradition, in his skepticism that the world can be changed any way but very, very slowly, Obama is deeply conservative.... It's not just that he thinks revolutions are unlikely," MacFarquhar added. It's also, she wrote, that, "He values continuity and stability for their own sake, sometimes even more than he values change for the good" ("The Conciliator," May 7, 2007).

According to liberal journalist Ryan Lizza in the *New Yorker* last summer: "Perhaps the greatest misconception about Barack Obama is that he is some sort of anti-establishment revolutionary. Rather, every stage of his political career has been marked by an eagerness to accommodate himself to existing institutions rather than tear them down or replace them" ("Making It," July 21, 2008).

Left, black political scientist Adolph Reed, Jr., who once lived in Obama's Illinois state-legislative district, described Obama in the *Village Voice* in 1996, at the literal beginning of Obama's political career, as follows: "In Chicago, for instance, we've gotten a foretaste of the new breed of foundation-hatched black communitarian voices: one of them, a smooth Harvard lawyer with impeccable credentials and vacuous-to-repressive neoliberal politics, has won a state senate seat on a base mainly in the liberal foundation and development worlds. His fundamentally bootstrap line was softened by a patina of the rhetoric of authentic community, talk about meeting in kitchens, small-scale solutions to social problems, and the predictable elevation of process over program—the point where identity politics converges with old-fashioned middle class reform in favoring form over substance. I suspect that his ilk is the wave of the future in U.S. black

"In Chicago, for instance, we've gotten a foretaste of the new breed of foundation-hatched black communitarian voices: one of them, a smooth Harvard lawyer with impeccable credentials and vacuous-to-repressive neoliberal politics, has won a state senate seat on a base mainly in the liberal foundation and development worlds...."

politics here, as in Haiti and wherever the International Monetary Fund has sway."

Consistent with these reflections, Obama's guaranteed choice health care plan amounts to a probably unworkable "half-way solution" that falls short of the public's longstanding desire for universal national health insurance. It preserves the power and profits of the institutions most responsible for the health care crisis—private insurance and pharmaceutical corporations. "Despite Barack Obama's avowed hopes for change," Roger Bybee notes, the president's health reform "manacled to private insurers, may ultimately deepen public cynicism of the possibility of meaningful reform" (*Z Magazine*, December 2008).

In a similar vein, "Obamanomics" falls short of the progressive initiatives and challenges to financial and corporate power required to spark equitable domestic development. As adjusted in response to the banking crisis and deepening recession, moreover, Obama's economic program may well amount to "something akin to a national austerity program...." Instead of forward movement on jobs, education, retirement, and health care, Jack Rasmus finds, "what me may well get is 'Let's all tighten our belts to get through this crisis'" (*Z Magazine*, December 2008).

But like most of the nation's elected office-holders, Obama supports a massive taxpayer-funded bailout of leading Wall Street financial and insurance firms deemed "too big [and powerful] to fail"—a curious government payout for parasitic enterprises that have driven the national and global economy into the ground. Morgan Stanley alone is slated to receive tens of billions of federal dollars, a giant state capital dividend approved by Obama even as the firm's analysts observe Obama's conventional establishment wisdom holding that "there is no peace dividend."

Obama's "economic team," including Lawrence Summers (top economic advisor) and Treasury Secretary Timothy Geithner, is full of reigning neoliberals calling for the socialization of the market economy's losses and the upward privatization of its gains.

Holding Constituencies in Check

Obama's business-friendly centrism helped him garner record-setting corporate campaign contributions during the last election cycle. He received more than $33 million from "FIRE" (the finance-real-estate and insurance sector), including $824,202 from Goldman Sachs. He has been consistently backed by the biggest and most powerful Wall Street firms. At the same time, and by more than mere coincidence, candidate Obama enjoyed a remarkable windfall of favorable corporate media coverage—the key to his success in winning votes and small donations from middle-class and non-affluent people.

As many of his elite sponsors certainly understand, Obama's outwardly progressive persona is perfectly calibrated to divert, capture, control, and contain popular rebellions. He is uniquely qualified to simultaneously surf, de-fang, and "manage" the U.S. and world citizenry's rising hopes for democratic transformation in the wake of the long national Bush-Cheney nightmare. As John Pilger noted last May, "By offering a 'new,' young and apparently progressive face of the Democratic Party—with the bonus of being a member of the black elite—he can blunt and divert real opposition," bringing "intense pressure on the U.S. antiwar and social justice movements to accept a Democratic administration for all its faults."

Sadly enough, Obama's race is part of what makes him so well matched to the tasks of mass pacification and popular "expectation management" (former Obama advisor Samantha Power's revealing phrase). As Aurora Levins Morales noted in Z Magazine last April, "This election is about finding a CEO capable of holding domestic constituencies in check as they are further disenfranchised and...[about] mak[ing] them feel that they have a stake in the military aggressiveness that the ruling class believes is necessary. Having a black man and a white woman run helps to obscure the fact that...decline of empire is driving the political elite to the right.... Part of the cleverness of having such candidates is the fact that they will be attacked in ways that make oppressed people feel compelled to protect them."

Imperial "Re-branding"

The logic works at the global level. A considerable segment of the U.S. foreign policy establishment thinks that Obama's race, name (technically Islamic), experience living in (Muslim Indonesia, as a child) and visiting (chiefly his father's homeland, Kenya) poor nations, and his nominally "anti-war" history will help them repackage U.S. world power in more politically correct wrapping. John F. Kerry, who ran for the presidency four years earlier largely on the claim that he would be a more effective imperial manager than George W. Bush, was thinking of these critical "soft power" assets when he praised Obama as someone who could "reinvent America's image abroad." So was Obama when he said to reporters aboard his campaign plane in 2007: "If I am the face of American foreign policy and American power...you can tell people, 'We have a president in the White House who still has a grandmother living in a hut on the shores of Lake Victoria and has a sister who's half-Indonesian married to a Chinese-Canadian,' then they're going to think that 'he may have a better sense of what's going on in our lives and country.'"

Obama's global biography, ethno-cultural nomenclature, and charisma are great attractions to a predominantly caucasian U.S. foreign policy elite hoping to restore American legitimacy in a majority non-white world that has been provoked and disgusted by U.S. behavior in the post-9/11 era (and truthfully before). He is in many ways an ideal symbol of imperial "re-branding." According to centrist *New York Times* columnist Nicholas Kristof just before the election, the ascendancy of a black president "could change global perceptions of the United States, redefining the American 'brand' to be less about Guantanamo and more about equality."

The leading advertising trade journal *Advertising Age* agreed. Last October it hailed Obama as "Marketer of the Year" and praised him for producing "An Instant Overhaul for Tainted Brand America." The journal quoted David Brain, CEO of the global public relations firm Edelman Europe, Middle East and Africa, on how "the election and nomination process is the brand relaunch of the year. Brand USA. It's just fantastic."

According to Nick Ragone, the senior VP of client development at the global advertising firm Omnicom Group's Ketchum, "We've put a new face on [America] and that face happens to be African American." Ragone told *Advertising Age* that "it takes a lot of the hubris and arrogance of the last eight years and starts to put it in the rearview mirror for us."

Harvard Business School professor and former WWP Group (a global advertising firm) board member John Quelch (co-author of *Greater Good: How Good Marketing Makes for Better Democracy*) told *Advertising Age* that, "The election result zero-bases the image of the United States worldwide. We have a clean slate with which to work."

Carolyn Carter, the London-based president and CEO of Grey Group Europe, Middle East and Africa (creator of the teeth-rotting "Coke Zero" ad campaign in Northern

Europe) agreed, adding, "The last eight years broke faith in Brand America, and people want that faith restored."

Enter Obama, who is "almost like Che Guevera, in a good way," according to *Foreign Policy* magazine's web editor Blake Hounshell. "He has icon status," Hounshell explains, "with all the art around the world of his face." The difference is that Che roused independent left and Third World challenges to the American Empire while Obama inspires cap-

> *Vast swaths of suffering humanity are increasingly desperate for true progressive change and a peace dividend beneath and beyond quadrennial corporate-crafted and candidate-centered U.S. "election extravaganzas"*

tivation with the corporate-imperial U.S. According to Scott Kronick, global marketing firm Ogilvy PR's Beijing-based president, Obama's triumph "sends a strong message to the world that despite what many people believe and feel...America can be very open, democratic, and progressive."

Call it the identity politics of foreign policy. The old empire wants new, faux-progressive clothes and Obama is just the person to wear them. According to the former Clinton administration official and Kissinger Associates director David J. Rothkopf, Obama's cabinet picks epitomize "the violin model: hold power with the left hand and play the music with your right" (*NYT*, November 21, 2008).

Meanwhile, the poverty population's ranks are rising and the poor are getting poorer at home and abroad. Vast swaths of suffering humanity are increasingly desperate for true progressive change and a peace dividend beneath and beyond quadrennial corporate-crafted and candidate-centered U.S. "electoral extravaganzas" (Noam Chomsky's phrase). Obama will deliver only as much change as he can be compelled to by popular resistance and rebellion.

It is wonderful and historic that the American electorate put a black family in the White House. Still, Barack Obama is no magical exception to the rule observed last spring by Howard Zinn: "Let's remember that even when there is a 'better' candidate (yes, better Roosevelt than Hoover, better anyone than George Bush), that difference will not mean anything unless the power of the people asserts itself in ways that the occupant of the White House will find it dangerous to ignore...."

From Z Magazine, *January 2009*
Volume 22, Number 1

25.

We Own The World

From a Z Media Institute talk

By Noam Chomsky

YOU ALL KNOW, of course, there was an election—what is called "an election" in the United States. There was really one issue in the election, what to do about U.S. forces in Iraq and there was, by U.S. standards, an overwhelming vote calling for a withdrawal of U.S. forces on a firm timetable.

> *This poll found that two-thirds of the people in Baghdad wanted the U.S. troops out immediately; the rest of the country—a large majority—wanted a firm timetable for withdrawal, most of them within a year or less*

As few people know, a couple of months earlier there were extensive polls in Iraq, U.S.-run polls, with interesting results. They were not secret here. If you really looked, you could find references to them so it's not that they were concealed. This poll found that two-thirds of the people in Baghdad wanted the U.S. troops out immediately; the rest of the country—a large majority—wanted a firm timetable for withdrawal, most of them within a year or less.

The figures are higher for Arab Iraq in the areas where troops were actually deployed. A very large majority felt that the presence of U.S. forces increased the level of violence and a remarkable 60 percent for all of Iraq, meaning higher in the areas where the troops are deployed, felt that U.S. forces were legitimate targets of attack. So there was a considerable consensus between Iraqis and Americans on what should be done in Iraq, namely troops should be withdrawn either immediately or with a firm timetable.

Well, the reaction of the post-election U.S. government to that consensus was to violate public opinion and increase the troop presence by maybe 30,000 to 50,000. Predictably, there was a pretext announced. It was pretty obvious what it was going to be. "There is outside interference in Iraq, which we have to defend the Iraqis against. The Iranians are interfering in Iraq." Then came the alleged evidence about finding IEDs, roadside bombs with Iranian markings, as well as Iranian forces in Iraq. "What can we do? We have to escalate to defend Iraq from the outside intervention."

Then came the "debate." We are a free and open society, after all, so we have "lively" debates. On the one side were the hawks who said, "The Iranians are interfering, we have to bomb them." On the other side were the doves who said, "We cannot be sure the evidence is correct, maybe you misread the serial numbers or maybe it is just the revolutionary guards and not the government."

So we had the usual kind of debate going on, which illustrates a very important and pervasive distinction between several types of propaganda systems. To take the ideal types, exaggerating a little: totalitarian states' propaganda is that you better accept it, or else. And "or else" can be of various consequences, depending on the nature of the state. People can believe whatever they want as long as they obey.

Democratic societies use a different method: they don't articulate the party line.

Democratic societies use a different method: they don't articulate the party line. What they do is presuppose it, then encourage vigorous debate within the framework of the party line.

What they do is presuppose it, then encourage vigorous debate within the framework of the party line. This serves two purposes. For one thing it gives the impression of a free and open society because, after all, we have lively debate. It also instills a propaganda line that becomes something you presuppose, like the air you breathe.

That was the case here. This is a classic illustration. If you look at the debate that took place and is still taking place about Iranian interference, no one points out that this is in-

sane. How can Iran be interfering in a country that we invaded and occupied? It's only appropriate on the presupposition that we own the world. Once you have that established in your head, the discussion is perfectly sensible.

You read a lot of comparisons now about Vietnam and Iraq. But almost everything is totally different except in one respect: how they are perceived in the United States. In both cases there is what is now sometimes called the "Q" word, quagmire. Is it a quagmire? It is now recognized that Vietnam was a quagmire. There is a debate on whether Iraq, too, is a quagmire. In other words, is it costing us too much? That is the question you can debate.

So in the case of Vietnam, there was a debate. Not at the beginning—in fact, there was so little discussion in the beginning that nobody even remembers when the war began—1962, if you're interested. That's when the U.S. attacked Vietnam. But there was no discussion, no debate, nothing.

By the mid-1960s, mainstream debate began and it was the usual range of opinions between the hawks and the doves. The hawks said, if we send more troops, we can win. The doves, well, Arthur Schlesinger, historian and Kennedy advisor, said in his book (1966) that we all pray that the hawks will be right and that the current escalation of troops, which by then was approaching half a million, will work and bring us victory. If it does, we will all be praising the wisdom and statesmanship of the American government for winning victory—in a land that we're reducing to ruin and wreck.

You can translate that word by word to the doves today. We all pray that the surge will work. If it does, contrary to our expectations, we will be praising the wisdom and statesmanship of the Bush administration in a country, which, if we're honest, is a total ruin, one of the worst disasters in military history for the population.

If you get way to the left end of mainstream discussion, you get somebody like Anthony Lewis who, at the end of the Vietnam War in 1975, wrote, in retrospect, that the war began with benign intensions to do good; that is true by definition, because it's us, after all. But by 1969, he said, it was clear that the war was a mistake. For us to win a victory would be too costly—for us—so it was a mistake and we should withdraw. That was the most extreme criticism.

Very much like today. We could withdraw from Vietnam because the U.S. had already essentially obtained its objective by then.In Iraq we can't because we haven't obtained our objectives. For those of you who are old enough to remember—or have read about it—you will note that the peace movement pretty much bought that line. Just like the mainstream discussion, the opposition to the war, including the peace movement, was mostly focused on the bombing of the North. When the U.S. started bombing the North regularly in February 1965, it also escalated the bombing of the South to triple the scale—and the South had already been attacked for three years by then. A couple of hundred thousand South Vietnamese were killed and thousands, if not tens of thousands, had been driven into concentration camps.

The U.S. had been carrying out chemical warfare to destroy food crops and ground cover. By 1965, South Vietnam was already a total wreck.

Bombing the South was costless for the United States because the South had no defense. Bombing the North was costly—you bomb the North, you bomb the harbor, you might hit Russian ships, which begins to become dangerous. You're bombing an internal Chinese railroad—the Chinese railroads from southeast to southwest China happen to go through North Vietnam—who knows what they might do.

In fact, the Chinese were accused, correctly, of sending Chinese forces into Viet-

nam, namely to rebuild the railroad that we were bombing. So that was "interference" with our divine right to bomb North Vietnam. So most of the focus was on the bombing of the North. The peace movement slogan, "Stop the bombing" meant the bombing of the North.

In 1967 the leading specialist on Vietnam, Bernard Fall, a military historian and the only specialist on Vietnam respected by the U.S. government—who was a hawk, incidentally, but who cared about the Vietnamese—wrote that it's a question of whether Vietnam will survive as a cultural and historical entity under the most severe bombing that has ever been applied to a country this size. He was talking about the South. He kept emphasizing it was the South that was being attacked. But that didn't matter because it was costless, therefore it's fine to continue. That is the range of debate, which only makes sense on the assumption that we own the world.

If you read, say, the *Pentagon Papers*, it turns out there was extensive planning about the bombing of the North—very detailed, meticulous planning on just how far it can go. What happens if we go a little too far, and so on. There is no discussion at all about the bombing of the South, virtually none. Just an occasional announcement, okay, we will triple the bombing or something like that.

If you read Robert McNamara's memoirs of the war—by that time he was considered a leading dove. He reviews the meticulous planning about the bombing of the North, but does not even mention his decision to sharply escalate the bombing of the South at the same time that the bombing of the North was begun.

I should say, incidentally, that with regard to Vietnam what I have been discussing is articulate opinion, including the leading part of the peace movement. There was also public opinion, which it turns out is radically different and that is of some significance. By 1969 around 70 percent of the public felt that the war was fundamentally wrong and immoral. That was the wording of the polls, and that figure remains fairly constant up until the most recent polls just a few years ago. The figures are pretty remarkable because people who say that in a poll almost certainly think, I must be the only person in the world that thinks this. They certainly did not read it anywhere, they did not hear it anywhere. But that was popular opinion.

The same is true with regard to many other issues. But for articulate opinion it's pretty much the way I've described—largely vigorous

> By 1969 around 70 percent of the public felt that the war was fundamentally wrong and immoral. That was the wording of the polls, and that figure remains fairly constant up until the most recent polls just a few years ago.

debate between the hawks and the doves, all on the unexpressed assumption that we own the world. So the only thing that matters is how much is it costing us or for some more humane types, are we harming too many of them?

Re-Missioning

Getting back to the election, there was a lot of disappointment among anti-war people—the majority of the population—that Congress did not pass any withdrawal legislation. There was a Democratic resolution that was vetoed, but if you look at the resolution closely it was not a withdrawal resolution. There was a good analysis of it by General Kevin Ryan, who was a fellow at the Kennedy School at Harvard. He went through it and he said it really should be called a re-missioning proposal. It leaves about the same number of American troops, but with a slightly different mission.

He said, first of all, it allows for a national security exception. If the president says there is a national security issue, he can do whatever he wants—end of resolution. The second gap

is it allows for anti-terrorist activities. Okay, that is whatever you like. Third, it allows for training Iraqi forces. Again, anything you like.

Next, it says troops have to remain for protection of U.S. forces and facilities. What are U.S. forces? Well, U.S. forces are those embedded in Iraqi armed units where 60 percent of their fellow soldiers think that they—U.S. troops, that is—are legitimate targets of attack. Incidentally, those figures keep going up, so they are probably higher by now.

Well, okay, that is plenty of force protection. What facilities need protection was not explained in the Democratic resolution, but facilities include what is called "the embassy." The U.S. embassy in Iraq is nothing like any embassy that has ever existed in history. It's a city inside the green zone, the protected region of Iraq, that the U.S. runs. It's got everything from missiles to McDonalds, anything you want. They didn't build that huge facility because they intend to leave.

That is one facility, but there are others. There are "semi-permanent military bases," which are being built around the country. "Semipermanent" means as long as we want. General Ryan omitted a lot of things. He omitted the fact that the U.S. is maintaining control of logistics and logistics is the core of a modern Army. Right now about 80 percent of the supply is coming in though the south, from Kuwait, and it's going through guerilla territory, easily subject to attack, which means you have to have plenty of troops to maintain that supply line. Plus, of course, to keep control over the Iraqi Army.

The Democratic resolution excludes the Air Force. The Air Force does whatever it wants. It is bombing pretty regularly and it can bomb more intensively. The resolution also excludes mercenaries, which is no small number—sources such as the *Wall Street Journal* estimate the number of mercenaries at about 130,000, approximately the same as the number of troops, which makes some sense. The traditional way to fight a colonial war is with mercenaries, not with your own soldiers—that is the French Foreign Legion, the British Ghurkas, or the Hessians in the Revolutionary War. That is part of the main reason the draft was dropped—so you get professional soldiers, not people you pick off the streets.

So, yes, it is re-missioning, but the resolution was vetoed because it was too strong, so we don't even have that. And, yes, that did disappoint a lot of people. However, it would be too strong to say that no high official in Washington called for immediate withdrawal. There were some. The strongest one I know of—when asked what is the solution to the problem in Iraq—said it's quite obvious, "Withdraw all foreign forces and withdraw all foreign arms." That official was Condoleeza Rice and she was not referring to U.S. forces, she was referring to Iranian forces and Iranian arms. And that makes sense, too, on the assumption that we own the world because, since we own the world and, therefore, U.S. forces cannot be foreign forces anywhere. If we invade Iraq or Canada, say, we are the indigenous forces. It's the Iranians that are foreign forces.

I waited for a while to see if anyone, at least in the press or journals, would point out that there was something funny about this. I could not find anyone who said, wait a second, there are foreign forces there, 150,000 American troops, plenty of American arms. So, when British sailors were captured in the Gulf by Iranian forces, there was debate, "Were they in Iranian borders or in Iraqi borders?" Actually, there is no answer to this because there is no territorial boundary, and that was pointed out. It was taken for granted that if British sailors were in Iraqi waters, then Iran was guilty of a crime by intervening in foreign territory. But Britain is not considered guilty of a crime by being in Iraqi territory because Britain is a U.S. client state and we own the world, so Britain is there by right.

What about the possible next war—Iran? There have been very credible threats by the U.S. and Israel—essentially a U.S. client—to attack Iran. There happens to be something called the UN Charter which says in Article 2

> *It was anticipated by U.S. intelligence and other intelligence agencies and independent experts that an attack on Iraq would probably increase the threat of terror and nuclear proliferation. But that went way beyond what anyone expected.*

that the "threat or use of force" in international affairs is a crime. Does anybody care? No, because we're an outlaw state by definition or, to be more precise, our threats and use of force are not foreign, they're indigenous because we own the world. So there are threats to bomb Iran—maybe we will and maybe we won't. That is the debate that goes on. Is it legitimate if we decide to do it? People might argue it's a mistake. But does anyone say it would be illegitimate? For example, the Democrats in Congress refused to include an amendment that would require the Executive to inform Congress if it intends to bomb Iran— to consult, inform. Even that is not accepted.

The whole world is aghast at this possibility. It would be monstrous. A leading British military historian, Correlli Barnett, wrote recently that if the U.S. does attack, or Israel does attack, it would be World War III. The attack on Iraq has been horrendous enough. Apart from devastating Iraq, the UN High Commission on Refugees reviewed the number of displaced people—they estimate 4.2 million, over 2 million fled the country, another 2 million fleeing within the country. That is in addition to the numbers killed, which if you extrapolate from the last studies, are probably approaching a million.

It was anticipated by U.S. intelligence and other intelligence agencies and independent experts that an attack on Iraq would probably increase the threat of terror and nuclear proliferation. But that went way beyond what anyone expected. Well known terrorism specialists Peter Bergen and Paul Cruickshank estimated —using mostly government statistics—that what they call "the Iraq effect" increased terror by a factor of seven, and that is pretty serious and gives you an indication of the ranking of protection of the population on the priority list of leaders. It's very low.

So what would the Iran effect be? Well, that is incalculable. It could be World War III. Very likely a massive increase in terror, who knows what else. Even in the states right around Iraq that don't like Iran—Pakistan, Saudi Arabia, and Turkey—even there the large majority would prefer to see a nuclear armed Iran to any U.S. military action, and they are right. Military action could be devastating. It doesn't mean we won't do it. There is very little discussion here of the illegitimacy of doing it, again on the assumption that anything we do is legitimate, it just might cost too much.

Is there a possible solution to the U.S./Iran crisis? Well, one possibility would be an agreement that allows Iran to have nuclear energy—like every signer of the non-prolifera-

> The problem in the United States is the inability of organizers to do something in a population that overwhelmingly agrees with them and to make that current policy. Of course, it can be done. Peasants in Bolivia can do it, we can obviously do it here.

tion treaty—but not to have nuclear weapons. In addition, it would call for a nuclear weapons free zone in the Middle East. That would include Iran, Israel (which has hundreds of nuclear weapons), and any U.S. or British forces deployed in the region. A third element of a solution would be for the United States and other nuclear states to obey their legal obligation, by unanimous agreement of the World

Court, to make good-faith moves to eliminate nuclear weapons entirely.

Is this feasible? Well, it's feasible on one assumption, that the United States and Iran become functioning democratic societies because what I have just quoted happens to be the opinion of the overwhelming majority of the populations in Iran and the United States. On everything that I've mentioned there is an overwhelming majority. So, yes, there would be a very feasible solution if these two countries were functioning democratic societies, meaning societies in which public opinion has some kind of effect on policy. The problem in the United States is the inability of organizers to do something in a population that overwhelmingly agrees with them and to make that current policy. Of course, it can be done. Peasants in Bolivia can do it, we can obviously do it here.

Can we do anything to make Iran a more democratic society? Not directly, but indirectly we can. We can pay attention to the dissidents and the reformists in Iran who are struggling courageously to turn Iran into a more democratic society. We know exactly what they are saying, they are very outspoken about it. They are pleading with the United States to withdraw the threats against Iran. The more we threaten Iran, the more we give a gift to the reactionary, religious fanatics in the government. The threats have led to repression, predictably.

Now the Americans claim they are outraged by the repression, which we should protest, but we should recognize that the repression is the direct and predictable consequence of the actions that the U.S. government is taking. So if you take actions and then they have predictable consequences, condemning the consequences is total hypocrisy.

Incidentally, in the case of Cuba about two-thirds of Americans think we ought to end the embargo and all threats and enter into diplomatic relations. That has been true ever since polls have been taken—for about 30 years. The figure varies, but it's roughly there. Zero effect on policy, in Iran, Cuba, and elsewhere.

So there is a problem and that problem is that the United States is not a functioning democracy. Public opinion does not matter and among articulate and elite opinion that is a principle—it shouldn't matter. The only principle that matters is we own the world and the rest of you shut up, whether you're abroad or at home.

So, there is a potential solution to a very dangerous problem, it's essentially the same solution: do something to turn our own country into a functioning democracy. But that is in radical opposition to the fundamental presupposition of all elite discussions, mainly that we own the world and that these questions don't arise and the public should have no opinion on foreign policy, or any policy.

Once, when I was driving to work, I was listening to National Public Radio (NPR) which is supposed to be the kind of extreme radical end of the spectrum. I read a statement somewhere, I don't know if it's true, but it was a quote from Obama, who is the hope of the liberal doves, in which he allegedly said that the spectrum of discussion in the United States extends between two crazy extremes, Rush Limbaugh and NPR. The truth, he said, is in the middle and that is where he is going to be, in the middle, between the "crazies."

NPR then had a discussion—it was like being at the Harvard Faculty Club—serious people, educated, no grammatical errors, who know what they're talking about, usually polite. The discussion was about the so-called missile defense system that the U.S. is trying to place in Czechoslovakia and Poland—and the Russian reaction. The main issue was, "What is going on with the Russians? Why are

they acting so hostile and irrational? Are they trying to start a new Cold War? There is something wrong with those guys. Can we calm them down and make them less paranoid?"

The main specialist they called in, I think from the Pentagon or somewhere, pointed out, accurately, that a missile defense system is essentially a first-strike weapon. That is well known by strategic analysts on all sides. If you

> *So, there is a potential solution to a very dangerous problem, it's essentially the same solution: do something to turn our own country into a functioning democracy. But that is in radical opposition to the fundamental presupposition of all elite discussions, mainly that we own the world*

think about it for a minute, it's obvious why. A missile defense system is never going to stop a first strike, but it could, in principle, if it ever worked, stop a retaliatory strike. If you attack some country with a first strike, and practically wipe it out, if you have a missile defense system, and prevent them from retaliating, then you would be protected, or partially protected. If a country has a functioning missile defense system it will have more options for carrying out a first strike. Okay, obvious, and not a secret. It's known to every strategic analyst. I can explain it to my grandchildren in two minutes and they understand it.

So on NPR it is agreed that a missile defense system is a first-strike weapon. But then comes the second part of the discussion. Well, say the pundits, the Russians should not be worried about this. For one thing because it's not enough of a system to stop their retaliation, so therefore it's not yet a first-strike weapon against them. Then they said it is kind of irrelevant anyway because it is directed against Iran, not against Russia.

Okay, that was the end of the discussion. So, point one, missile defense is a first-strike weapon; second, it's directed against Iran. Now, you can carry out a small exercise in logic. Does anything follow from those two assumptions? What follows is it's a first- strike weapon against Iran. Since the U.S. owns the world, what could be wrong with having a first-strike weapon against Iran. So the conclusion is not mentioned. It is not necessary.

A year ago or so, Germany sold advanced submarines to Israel, which were equipped to carry missiles with nuclear weapons. Why does Israel need submarines with nuclear armed missiles? There is only one imaginable reason and everyone in Germany with a brain must have understood that—certainly their military system did—it's a first-strike weapon against Iran. Israel can use German submarines to illustrate to Iranians that if they respond to an Israeli attack they will be vaporized.

The fundamental premises of Western imperialism are extremely deep. The West owns the world and now the U.S. runs the West, so, of course, they go along. The fact that they are

> *The fundamental premises of Western imperialism are extremely deep. The West owns the world and now the U.S. runs the West, so, of course, they go along. The fact that they are providing a first-strike weapon for attacking Iran—I'm guessing now—probably raised no comment because why should it?*

providing a first-strike weapon for attacking Iran—I'm guessing now—probably raised no comment because why should it?

You can forget about history, it does not matter, it's kind of "old fashioned," boring stuff we don't need to know about. But most countries pay attention to history. So, for example, for the United States there is no discussion of the history of U.S./Iranian relations. Well, for the U.S. there is only one event in Iranian history—in 1979 Iranians overthrew the tyrant that the U.S. was backing and took some hostages for over a year. That happened and they had to be punished for that.

But for Iranians their history is that for over 50 years, literally without a break, the U.S. has

been torturing Iranians. In 1953, the U.S. overthrew the parliamentary government and installed a brutal tyrant, the Shah, and kept supporting him while he compiled one of the worst human rights records in the world—torture, assassination, anything you like. In fact, President Carter, when he visited Iran in December 1978, praised the Shah because of the love shown him by his people, and so on and so forth, which probably accelerated the overthrow. Of course, Iranians have this odd way of remembering what happened to them and who was behind it. When the Shah was overthrown, the Carter administration immediately tried to instigate a military coup by sending arms to Iran through Israel to try to support military force to overthrow the government. We immediately turned to supporting Iraq, that is Saddam Hussein, and his invasion of Iran.

Saddam was executed for crimes he committed in 1982, by his standards not very serious crimes—complicity in killing 150 people. Well, there was something missing in that account—1982 is a very important year in U.S./Iraqi relations. That is the year in which Ronald Reagan removed Iraq from the list of states supporting terrorism so that the U.S. could start supplying Iraq with weapons for its invasion of Iran, including the means to develop weapons of mass destruction, chemical and nuclear weapons. That is 1982.

A year later Donald Rumsfeld was sent to firm up the deal. Well, Iranians may very well remember that this led to a war in which hundreds of thousands of them were slaughtered with U.S. aid going to Iraq. They may well remember that the year after the war was over, in 1989, the U.S. government invited Iraqi nuclear engineers to come to the United States for advanced training in developing nuclear weapons.

What about the Russians? They have a history, too. One part of the history is that in the last century Russia was invaded and practically destroyed three times through Eastern Europe. You can look back and ask, when was the last time that the U.S. was invaded and practically destroyed through Canada or Mexico? That doesn't happen. We crush others and we are always safe, but the Russians don't have that luxury. In 1990, a remarkable event took place. I was kind of shocked, frankly. Gor- bachev agreed to let Germany be unified, meaning join the West and be militarized within a hostile military alliance. This is Germany, which twice in that century practically destroyed Russia. That's a pretty remarkable agreement.

There was a quid pro quo. Then-president George Bush I agreed that NATO would not expand to the East. The Russians also demanded, but did not receive, an agreement for a nuclear-free zone from the Artic to the Baltic, which would give them a little protection from nuclear attack. That was the agreement in 1990. Then Bill Clinton came into office, the so-called liberal. One of the first things he did was to rescind the agreement, unilaterally, and expand NATO to the East.

For the Russians that's pretty serious, if you remember the history. They lost 25 million people in the last World War and over 3 million in World War I. But since the U.S. owns the world, if we want to threaten Russia, that is fine. It is all for freedom and justice, after all, and if they make unpleasant noises about it, we wonder why they are so paranoid. Why is Putin screaming as if we're somehow threatening them, since we can't be threatening anyone, owning the world.

One of the other big issues on the front pages now is Chinese "aggressiveness." There is a lot of concern about the fact that the Chinese are building up their missile forces. Is China planning to conquer the world? Big debates about it. Well, what is really going on? For years, China has been in the lead in trying to prevent the militarization of space. If you look at the debates and the Disarmament Commission of the UN General Assembly, the votes are 160 to 1 or 2. The U.S. insists on the militarization of space. It will not permit the outer space treaty to explicitly bar military relations in space.

Clinton's position was that the U.S. should control space for military purposes. The Bush administration was more extreme. Their position is the U.S. should own space, their words.

> *It's a pretty remarkable comment on the impossibility of achieving democracy in the United States. Again, the logic is pretty elementary. Steinbrunner and Gallagher are assuming that the United States cannot be a democratic society; it's not one of the options.*

We have to own space for military purposes. So that is the spectrum of discussion here. The Chinese have been trying to block it and that is well understood. You read the most respectable journal in the world, I suppose, the *Journal of the American Academy of Arts and Sciences*, and you find leading strategic analysts, John Steinbrunner and Nancy Gallagher, a couple of years ago, warning that the Bush administration's aggressive militarization is leading to what they call "ultimate doom." Of course, there is going to be a reaction to it. You threaten people with destruction, they are going to react. These analysts call on peace-loving nations to counter Bush's aggressive militarism. They hope that China will lead peace-loving nations to counter U.S. aggressiveness. It's a pretty remarkable comment on the impossibility of achieving democracy in the United States. Again, the logic is pretty elementary. Steinbrunner and Gallagher are assuming that the United States cannot be a democratic society; it's not one of the options, so therefore we hope that maybe China will do something.

Well, China finally did something. It signaled to the United States that they noticed that we were trying to use space for military purposes, so China shot down one of their satellites. Everyone understands why—the militari- zation and weaponization of space depends on satellites. While missiles are very difficult or maybe impossible to stop, satellites are very easy to shoot down. You know where they are. So China is saying, "Okay, we understand you are militarizing space. We're going to counter it not by militarizing space, we can't compete with you that way, but by shooting down your satellites."

That is what was behind the satellite shooting. Every military analyst certainly understood it and every lay person can understand it. But take a look at the debate. The discussion was about, "Is China trying to conquer the world by shooting down one of its own satellites?"

About a year ago, there was a new rash of articles and headlines on the front page about the "Chinese military build-up." The Pentagon claimed that China had increased its offensive military capacity—with 400 missiles, which could be nuclear armed. Then we had a debate about whether that proves China is trying to conquer the world or the numbers are wrong, or something.

Just a little footnote. How many offensive nuclear armed missiles does the United States have? Well, it turns out to be 10,000. China may now have maybe 400, if you believe the hawks. That proves that they are trying to conquer the world? It turns out, if you read the international press closely, that the reason China is building up its military capacity is not only because of U.S. aggressiveness all over the place, but also the fact that the United States has improved its targeting capacities so it can now destroy missile sites in a much more sophisticated fashion wherever they are, even if they are mobile. So who is trying to conquer the world? Well, obviously the Chinese because, since we own it, they are trying to conquer it.

It's all too easy to continue with this indefinitely. Just pick your topic. It's a good exercise to try. This simple principle, "we own the world," is sufficient to explain a lot of the discussion about foreign affairs.

I will finish with a word from George Orwell. In the introduction to *Animal Farm* he said, England is a free society, but it's not very different from the totalitarian monster I have been describing. He says, in England, unpopular ideas can be suppressed without the use of force. Then he goes on to give some dubious examples. At the end, he turns to a very brief explanation, actually two sentences, but they are to the point. He says, one reason is the press is owned by wealthy men who have every reason not to want certain ideas to be expressed. And the second reason—and I think a more important one—is a good education. If you have gone to the best schools and graduated from Oxford and Cambridge, and so on, you have instilled in you the understanding that there are certain things it would not do to say; actually, it would not do to think. That is the primary way to prevent unpopular ideas from being expressed.

In contrast, the ideas of the overwhelming majority of the population, who don't attend Harvard, Princeton, Oxford and Cambridge, enable them to react like human beings, as they often do.

From a talk at Z Media Institute 2007
Printed in Z Magazine, January 2008
Volume 21, Number 1

Contributor Biographies

DAVID BARSAMIAN *is founder and director of Alternative Radio. He is the author of numerous books with Noam Chomsky, Howard Zinn, Tariq Ali, and Edward Said. His latest are* What We Say Goes *and* Targeting Iran.

HERBERT P. BIX *is a professor of history at Binghamton University and the author of* Hirohito and the Making of Modern Japan, *an acclaimed account of the Japanese Emperor and the events which shaped modern Japanese imperialism.*

NOAM CHOMSKY *is a linguist, philosopher, political critic, and activist. He is an Institute Professor and Professor (Emeritus) in the Department of Linguistics & Philosophy at MIT where he has worked for over 50 years. In addition to his work in linguistics, he has written on war, politics, and mass media, and is the author of over 100 books.*

WARD CHURCHILL *is an author and political activist. He was a professor of ethnic studies at the University of Colorado at Boulder from 1990 to 2007. The primary focus of his work is on the treatment of Native Americans by the U.S. government.*

TIM COLES *is a writer and filmmaker whose articles have appeared in* Z *and* Peace Review.

NICOLAS J. S. DAVIES *is the author of* Blood On Our Hands: the American Invasion and Destruction of Iraq *(Nimble Books).*

JANE FRANKLIN *is author of* Cuban Foreign Relations 1959-1982 *and* Cuba and the U.S.: A Chronological History. *She has published numerous articles and has lectured about Cuba, Vietnam, Nicaragua, El Salvador, and Panama.*

ZOLTAN GROSSMAN *is a faculty member in Geography and Native American & World Indigenous Peoples Studies at Evergreen State College in Olympia, Washington.*

A.K. GUPTA *is a co-founder of* The Indypendent *and the* Occupied Wall Street Journal. *He is*

writing a book on the decline of the American empire for Haymarket.

EDWARD S. HERMAN *is an economist and media analyst. He co-edited, with Philip Hammond,* Degraded Capability: The Media and The Kosovo Crisis.

M.L. RANTALA *is a freelance writer and editor of The* Evergreen, *the newspaper of the Hyde Park Cooperative Society (Chicago). She edited, with Arthur J. Milgram,* Cloning: For and Against *(Open Court, 1999).*

STEPHEN ROBLIN *is an activist and researcher from Baltimore, Maryland. His articles have appeared in* Z *and other publications.*

STEPHEN ROSSKAMM SHALOM *is a professor of political science at William Paterson University in New Jersey. He is the author of numerous publications including* Which Side Are You On?: An Introduction to Politics, Imperial Alibis: Rationalizing U.S. Intervention After the Cold War, *and* The United States and the Philippines: A Study of Neocolonialism.

MARESI STARZMANN *is an anthropologist working and writing at the Free University Berlin, Germany. She engages with the history and politics of anthropology, and more recently has started writing about pop culture responses to anthropological research.*

PAUL STREET *is a writer, speaker, and activist based in Iowa City, Iowa and Chicago, Illinois. He is the author of* Empire and Inequality: America and the World Since 9/11; Racial Oppression in the Global Metropolis; *and* Segregated Schools: Educational Apartheid in Post-Civil Rights America.

MATTHEW WILLIAMS *is a peace activist who works with Boston Mobilization for Survival's Campaign for the Iraqi People.*

Other Z Books

Fanfare for the Future Series: Volume 1 develops a shared set of concepts for a new society (109 pp). Volume 2 addresses economics, politics, kinship, culture, ecology, and international relations (178 pp). Volume 3 addresses tactics and strategy relevant to a participatory society (234 pp).

The Z Reader on Patriarchy: 37.7 Seconds contains essays (from 1988-2011) on a wide range of topics relevant to understanding the many manifestations of patriarchy in society. Writers include bell hooks, Sheila Rowbotham, Lydia Sargent, Midge Quandt, and many others. These essays all appeared either in Z Magazine, ZNet, Z Papers, or as a Z Media Institute handout (220 pp).